# THE MANUAL OF MUSEUM MANAGEMENT

# THE MANUAL OF MUSEUM MANAGEMENT

BARRY LORD
and
GAIL DEXTER LORD

London: The Stationery Office

© Barry Lord and Gail Dexter Lord 1997

Applications for reproduction should be made in writing to The Stationery Office Limited, St Crispins, Duke Street, Norwich NR3 IPD

ISBN 0 11 290518 8

British Library cataloguing in Publication Data

A CIP catalogue record for this book is available from the British Library

Barry Lord and Gail Dexter Lord have asserted their right under the Copyright, Designs and Patents Act 1988 to be identified as the authors of this work

Edited, designed and produced by The Stationery Office

Printed in the UK for The Stationery Office
0112905188/1 4/97 C15 G559 10170

# Contents

3709

F (LOR)

# Case Studies

# Figures

# Tables

# Contributors

**Dr Robert P Bergman** has been Director of the Cleveland Museum of Art since 1 July 1993, having previously served as Director of Baltimore's Walters Art Gallery from 1981 to 1993. A scholar of medieval art and architecture, Dr Bergman participates widely in national cultural affairs, having served as Chairman of the American Arts Alliance and President of the Association of Art Museum Directors, and currently serves as Chairman of the American Association of Museums.

**Dr Patrick J Greene**, in addition to his role as Director of the Museum of Science and Industry in Manchester, participates in a number of organisations. He chairs the Board of the Greater Manchester Visitor and Convention Bureau, and the advisory and fundraising panels of the North West Museums Service. He is also President of the International Council of Museums of Science and Technology (CIMUSET). He received an OBE in 1991.

**Janet Kamien** is currently the Vice President for the Science Museum of The Franklin Institute in Philadelphia, Pennsylvania. Before this she served as Director of Exhibits at the Field Museum, Chicago, and as an exhibit developer and an administrator at the Boston Children's Museum. Her primary interest is the continuing improvement of exhibits, both as product and process.

**Erika Langmuir** was Head of Education at the National Gallery in London from 1988 to 1995. She was Professor of Art History at the University of Sussex between 1982 and 1988 and has also held a Chair of Art History for the Open University.

**Mike Leber** currently leads the team that operates the City of Salford Museums and Art Galleries. He has over twenty-five years' experience of collections management and exhibition work and is an acknowledged expert and author on the life and works of L S Lowry. Having 'risen through the ranks', Mike places great value in encouraging and enhancing the contribution of staff at all levels.

**Barry Lord** is co-founder and a Managing Director of Lord Cultural Resources Planning & Management Ltd., a world-wide company specialising in the planning and management of museums, heritage sites, public art galleries, science centres and related attractions, as well as the government, non-profitmaking or private sector agencies that operate museums and other related institutions. With over thirty-five years' experience in the museum field, Barry is co-author of *The Cost of Collecting* (HMSO, 1989) and was co-editor of *The Manual of Museum Planning* (HMSO, 1991). Barry has led hundreds of museum planning and management studies in the United Kingdom, continental Europe, South-East and East Asia, Australia and North America.

**Gail Dexter Lord** is co-founder and a Managing Director of Lord Cultural Resources Planning and Management Ltd. She is also co-editor of *The Manual of Museum Planning* (HMSO, 1991) and co-author of *The Cost of Collecting* (HMSO, 1989). She has directed planning and management studies and visitor analyses for hundreds of museums and galleries throughout the United Kingdom, continental Europe, North America Asia and Australia.

**Terence Measham** is Director of the Powerhouse Museum, Sydney. He is the author of a number of publications on art and design. His latest book, *Treasures of the Powerhouse Museum*, was published in 1994. Its successor, *More Treasures – Director's Selection*, was published in 1996.

**Christine O'Neill**, Vice President for Development, The Art Institute of Chicago, has worked in institutional advancement for twenty-four years. She has served the Art Institute for eleven years, overseeing membership and audience development.

**Marjorie L Schwarzer** teaches in the Department of Museum Studies at John F Kennedy University in Orinda, California. She was previously Director of Education at the Chicago Children's Museum.

**Damien Whitmore** began his career as an education researcher for Granada Television before teaching at a comprehensive school in Oxford. He was Education Officer at the Arts Council of Great Britain from 1985 to 1988 and a producer for BBC Radio 5 from 1989 to 1990. In 1990 he joined the Design Museum as Head of Marketing and Development. Since July 1992 he has been Head of Communications at the Tate Gallery and manages the gallery's public relations, marketing, press, information, visitor services, political lobbying and interpretational activities.

**Simon Wilson** is a member of the Tate Gallery's Communications Department where he is responsible for editing or writing all of the Tate's interpretational material for the general public, including soundguides. He joined the Tate Gallery in 1967 as its first Official Lecturer and was Head of Education at the Tate from 1980 to 1991. He is the author of a number of books, including the Tate's *Illustrated Companion*.

**Hilary Young** has worked at the Victoria and Albert Museum since 1981. He is currently the Derby Fellow in Ceramic History.

# Foreword

I am delighted to have been asked to write the foreword for *The Manual of Museum Management*. This book provides invaluable advice and guidance for everyone involved in the creation, development and management of museums today.

It is of particular relevance to the Tate as it enters one of the most important phases in its history. The creation of the new Tate Gallery of Modern Art at Bankside in London and the development of the Tate Gallery of British Art on the current Tate Gallery site represent a considerable challenge. The effective management of valuable resources including money, space, time and staff will play a vital role in ensuring that the Tate realises its plans on time and within budget.

Museums and galleries throughout the world are changing and as we enter the 3rd millennium it is interesting to note that the numbers of visitors are growing and our profession is expanding. Increased visitor figures, however, bring with them greater challenges, more demands and added accountability. Today's museum visitor expects excellence not only in terms of exhibition and display, but in information, interpretation, catering, retail and all other services. If we are to keep our existing visitors and continue to attract new ones, then we must plan with their needs and expectations at the forefront of our thinking.

In these circumstances the conservation and care of museum collections assumes an ever greater importance. New approaches to storage will provide better conditions for objects and increased public access. There will be an increasing emphasis on preventive care, ensuring that all the works are at all times fit for study, display or loan. Access will also be improved by the development of more effective systems for both tracking and documenting museum collections.

This book contains a number of remarkable case studies from museums and galleries around the world, including two from the Tate Gallery. These provide a fascinating insight into the planning, development and realisation of a range of initiatives in very different environments. What they all reveal, however, is the need for collaboration, commitment and strategic planning.

Expanding audiences suggest that museums are playing an increasingly important role in meeting the need for intellectual and emotional stimulation that is common to us all. It is more than ever a privilege, pleasure and responsibility among museum professionals to ensure that inspiration, enjoyment and education await those who step through our doors.

Nicholas Serota
Director, Tate Gallery

# Preface

Museums are one of the most successful cultural institutions of our time. Whether devoted to art, science or history, their acquisitions and exhibitions are exciting and illuminating to an ever widening range of interested visitors around the world. Nations, states, provinces, counties, cities and towns all want museums, as do many universities. Increasingly, industries and even leisure pursuits – from embroidery to balloon flying – aspire to set up a museum of their own.

It might therefore be thought that the management of these successful institutions should be a relatively straightforward matter of pleasing a known public with a popular product, while pursuing the underlying goals of scholarship and preservation. But, as almost everyone knows who is involved with the management of museums, this is no longer true, if it ever was. In the past few decades especially, the pace of change in philosophy, in technology, in funding and in public expectations has required those responsible for museums to adapt rapidly and continuously, while attempting to maintain the museum's fundamental objectives.

This guide to the management of museums in the 21st century therefore begins in Chapter 1 with the question WHY? Why do we need museum management, and what is its appropriate role? We then turn in Chapter 2 to the people who animate museums and the structure of museum organisation (the WHO of museum management); and in Chapter 3 we examine the tools available to museum leadership – the HOW of museum management.

This manual is for all those involved or interested in the challenge of managing and leading museums in the 21st century: both those inside museums (museum management and staff, trustees, volunteers and committee members) and those outside museums, such as government and foundation staff and personnel in other agencies responsible for museums or grant-aid to them, designers and other museum service providers, and teachers and students in museum studies and related programmes. Our purpose is a practical one: to provide an easy-reference manual for the museum manager, including the director, president, and chief executive, for all those who are called on to perform management functions, including curators, department heads, project managers and team leaders, and for museum workers who wish to take management responsibility in the future. It is our hope that this book, and the case studies in it, will help to guide the way to still better museums in the 21st century.

# Acknowledgements

This Manual has its origins in a certificate course on Museum Organisation and Management that the authors prepared over a decade ago for the Ontario Museum Association. The course has travelled with us over the years and has developed through seminars, courses and presentations we have made to museum professionals – including Museum Association seminars in London, the museum training programme at the *Niederoesterreichisches Landesakademie* in Austria, the Cultural Resources Management programme at the University of Victoria, and museum training seminars at the Urban Council Training School in Hong Kong and the Singapore Philatelic Museum. Our appreciation is extended to the many students and colleagues who continually challenged our thinking and stimulated us to develop the course and eventually this Manual.

This book reflects, too, our international experience in the management of museums, both directly and in our role as consultants to museum professionals and Trustees around the world. Our thanks go as well to all of our clients and colleagues for their creativity and professionalism in the hopes that this book reflects the best of their intention, as well as the measure of their accomplishment.

Special thanks are due to Nicholas Serota, Director of the Tate Gallery, for writing the foreword to this book; and to Damien Whitmore, Head of Communications at the Tate, who worked through the book with us from concept to conclusion. We wish to thank also the authors of the case studies, who are listed elsewhere in the book, for their lively and cogent contributions.

Colleagues and associates of Lord Cultural Resources Planning & Management around the world have also contributed to the book's development. In particular we would like to acknowledge the contributions of Cultural Building Consultant Murray Frost regarding technical details pertaining to accommodations; of Ted Silverberg who reviewed the chapter on museum finances; of Hugh Spencer who cast a practised eye on sections pertaining to exhibition development; of Heather Maximea who assisted with many of the technical glossary entries; of Louise Rowe who commented on the budget cycle; and of Kathleen Brown who focused on issues of museum leadership. Debbie Knight and Kevin Proulx of the Lord production staff are owed many thanks for their technical work with the manuscript in readying it for our publisher. Our thanks, also, to Lia Baschiribod for her dedication and care in handling the manuscript and arranging the book's launch.

We would also like to thank those publishers, formerly HMSO and now called The Stationery Office, for their patience and commitment in bringing this book to the press. Special thanks go to Kim Anne Yarwood for her editorial acumen.

Finally, we wish to thank our daughter Beth and our son Ben for their patience during the writing and preparation of this book.

Gail Dexter Lord and Barry Lord

# 1

# WHY

## The Objectives of Museum Management

Almost everyone working in museums – including the directors – sometimes asks themselves: 'Why do we need management anyway. . . What is it good for?'

Unfortunately, the answer is frequently unclear. Too often management merely makes bureaucratic demands on the time of museum professionals who could be providing the collection or the public with valuable services instead of attending another meeting, filling out a form or writing another report. Lack of leadership affects both staff and public when exhibitions lack creativity, education lacks focus or the collection is presented without vision.

What is 'leadership' . . . Why do museums need it?

Although entire books have been written on the theory and practice of management and leadership, we are going to risk defining both in one chapter. And, in the spirit of a manual, we will be building a comprehensive diagram of museum management to help readers sort, remember and apply key management terms.

# 1.1 | The Purpose of Management

Contrary to popular belief, the purpose of management is to make it easier for the staff of the organisation to do their jobs by *facilitating decisions*.

To 'facilitate' means to make things easier than they would otherwise be:

*The purpose of management in museums is to facilitate decisions that lead to the achievement of the museum's mission, the fulfilment of its mandate, and the realisation of the goals and objectives for all of its functions.*

*Figure 1.1    The Purpose of Management*

This understanding of the purpose of museum management implies a very simple but effective means of *evaluation* of museum management:

*Is the museum's management facilitating decisions that lead to the achievement of its mission, mandate, goals and objectives for all of its functions?*

If so, management is doing its job. If not, changes are needed. And, since life is almost always a matter of degree, the quality of management may be evaluated by the extent to which it facilitates decisions that lead to the achievement of the museum's MISSION, MANDATE, GOALS and OBJECTIVES in fulfilment of the museum's functions.

| # Statements of Purpose

Museums are not the buildings that house them, nor even the collections they protect – important as these are. Museums are complex cultural institutions uniquely concerned both with collecting and preserving the material cultural heritage, and at the same time *communicating its meaning* – whether that meaning arises from works of art, archaeological and historical artefacts or scientific specimens. The social and even political dimensions of the communication of meaning result in an institution that combines those aspects with the 'hardware' functions of housing and caring for a collection.

The purpose of a particular museum is expressed in terms of:

- mission
- mandate
- goals
- objectives

The MISSION STATEMENT of a cultural institution is an objective, brief and hopefully inspiring assertion of its *raison d'être* or relevance. It should answer the question, 'Why should people care about this museum?' The mission statement directs our sights toward the long-range reason for the museum's existence. It is the foundation of all policy development. An example might be:

> *The mission of the County Museum is to preserve and communicate to residents and visitors the history and creative spirit of those who have lived here from the beginning of human habitation.*

The MANDATE of a cultural institution is the range of material culture for which it assumes responsibility. This may be stated in terms of:

- an academic discipline
- geographical range
- chronological range
- specialisation
- the relationships of the mandate to other institutions concerned with the same subject

An example of a mandate statement, which distinguishes our exemplar county museum from another institution, might be:

> *'The mandate of the County Museum is the archaeology, history and both fine and decorative art of the inhabitants of what is now – County from the first human occupation of the area to the present day; the natural history of the county is the mandate of the University Museum, and will therefore be included in County Museum exhibits only to the extent necessary to support the human history displays.'*

The mandate not only establishes the museum's mission in the objective world of public responsibilities, but also lays the foundation for the museum's relations with other institutions – governmental, educational and private sector, as well as with other museums.

The GOALS of a museum may be defined as the long-range, qualitative levels of collection development, collection care and visitor service towards which the institution is striving. They may be articulated for a given period of the museum's development in a strategic plan or master plan. Achieving them may take years.

By contrast, a museum's OBJECTIVES may be described as short-range, quantified expressions of particular steps on the way to the longer-range goals. Goals are placed on a timetable or schedule for fulfilment, and are usually specific to a one-year or two-year planning period. They may be articulated as part of a one-year plan of action, or as part of a budget exercise.

In defining its mission, mandate, goals and objectives, it is important for a museum to focus these on museum FUNCTIONS. There are six main museum functions that, taken together, define what is unique about museums. Three are related to the museum's assets, the other three to its activities (see Table 1.1).

*Table 1.1   Museum Functions*

| Assets | Activities |
| --- | --- |
| *Collecting* | *Research* |
| *Documentation* | *Display* |
| *Preservation* | *Interpretation* |

The seventh function, pulling the other six together, is ADMINISTRATION. The relationship between all seven may be visualised as a triangle, with the functions affecting assets grouped to one side, those representing activities along the other, and administration endeavouring to reconcile these two dimensions:

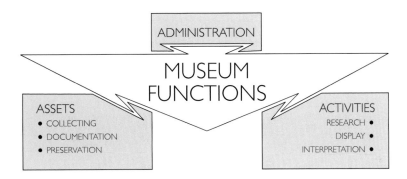

*Figure 1.2   The Triangle of Museum Functions*

The triangle is an appropriate image because (a) it is an inherently strong structural form, and (b) it points or suggests movement in a particular direction. Yet, at the same time, the inherent divergence of the two functions – assets-based and activity-related – is also made clear. The key role of administration in transforming this divergence into a creative rather than disabling tension is also indicated by the triangle. That role is described in section 1.3.

# 1.3 | The Roles of Management in Museums

In order for museum management to facilitate the achievement of mission, mandate, goals and objectives, it must be adept at playing not one but five roles:

- TO INSPIRE          with a sense of the museum's *mission*

- TO COMMUNICATE   the museum's *mandate*

- TO LEAD             towards the museum's *goals*

- TO CONTROL        the attainment of *objectives*

- TO EVALUATE       the fulfilment of museum *functions*

We can all identify with the fact that most managers cannot perform all five roles equally well. Yet understanding each of these roles in museum terms can help museum managers both to build on their strengths and to identify and strengthen those roles in which they may be weak. The diagram we are developing illustrates how these roles are mutually supportive.


## 1.3.1   TO INSPIRE WITH A SENSE OF MISSION

A former Director of the Corning Museum of Glass once told us: 'My mission is to get people excited about glass.' And because he was himself excited about glass, he was able to do so very well.

A good museum manager has a clear sense of the museum's mission, and inspires others to join in the fulfilment of that mission. This sense of mission is a well of creativity from which the manager derives original solutions to problems, redirects struggling staff towards the essential objectives, or sets challenges that lead the museum on to greater accomplishments. The manager's comprehension of the mission must be so infectious that people who meet him or her (from staff through volunteers and donors to visitors and the general public) want to get involved.

The manager must believe in the mission: it must matter emotionally, as well as intellectually, to him or her.

This role of management suggests a second criterion for the evaluation of museum management:

*Does management inspire staff, volunteers, supporters, visitors and others with a sense of the museum's mission?*

If inspiration is not forthcoming, it may be a weakness of management, or it may be that the mission is out of date, or has become irrelevant or less significant as we approach the 21st century. If this is the case, management should work with the museum's governing body to review and revise the mission statement. It is surprising how frequently trustees meeting to discuss the museum's mission discover

Figure 1.3   The Role of Management: Mission and Policies

divergent views despite prior confidence that everyone shared a common sense of purpose. Generally, major revisions to the mission statement are undertaken as part of a strategic planning process, as described in Chapter 3.

Getting the mission right may take time, but it is essential to the long-term direction of the institution, because the mission is the core around which *policies* should be formed. Without a fully understood mission, policies remain an empty form. However, when they are supportive of an agreed mission, policies can be directed more effectively towards a common end.

## 1.3.2   To communicate the mandate

A museum manager must understand the mandate of the institution, and be able to communicate it to others, both within the museum and beyond its walls. He or she must be aware of both the extent and the limitations of that mandate, and of its relationship with the mandates of other institutions. By exercising the mandate consciously, the manager and the museum may be said to be 'communicating' the mandate clearly to visitors, funders and the museum's own governing body and staff.

If a museum is not fulfilling its mandate, and if that mandate is of real interest and concern to others, then another institution – a new museum or an existing museum or related institution – may compete for or fulfil that mandate. Usually, it is not a question of a complete replacement, but of a gradual

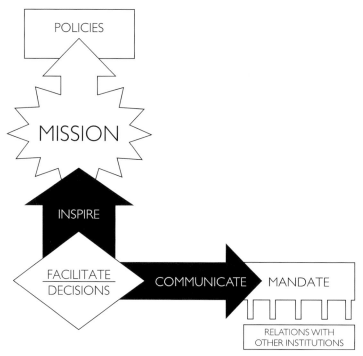

Figure 1.4    The Role of Management: Communicating the Mandate

encroachment from other institutions expanding their field of activity. If, for example, a museum of Asian art is not very active in exhibiting or collecting contemporary Asian art, then a museum of contemporary art in the same city might expand into that field, and effectively usurp the Asian art museum's mandate, leading to competition for collections and exhibitions. 'Use it or lose it' applies to mandate.

On the other hand, lack of clarity about the museum's mandate can lead the institution to distractions that interfere with the accomplishment of the museum's purposes. It may, for example, be tempting for the county history museum to offer an exhibition on dinosaurs because of their popularity, even though there were never any such creatures in what is now that county; this may be admissible as part of a temporary exhibition programme 'Opening a Window on the World', but if such exhibitions become a major activity, absorbing the energies of staff while the permanent collection of archaeological and historical artefacts is neglected, then the museum is losing sight of its mandate.

A third criterion of effective museum management could be phrased as follows:

*Are both the extent and the limitations of the museum's mandate understood? Are they being fully exercised and clearly communicated, both within the museum and outside? Do the museum's relations with other institutions – governmental, educational and private sector, as well as other museums – reflect a clear and complete understanding of this mandate?*

### 1.3.3  TO LEAD TOWARDS GOALS

Management and leadership are related, but are not identical. It is often said that management is about 'doing it right', while leadership is 'doing the right thing'. A leader is constantly aware of the institution's goals, and is therefore able to guide others towards their achievement.

For example, once it has been decided that one of the goals of the museum's documentation programme is the conversion of its records to an electronic form, it will require leadership as well as good management to steer towards that goal and to dedicate the necessary staff and resources to its achievement despite the many other demands on time, funds and facilities. It will also require leadership to balance the dedication to that goal with the requirements of a temporary exhibition programme that also needs attention from the same registrar who is responsible for the automation project.

Long-range institutional goals should be identified in plans such as strategic plans or master plans that link goals to the museum's mission (and therefore with its policies) and mandate.

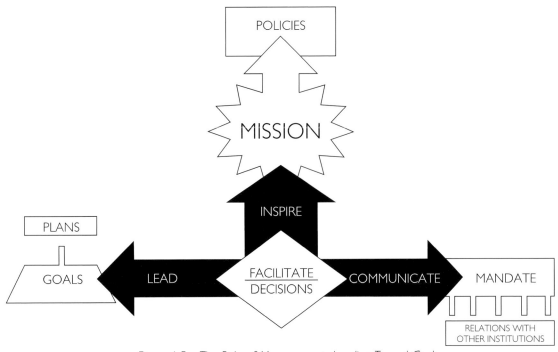

*Figure 1.5    The Role of Management: Leading Toward Goals*

*Leadership* is the fourth criterion for good management:

*Is management effectively leading the museum towards long-range goals articulated in plans that are consistent with the museum's mission, policies and mandate?*

## 1.3.4    To control the attainment of objectives

To achieve the broad institutional goals articulated in the museum's plans, management must break them down into short-range, measurable objectives which, taken together, will lead to the qualitative change that is expressed in the goals. Management is also responsible for assigning resources needed to achieve these objectives and to make sure they are accomplished on schedule and on budget.

Monitoring the BUDGET and the SCHEDULE – ensuring that resources of time and money are utilised in accordance with the allocations – is one of the key functions of management. This is essentially the CONTROL function of management.

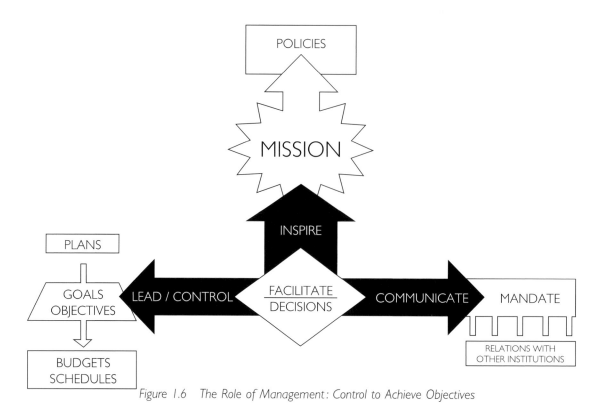

*Figure 1.6    The Role of Management: Control to Achieve Objectives*

This role of management suggests a fifth evaluation criterion:

*Are long-range goals being translated into short-range, measurable objectives? Is the attainment of annual objectives controlled by the monitoring of the budget and other resource allocation plans?*

## 1.3.5  TO EVALUATE THE FULFILMENT OF MUSEUM FUNCTIONS

The achievement of a museum's mission, the accomplishment of its mandate, and even the attainment of short-term objectives en route to long-range goals, are valuable to the museum only if all of these are related to the specific functions of a museum – the six functions ranged along the two diverging sides of the triangle in fig. 1.2. An important role of management, therefore, is to evaluate the fulfilment of these functions. How well is the museum collecting, documenting and preserving its collection? And how well is it studying, displaying and interpreting that collection to the public? This management role is often referred to as ADMINISTRATION.

The evaluation of these specifically museological functions should be made in terms of both EFFECTIVENESS and EFFICIENCY:

- EFFECTIVENESS measures the extent to which the museum's efforts achieve the intended result – which should have been quantified as far as possible in the work plan for that function.

- EFFICIENCY measures that effect in relation to the effort required – in person-hours, in money, in space (which is often at a premium in museums) or in the use of facilities or equipment. The term 'cost-effectiveness' is sometimes used, really to describe efficiency measured in financial terms; 'person-effectiveness' and 'space-effectiveness' would be equally useful concepts, but all three are really measures of efficiency.

Accurate and sensitive evaluation of the fulfilment of museological functions is a further measure of the success of museum management:

*Is management evaluating both the effectiveness and the efficiency of the museum's fulfilment of its functions?*

Figure 1.7 has been built from all the evaluation criteria discussed so far in this chapter. It illustrates the five roles of management in relation to museum functions and policies. And at the very heart of the diagram is the reminder that the purpose of management is to make it easier (for it will never be easy!) for people who work and volunteer in museums to do their jobs – which is the subject of Chapter 2.

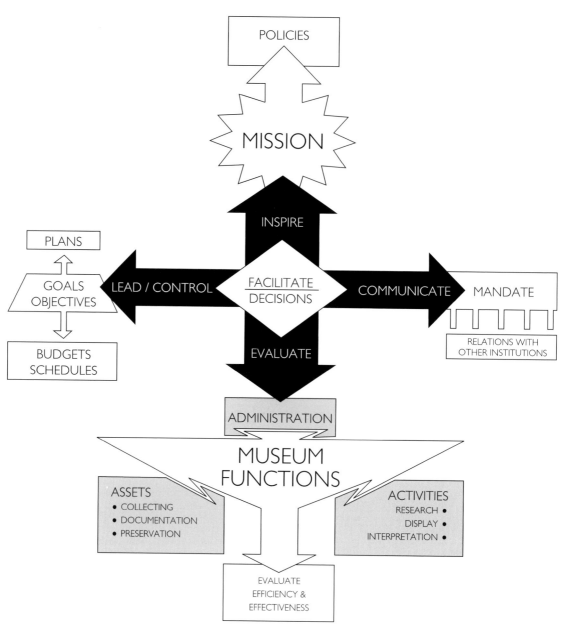

Figure 1.7 Summary of Museum Management

# 2

# WHO

## The Structure of Museum Organisation

Museums are governed, managed and operated by people: they are inherently social institutions in which people work together to achieve and sustain the mission, mandate, goals and objectives. Who these people are and how they work together are the subjects of this chapter. We consider first the alternative modes of museum governance, and then the three fundamental roles which people perform in the governance, management and operation of museums:

- trustees (2.2)

- staff (2.3)

- volunteers (2.4)

# 2.1 | Modes of Governance

The governing body of a museum assumes the ultimate legal and financial responsibility for it. Despite the wide variety of circumstances in which museums around the world have been established, there are only four principal modes of governance:

- line departments (2.1.1)
- arm's length institutions (2.1.2)
- non-profitmaking or charitable organisations (2.1.3)
- private ownership (2.1.4)

Those involved in establishing a new museum should carefully consider which mode of governance will best meet the long-term needs of the institution. Those responsible for existing museums should also review governance issues, because what was a suitable form of governance fifty years ago may no longer be appropriate. For example, as museums enter the 21st century, the societal trends toward decentralisation and privatisation are reflected in the tendency to transfer the governance of museums which were once part of government agencies or public authorities to the non-profitmaking or charitable sector. The process of reviewing and changing a museum's governance is called INSTITUTIONAL PLANNING.

This section outlines the characteristics, advantages and disadvantages of each of these modes, and concludes with Table 2.1, which summarises all four.

## 2.1.1 LINE DEPARTMENTS

National, state, provincial, county and local authority museums and galleries are often part of the cultural departments of the relevant level of government. This is equally true of specialised museums in their respective departments: a postal museum, for example, may be part of a national postal or telecommunications service; a geology museum may be part of a university's geology department, and an automotive museum may be established within the public relations department of a car manufacturer. These are all examples of LINE DEPARTMENT MUSEUMS.

Line department museums form part of a government, university or corporation department. Their employees are civil servants if the museum is a government line department, or employees of the university or corporation that operates the museum. The director of a government line department museum may be appointed by the departmental minister, or may be recruited through the civil service process; directors of university or corporate line department museums, and of some government museums, may be engaged in the same way as other departmental administrators. In any case, the governance of the line department museum is integrated with that of the larger body.

Line department museums are funded primarily through allocations from the budget of the governing organisation. This is usually not grant aid, but a line item in the department budget. Admission to some line department museums is therefore free of charge, while others charge admission and raise additional revenue in other ways, but all have a central allocation from their governing body to sustain them. The collection and the buildings of line department museums are often owned by the parent body.

Many government line department museums around the world share a common problem in the disposition of their earned revenues, which typically go to a central government finance department, and do not benefit the institution directly. As a result many of these museums have little incentive to provide retail or food services of good quality, and their shops and cafes sometimes reflect this. Amending this accounting principle so that line department museums can keep their earnings has resulted in vast improvements in catering, retailing and services in many national museums.

Since they are part of a larger departmental body, most line department museums do not have a membership organisation. In recent years some have recruited friends' groups, both as a means of retaining earned income and of obtaining financial support. Volunteers are also often more difficult to recruit in a line department museum, because of the perception that everything is being done by paid staff.

If a line department museum has a board, it will be an *advisory board* without governing authority. This advisory group (sometimes called a *visiting committee*) typically reports to the political authority in the case of government line department museums, or to the university or corporation president in other instances. Members of such boards or committees are usually said to represent the public or academic interest in the museum, although some may also be appointed to represent concerned interest groups. In some instances the advisory board or visiting committee may advise the minister of the department or the president of the university or corporation on the selection of the director.

Many governments – national, state, provincial, county or municipal – operate museum systems in which several museums are grouped together to form a *museums service*. These associations of multiple museums are cost-effective to administer, due to the centralisation of at least some functions. The constituent museums may share their governing authority's accounting, personnel, maintenance, security or other services, adding only the curatorial and programming staff that are unique to each museum. Many museum services have found it cost-effective to centralise conservation and documentation functions for all participating institutions, and in some cases to erect or renovate non-public collection stores and laboratories. The disadvantages of such services for the participating museums can be loss of independence and difficulty in maintaining a distinct image, which may affect fundraising; but if well managed, they can be both efficient and effective in providing a wide range of museum experiences for residents and visitors throughout the jurisdiction of the presiding government.

## 2.1.2   ARM'S LENGTH INSTITUTIONS

Although many levels of government, universities and corporations are content to operate their museums as line departments, some have discovered advantages to establishing (or re-establishing) them as ARM'S LENGTH INSTITUTIONS. ('Arm's length' refers to the distance between head and hand, which appears to allow the hand a certain degree of autonomy, even though it is ultimately controlled by the head.) The arm's length approach is intended to ensure that the museum is independent of partisan politics or corporate interest, and to encourage the institution to find additional means of support besides government, university or corporate funds.

Arm's length museums differ from line department museums in that they normally have a *governing board* appointed by the senior political authority within that jurisdiction, or by the president of the university or corporation. The government department, university or corporation is usually represented on this board, along with representatives of concerned interest groups and/or the general public. This governing board is not merely advisory, but determines policy and long-range plans and engages the museum's director. In museums at arm's length from government, such a governing board is said to hold its responsibility for the museum as a *public trust.*

Museum staff may either be considered civil servants or employees of the university or corporation, or else they may be employed directly by the arm's length museum. The collection and/or the land and buildings of an arm's length museum may be owned by either the government department or the museum itself. Owing to a heightened perception of their autonomy, arm's length museums are sometimes more successful in attracting donations of both funds and objects for their collection than line department museums. Volunteers may also be more likely to support an arm's length museum than a line department institution.

Government funding for arm's length museums may be an annual allocation (as in line department museums), but it often takes the form of annual, dedicated grant aid, rather than a departmental allocation. The amount of this annual grant is typically determined from year to year, thus making the arm's length institution less certain of its annual budget levels than the line department museum. On the other hand, the arm's length museums are usually at liberty to raise additional non-governmental funds, or even to attract grants from other levels or departments of government. Arm's length museums usually do not have the line department museums' problem of their earned revenues going to a general government finance department, but are able to access both government and earned revenues freely for their own benefit.

## 2.1.3   NON-PROFITMAKING OR CHARITABLE ORGANISATIONS

The boards of museums that are incorporated as NON-PROFITMAKING OR CHARITABLE ORGANISATIONS are governing bodies, not merely advisory bodies. The board may be self-perpetuating or elected from the membership of the organisation, or it may consist of both appointed and elected members. Whatever its specific form or size, the board collectively assumes legal and financial responsibility for the museum, subject to the laws governing this type of organisation in each country. To achieve charitable or non-profitmaking status, the museum organisation will usually have applied for and obtained registration, letters patent or a charitable tax number, allowing it to provide tax-deductible receipts for donations and to receive other benefits allowed by government policy in each jurisdiction. Consequently, the museum organisation must comply with a broad range of government regulations in order to maintain that status. For example, it may be necessary to establish a separate corporation to operate retail or catering, since the non-profitmaking museum itself may not be allowed to operate these directly.

The non-profitmaking or charitable organisation typically owns the museum collection, land and buildings, and employs the museum staff. However, there are many independent, non-profitmaking or charitable trusts that operate museums in government or local authority-owned buildings, and some that care for local authority-owned collections. The museum director is appointed by the trustees. Funding is likely to be a mixture of public and private funds, including income from endowments, donations and visitor spending in the museum. Volunteers generally play a prominent role in these museums.

## 2.1.4   PRIVATE OWNERSHIP

One or another of the three previous modes of governance are found in virtually all public museums around the world. In addition, there are a number of museums that are owned and directly operated by private individuals, foundations or companies. These museums may be operated as private charities, or may be intended to earn a profit for their owners. However, it should be noted that profitmaking museums would not be classified as museums under the UNESCO definition of 'museum' nor the definitions of the British Museums Association and the American Association of Museums, all of which define museums as non-profitmaking institutions.

The individuals or the incorporated companies that operate private museums normally own the collections and own or lease the buildings. The funding for private museums comes directly from their owners and from earned revenues. The director is usually employed by the owner, who may also appoint an advisory board or committee. Staff are employees of the individual or the private company. Volunteers are rare.

## 2.1.5   SUMMARY OF MODES OF GOVERNANCE

Table 2.1 (overleaf) summarises the four modes of governance of museums and galleries in relation to the six key factors identified.

*Table 2.1   Modes of Museum Governance*

| Factor | Line Departments | Arm's Length | Non-profitmaking | Private |
|--------|------------------|--------------|------------------|---------|
| *Ownership* | Government, university or corporation | Government, university or corporation | Association or public company | Individual or private company |
| *Board or Trust* | Advisory | Governing or advisory | Governing | Advisory |
| *Funds* | Annual allocation | Granted and earned | Earned, with grants and endowment | Private and earned |
| *Donations* | Less likely | More likely | Most likely | Not likely |
| *Staff* | Civil service or university or corporation staff | May be civil service or museum staff | Association employees | Company employees |
| *Volunteers* | Difficult | Possible | Important | Rare |

Any change in the museum's institutional status must be carefully considered: a government line department museum may envy the freedom of an arm's length institution, but is it prepared for uncertainty in its annual funding? On the other hand, a non-profitmaking or charitable organisation struggling to finance the local public art gallery may find advantages in moving to arm's length status by appointing civic representatives to its board. These decisions are best taken as the result of a careful INSTITUTIONAL PLANNING process.

# 2.2 | The Board

Trusts and boards around the world hold their museums' collections and other assets in *public trust,* not only for the public of today but also for their descendants. They are *fiduciary* in character – a word describing trusteeship of property for others – meaning, in the case of museums, that trustees have an obligation to manage the property of others (in this case, the public) with the same diligence, honesty and discretion as prudent people would exercise in managing their own affairs.

## 2.2.1 BOARD ROLES AND RESPONSIBILITIES

As a consequence, although there may be many specific differences in the constitutions of museum boards around the world, governing boards have the following ten responsibilities in common. Advisory boards are generally expected to make recommendations on these issues to a higher body.

1   to ensure the continuity of the museum's mission, mandate and purposes;

2   to act as an advocate in the community (national, international, state, province, county, local, or community of interest) for public involvement in the museum;

3   to provide for the present and long-term security and preservation of the collection, and the safety of staff and visitors, at a level consistent with the museum's mission and mandate;

4   to ensure that the museum serves as wide a public as possible;

5   to ensure that the museum undertakes research to create and disseminate accurate and objective knowledge relevant to its collection;

6   to review and approve policies consistent with the museum's mission and mandate, and to monitor staff implementation of these policies;

7   to plan for the future of the museum, including reviewing and approving a CORPORATE PLAN (or STRATEGIC PLAN or BUSINESS PLAN) that identifies the museum's goals and ways to attain them, and monitoring implementation of the plan;

8   to assure the financial stability of the museum through reviewing, approving and monitoring budgets and financial reports, arranging for regular audits, investing the museum's financial assets wisely and raising funds as required to allow the museum to meet its current and future financial responsibilities;

9   to recruit and negotiate a contract with the museum's director, to evaluate his or her performance, and to terminate his or her employment if necessary;

10  to ensure that the museum has adequate staff to undertake all museum functions.

Thus the board appoints the director and delegates to her or him the responsibility to recruit, evaluate and, if necessary, dismiss all other museum staff. The director is not generally a board member, but attends all board meetings *ex officio* and recommends policies and plans to the board consistent with the museum's mission and mandate. The board is responsible for raising money so that the museum can achieve the plans it has approved. This fundraising role may encompass: support of staff fundraising and revenue generation activities; acting as an advocate on behalf of the museum to public and private funders, including government, corporations and foundations, as well as making donations and inviting others to make donations. Trustees are both formal and informal advocates for the museum in the community, which includes the political arena as well as the private sector.

The board's role, as indicated above, is that of guiding and monitoring policies, rather than policy formulation, which is a management function. However, there can be a fine line between the board fulfilling its monitoring role and being a 'rubber stamp' for management. When a board is a 'rubber stamp', it is unlikely to be effective in fundraising or museum advocacy. Conversely, there may be very serious problems when boards interfere with management functions by trying to write policies, frame budgets or decide on procedures.

Balancing the role of the board and the responsibilities of management so that both are able to perform their jobs well is one of the main challenges facing museum leadership in the new century. Another major challenge centres on the board's advocacy functions and the degree to which trustees should reflect the diversity of the community in order to be more effective in acting as advocates for the museum in the community. How will these two major challenges be met? – through extensive discussion and dialogue among people, both within the museum community, and between museums and the communities they serve. Museum directors need to spend considerable time keeping trustees fully informed of the issues behind the policies so that the board may make informed decisions. One approach is for the director to present policy options to the board for discussion and evaluation so that board members can truly fulfil their governance responsibilities. Board members need to be scrupulous in separating governance from management functions. An effective nominating committee that continuously evaluates board performance and which involves the director in the recruitment and training of new board members can be enormously helpful in clarifying governance and management roles and in addressing issues of board diversity. The president or chair of the board and the director have important and mutually supportive roles to play in maintaining an atmosphere of open discussion, access to information, and collegiality.

The director's management role with respect to the board is so critical to the success of the museum that it suggests a seventh management evaluation criterion:

*Does the director facilitate the flow of information between board and management? Does she or he provide leadership to the board in policy formulation and planning by presenting policy options to the board for discussion and decision, and by establishing planning processes in which board and management work together to set institution-wide goals?*

The roles and responsibilities of the board are usually regulated by a *constitution* or equivalent document that establishes, for example:

- the number of trustees and their means of appointment or election;
- public trust commitments and degree or limitation of personal responsibility;
- length of trustees' terms of office;

- frequency, location, quorum and minuting of meetings;
- policy on public access to board meetings or minutes;
- financial accounting practices, spending and borrowing rules;
- responsibilities and means of selection of officers of the board;
- board committees;
- remuneration of board members and provision for expenses;
- procedures in the event of dissolution of the board.

## 2.2.2  BOARD COMMITTEES

There are many sizes of museum boards. A large board of sixty to seventy people is often considered desirable for fundraising and community representation. Smaller boards with twenty to thirty members are sometimes considered to be more involved. Smaller museums in smaller communities may find even fewer members – seven to fifteen people – more efficient.

Most boards find it advisable to appoint their members to *committees*, so that the board can work on a wide range of issues simultaneously. In doing so, boards should set TERMS OF REFERENCE to establish the mandate of the committee and its limitations. It is an important principle that while boards work through committees, it is the board as a whole that makes policy decisions. Committees may recommend policies but should not approve them, and they should report to the board regularly on the implementation of policies or plans. The following are among the committees most commonly appointed:

- EXECUTIVE COMMITTEE: It may be advisable to appoint an executive committee to facilitate decisions between board meetings. This committee should normally include the board president or chair, the other senior officers and the museum director *ex officio*.
- NOMINATING COMMITTEE: This is a very important committee which has two main responsibilities: the ongoing evaluation of board performance, and making recommendations for changes in governance or board procedures; and identifying strengths and weaknesses of the board and recruiting trustees who will strengthen the board.
- FINANCE COMMITTEE: It is sometimes useful to set up a committee to focus exclusively on finances. This committee may have responsibility for capital fundraising as well, but is usually concerned only with ongoing operating funds. It normally works with staff to recommend the annual budget to the board, monitors financial reports and ensures that the museum's accounts are audited.
- DEVELOPMENT COMMITTEE: This committee addresses the board's fundraising role, such as annual giving, corporate sponsorship, planned giving and the many programmes and activities the board undertakes to raise money. Specific subcommittees may be formed to spearhead special areas such as endowment and capital funds.

- LONG-RANGE PLANNING COMMITTEE: Long-range planning is a board function that is frequently delegated to a committee that will work with museum management and planners to develop the strategic plan or the master plan as required by the board. This committee takes responsibility for the planning process, reports regularly to the board and recommends the resultant plan to the board for approval.

- ACQUISITION COMMITTEE: Curators have the professional responsibility for collection development, but since additions to the collection affect the long-term future of the institution, many museum boards have established acquisition committees to which curators present proposed acquisitions for approval. Such a committee can be instrumental in encouraging donations to the collection or finding sponsors for acquisitions that are beyond the museum's budget. The acquisitions committee is usually also responsible for approval of de-accessioning recommended by the curators through the director.

- MEMBERSHIP COMMITTEE: If the museum has a membership base, a dedicated committee of the board with its roots in the community can be very effective in recruiting new members, and in sustaining a lively level of membership participation in the museum. This committee may be concerned with corporate as well as individual or family memberships, and with encouraging members to increase their support of the museum by moving up to higher levels of membership.

Of course, boards may appoint additional committees as necessary. However, some committees are problematic – exhibition committees, for example, can be appropriate if they focus on exhibition policy and on sponsorship for proposed exhibitions, but too often go beyond the limits of a board's concern and make decisions on exhibition selection or priorities that should be delegated to staff.

The museum director is an *ex officio* member of all board committees and should give priority to the executive committee and the acquisition committee. The director may share or delegate this responsibility to other staff members in the case of committees that concern them: the chief financial officer may work with the finance committee, the head of development with the development and membership committees, the chief curator with the acquisitions committee, and so on.

## 2.2.3   BOARD PROCEDURES

Boards malfunction when they attempt to direct the day-to-day activities of the museum instead of delegating those decisions to staff. In some small museums, or in the early phases of a museum's development, it may be necessary for boards to undertake what are normally staff functions. When this is so, it should be explicitly understood and agreed that such activity is temporary, until staff can be recruited to fulfil those tasks.

Board members need training and development, just like staff and volunteers. Most museums find it useful to provide each incoming member with a *trustees' manual* that includes all the relevant mission, mandate and policy statements and the board constitution, as well as a history of the institution, current plans, staff organisation charts, budgets and financial reports, a list of board roles and responsibilities, and an outline of the committee structure. The new trustee should attend at least one *orientation session*, which should include a tour of the building and introduction to the division or department heads.

Board members need to be clear about the extent of their personal and collective liability for the museum's actions. This varies according to the legal provisions of each country, but in general, the incorporation of a non-profitmaking society or similar association should have the legal effect of placing liability on the institution collectively. As part of their fiduciary responsibility, trustees also need to be assured that the museum's insurance is adequate for its risks and resources.

Museum boards should adopt a *code of ethics*, both for themselves and for their museums. A code of ethics protects the trustee as well as the museum's interests, and is written in the spirit that 'Justice must not only be done, but must be seen to be done.' The code should subscribe to relevant international conventions and national, state, provincial or local laws relating to artefacts, specimens or works of art, as well as to the *Code of Professional Ethics* adopted by the International Council of Museums (ICOM) in 1986, and parallel guidelines promulgated by the museum profession in each country, such as the British Museums Association's Code of Practice (published in the 1994 *Museums Yearbook*). These codes of professional practice affect staff as well as trustees, and should be adopted as part of the board's code of ethics to govern the museum as a whole.

The board's code of ethics should also aim to eliminate conflicts of interest for trustees with collecting activities related to those of the museum. Evidently, it is an advantage for the museum to have trustees who are also collectors in its field, especially as it may result in future donations; however, since the museum itself is involved in the collecting field, it is important that the trustee should declare to the board his or her collecting activity and, of course, any related business interests. A record should be kept of any advice given to the trustee by staff members affecting his or her collecting activity, and the trustee should normally be expected to give the museum first refusal on collecting opportunities that arise. The code should require a trustee to withdraw from any deliberations affecting his or her business interests, or from which he or she might benefit, directly or indirectly. The code should also require confidentiality of the trustee, and collegiality with fellow trustees in pursuing the interests of the museum, as well as minimal requirements for attendance at meetings and museum functions.

It is important for the board to maintain appropriate relations with the museum director. The director recommends policies and plans to the board, implements approved policies and plans, and is responsible for the day-to-day management of the museum. The board should give the director unflinching support as long as its policies and plans are being implemented in a professional manner, and should not be involved in day-to-day administration. The board should expect from its director timely reports and recommendations, full disclosure of relevant information, and a commitment to the museum's mission that goes beyond personal enthusiasms or career goals.

Board relations with staff should be regulated by a board policy statement that may be included in the board's code of ethics. Normally, staff should report to the director, and the director should report to the board, except for staff who are delegated by the director to report to board committees. In a unionised museum there will be provisions for resolving grievances in a collective bargaining agreement. However, the code of ethics should provide for occasions of disagreement or conflict, whether these are professional concerns or grievances over employment conditions, so that the board may serve as an ultimate level of appeal within the institution. In such cases the policy should provide procedures so that the board can help to resolve the dispute in a constructive way that does not undermine the director, but responds judiciously to staff concerns in the light of the museum's mission and objectives.

# 2.3 | Museum Staff

In this section we describe the roles and responsibilities of the people who conduct the functions of the museum, define three alternative models of staff organisation, and consider issues of working conditions and job satisfaction.

## 2.3.1 THE ORGANISATION OF STAFF BY MUSEUM FUNCTION

The traditional organisation of museum staff, still found in some older museums, focused on curatorial departments determined by the academic disciplines represented within the collection. Each department might have not only its own curators, but also its own conservators, preparators and technicians. Such an approach resulted in the identification some years ago of as many as forty-five different systems of documentation in use at that time in the Victoria and Albert Museum.

The organisation of museum staff today usually responds to a wider range of functions than the curatorial, and relieves the curator of responsibility for many administrative and programming functions. In Figure 1.2 we presented the six museological functions as two sides of a triangle, or as two divergent directions, held together by an administrative hypotenuse. Directional arrows added to the lines of the triangle may serve to indicate the inherent stresses in this model, which the museum administration must strive to make a creative rather than a destructive tension:

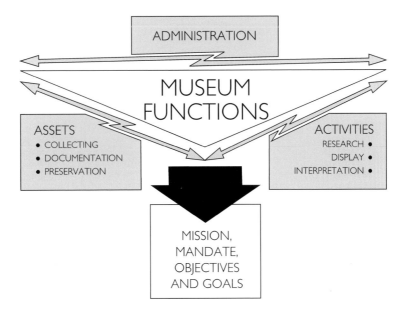

*Figure 2.1    The Dynamics of Museum Management*

Allowed to follow their own bent, each of the two divergent directions within the museum would contradict the other. The safety, preservation and documentation of the collection could best be accomplished in a building closed to the public, with large areas kept in the dark for most of the time; while the study, display and dissemination of information about the collection takes us in the opposite direction, toward maximising public access in brightly-lit, open displays, including hands-on programmes where possible. The task of the administration is to reconcile these two divergent aspects of the museum's functions, and to give their conjunction a positive and stimulating direction.

The triangle of museum functions suggests organisation of staff into three divisions – one concerned with the museum's assets, another with its activities, and the third with the administration of the other two. While the titles applied to such divisions vary, these are commonly used:

- collections
- public programmes
- administration

However, the existence of three distinct 'divisions' implies the need for cross-divisional and interdepartmental collaboration, as the examples below demonstrate.

- Limiting the 'assets' division to collection management functions tends to relegate site and building operations and maintenance to the administrative division. Since the security division is concerned with site and building operation, responsibility for this function is often located there as well. This means that curators and conservators must rely on these administrative departments to control the environment and safety of their collections, and they need to establish ways of working effectively with administration.

- Exhibitions are one of the principal activities or programmes of most museums. A few decades ago, they were almost exclusively developed – and certainly always directed – by curators. They evidently require significant participation by curators, registrars and conservators from the collection management division, as well as the involvement of designers, educators and others from the public programmes division. This has sometimes resulted in the creation of such posts as curator of exhibitions, or exhibition departments, where exhibition planners and designers work together but curators are consulted only when absolutely necessary. The administrative division is also concerned with exhibition development, ranging from security implications through cost controls to sponsorship and the provision of stock specific to the exhibition in the museum shop. Educational and publications programmes similarly require curatorial input, and administrative controls.

This issue of enabling staff to work across departments and divisions to fulfil museum functions is pervasive and significant enough to form an eighth criterion of museum management:

*Does management facilitate interdepartmental co-operation and teamwork to conduct museum functions and create programmes such as exhibitions?*

## 2.3.2 ORGANISATIONAL MODELS

The following alternative organisational models for museum staff highlight different ways in which museum management can overcome compartmentalisation and facilitate teamwork among museum staff:

- hierarchical pyramid
- matrix organisation
- task forces

These models are by no means exclusive, and may be used in combination as required in the life of the museum. Thus the organisation chart may be drawn as a hierarchical pyramid, with matrix organisation and/or task forces being introduced as necessary for specific functions or projects.

### 2.3.2.1 HIERARCHICAL PYRAMID

The HIERARCHICAL PYRAMID of authority is the form of organisation found in most museums around the world. Figure 2.2 illustrates the three-division museum organisation discussed in subsection 2.3.1.

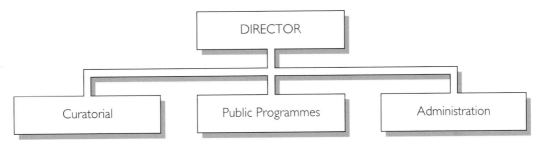

*Figure 2.2    Typical Three-division Organisation*

In a small museum, one or two persons may perform all functions. If only three or four staff can be hired, these functions must be distributed among them. In a larger museum, each division will have its own departments arranged to continue the hierarchy, as in the generic examples in Figures 2.3–2.5.

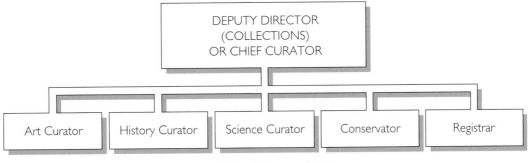

*Figure 2.3    Collections Division*

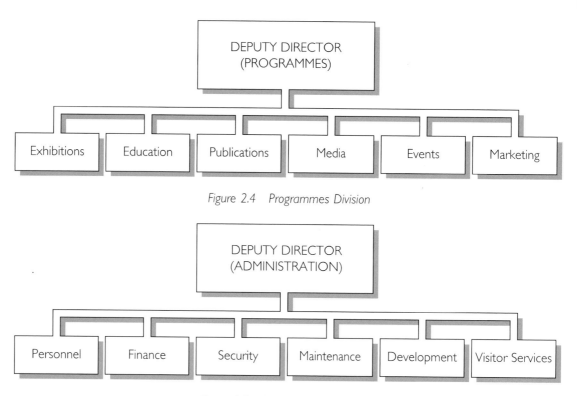

Figure 2.4 *Programmes Division*

Figure 2.5 *Administration Division*

Museums with smaller staffs will assign more than one of these responsibilities (and others in each division) to individuals, whereas larger museums will continue the hierarchical pyramid of each department as required. The following ORGANISATION CHARTS shown in Figures 2.6–2.9 assume a relatively large staff, but may, of course, be adapted for smaller organisations:

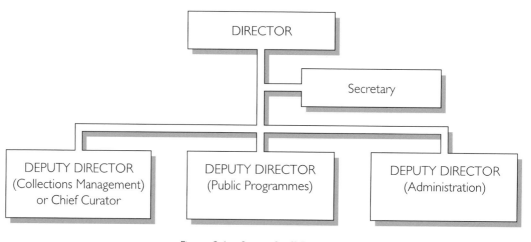

Figure 2.6 *Senior Staff Executive*

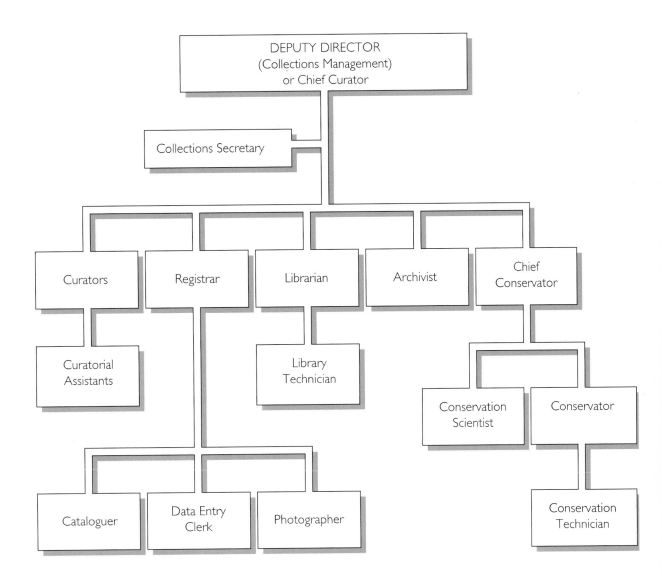

*Figure 2.7   Collections Division Organisation Chart*

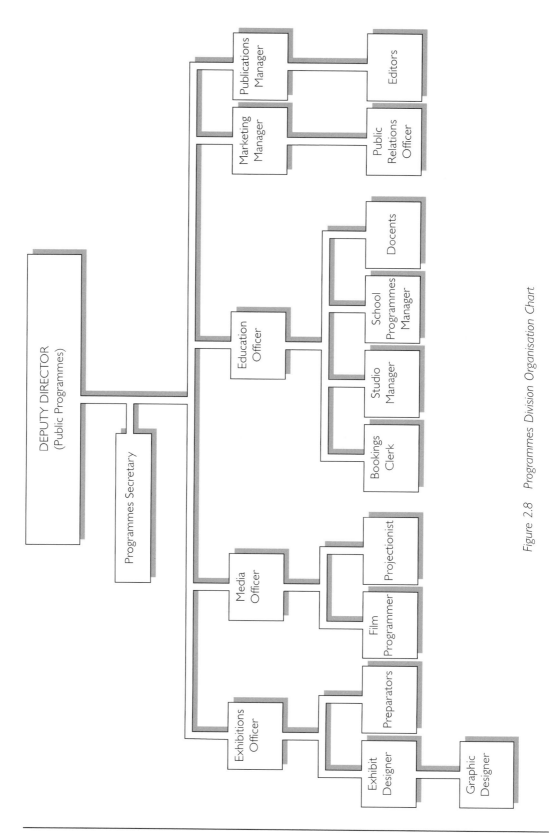

Figure 2.8  Programmes Division Organisation Chart

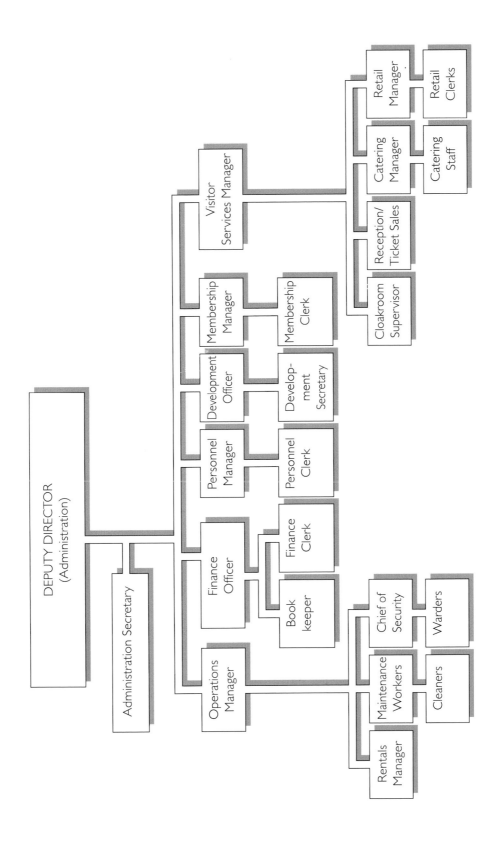

Figure 2.9   Administration Division Organisation Chart

## 2.3.2.2 MATRIX ORGANISATION

A matrix is a format in which functions are arranged as axes of interaction. Since administration serves the other two divisions, one application of MATRIX ORGANISATION to museum management could be expressed in the matrix in Table 2.2, with the provision of administrative services to each of these divisions marked with a solid bar.

Table 2.2   Administration Matrix

| Division | Personnel | Finance | Security | Maintenance |
|----------|-----------|---------|----------|-------------|
| Curatorial | | | | |
| Programmes | | | | |

Another application of matrix organisation to museum staff is the correlation of public programmes and collection management staff. Table 2.3 shows this matrix for three public programming functions, with a solid bar again indicating primary areas of intersecting service provision:

Table 2.3   Collection Management Matrix

| Programmes | Curators | Conservators | Registrar |
|------------|----------|--------------|-----------|
| Exhibitions | | | |
| Education | | | |
| Publications | | | |

Combining the two matrices would give the complete image of a cube, with all three divisions shown as three interacting axes, as in Figure 2.10 (see next page).

The successful interaction of all three visible sides of the cube provides for the most effective and efficient combination of the operative staff of a museum.

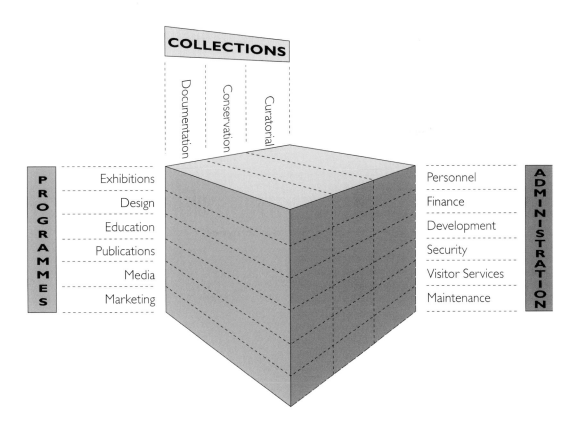

## 2.3.2.3 TASK FORCES

As subsection 2.3.2.2 on matrix organisation indicates, many museum activities, including such important ones as exhibition development, require the co-operation of departments from all three divisions. This can best be achieved by combining representatives of each department in *task forces* dedicated to particular projects.

Thus each major exhibition should be the task of a specific exhibition committee, a task force or project team that combines the talents of all those responsible for the many aspects of the exhibition project. (These are *staff* exhibition committees, not to be confused with the *board* exhibition committees discussed in subsection 2.2.2.)

Each exhibition committee should include representatives of the following divisions and departments:

- **Collection Management:**
- curation
- conservation
- documentation

- **Public Programmes:**
- exhibitions
- design
- education
- publications
- media
- marketing

- **Administration:**
- finance
- development
- security
- visitor services

Each department should be asked to nominate its representative. More important projects might require the attention of department chairpersons, whereas less critical projects should be seen as training opportunities in which junior members of each department can participate. Contracted participants – such as an exhibition designer engaged for a particular show – should also be nominated to the committee.

The museum director should have final approval on the composition of the task force, and should appoint the chair of the exhibition committee from among its members. Although the relevant curator might be the obvious nominee to chair many exhibition committees, some should be chaired by the exhibitions department representative, by the education representative or by the marketing or development representatives if audience development or membership recruitment are major focuses of the project. The committee may begin meeting monthly, should receive regular reports from all participants – so that security concerns, for example, are not left to the last minute – and should increase the frequency of its meetings as opening day nears. Crediting the members of the committee on exhibition literature or signage is an excellent way to inspire dedication to an outstanding result.

Similar task forces may be developed for projects in documentation, education, information technology, visitor services and audience development. The task force has proved to be a most useful way for museums to address their complex tasks, ensure that their professional expertise is well deployed, and provide opportunities for growth in staff members' responsibility and confidence.

### 2.3.3 JOB TITLES AND JOB DESCRIPTIONS

Many museums are operated entirely by volunteers, and many more have only one or a few paid staff. The functions outlined in this manual will have to be performed by these smaller numbers of personnel. Thus if only three paid personnel are provided, it is very likely that one will focus on collection management, one on public programmes and one on administration. The addition of staff to one division or another will reflect the museum's priorities.

The outline of job titles and job descriptions provided in the Appendix, however, assumes the appointment of all the posts listed in the organisation charts in subsection 2.3.2.1. It is unlikely that any museum would need all of these positions – it may be efficient to combine several posts into one – but the Appendix is intended to give a reasonably complete checklist.

Job titles vary around the world. In China, for example, one is likely to find 'researchers' doing what 'curators' do in a Western museum. One may also find 'box makers' fabricating the storage boxes for artefacts, a position not known in the West. The job titles listed in this subsection do not include such specialised employment, but are limited to the positions most commonly found internationally, with the job titles most commonly used in English in Western museums.

Even within these limits, there is considerable variation in terminology. The museum's chief executive, for instance, is usually called a 'director', but in some institutions may be called 'executive director', 'president', 'chief curator', 'curator', or even 'curator/director'. In the Appendix we have tried to list some of the variants, and have assumed that the museum is organised into the three divisions discussed in subsection 2.3.1, plus the director's office, assuming further that each division is headed by a deputy director, with the provision that the deputy director (collections) will in many instances be called 'chief curator'.

The number of positions also varies. Even in larger museums, some of the posts listed in the Appendix will not be needed, or will be filled by persons who also occupy other posts. In other places there will be more gradations, such as Assistant Curator positions between the rank of Curator and Curatorial Assistant. Notwithstanding all these qualifications, we hope that the list of job titles and job descriptions in the Appendix will be useful.

### 2.3.4 WORKING CONDITIONS

In the first part of the 20th century most people who worked in museums were amateurs in the best sense of the word, and many neither requested nor required payment for their work. In recent decades museum staff have struggled to be recognised as a profession, with commensurate working conditions and remuneration. While, in many parts of the world, museum staff have made significant advances in both pay and conditions of work, progress has been uneven. Many people who preserve and interpret the world's cultural and artistic heritage are still unable to earn a living wage, and struggle with poor working conditions.

No matter how financially constrained the museum may be, it should recognise the value of its staff by adopting a *personnel policy* that addresses, within the museum's means, such issues as:

- statutory regulations
- salaries
- benefits
- expenses provisions
- probationary periods
- hours of work and overtime
- statutory holidays, vacation, sick leave, maternity or paternity leave, and leave of absence
- training and professional development
- intellectual property provisions
- grievance and harassment procedures
- performance review
- termination conditions

CONTRACTING (sometimes referred to as 'contracting out') is often proposed as an alternative to permanent employment by the museum. It has worked well in catering, and some museums have used it successfully for cleaning, maintenance and security. A few local authorities have recently considered contracting out even the management of their museums. However, the museum's concern for long-term preservation of its collection and for dependable security means there are limits to this approach. Difficulties arise, especially if the museum must adhere to a government, university or corporation policy to select the lowest bidder on every contract. The lowest bidder for a security contract may be the most dangerous for a museum! Low-bid security contracts often result in poorly-paid, ill-trained and indifferently motivated warders or guards – with potentially disastrous consequences for the collection, and often enough for the visitors as well.

### 2.3.4.1 DIVERSITY

A particular concern for museums in multicultural or multiracial societies is to provide for a demographic distribution among museum employees that reflects the population distribution of the museum's community. Policies should be developed to encourage employment and promotion opportunities for women and members of minority groups. The result should be to make visitors of all ethnic backgrounds feel welcome, as well as providing a socially healthy basis for the museum profession.

Museums that preserve and display the culture of living societies must be particularly concerned to include members of those communities among their staff. In the case of disadvantaged groups, this may require special training programmes aimed at enhancing the opportunities for members of those communities to acquire the necessary professional or technical skills. The museums of South Africa, for instance, currently face the challenge of developing such training programmes for people who have only recently had the opportunity to take charge of the preservation and interpretation of their own culture.

## 2.3.4.2   TRAINING

TRAINING PROGRAMMES instruct employees in how to do their job, whereas EMPLOYEE DEVELOPMENT PROGRAMMES open up new opportunities for staff. Both may be organised in-house or may be provided by sponsoring (partially or fully) employee participation in courses run elsewhere. These may be museum training programmes from the introductory to the postgraduate level, or courses in a wide variety of professional pursuits, technical or management skills that may be useful to museum staff members in all posts. In the UK, the Museum Training Institute has been established as one of the institutions where relevant training is offered, whereas postgraduate programmes in museum studies at the University of Leicester or the University of London might be seen as either training or development opportunities.

Instituting a TRAINING AND DEVELOPMENT STRATEGY has always been important, but will become essential in the 21st century, as museums meet the challenge of constant change, ranging from museum philosophy through technology to public expectations and marketing requirements. The successful museum of the 21st century will provide a constant learning environment for its staff as well as its visitors. An important requirement of professional museum management is therefore to provide a training and development strategy that establishes general policies of support and is related to the specific needs of each individual, from the director to the maintenance staff. The strategy, updated annually, should identify the training needs of the museum, including provision for planned changes in direction, as well as the PERSONAL DEVELOPMENT PLANS of each individual, agreed in a consultative (and confidential) process of mutual identification of needs and resources. It is important for the director or the training officer (whoever is representing the museum) to ensure that the personal development plan meets the institution's requirements, rather than merely serving the career goals or enthusiasms of the individual employee.

One group who can benefit personally from a training and development strategy, and can then contribute far more to the employing museum, is the largest single sector on most museum rosters – the warders or security guards. Museums are only now beginning to recognise that these very numerous employees are also the ones who have the most frequent and prolonged contact with visitors: it is therefore most important that museums ensure that they understand what they are guarding, as well as how to guard it, and that they see a future for themselves within the institution.

Patrick Greene, Director of the Museum of Science and Industry in Manchester, has contributed Case Study 2.1, which describes the excellent staff training and development programmes related to customer care that he has developed there.

# The Culture of Change and Staff Training at the Museum of Science and Industry in Manchester

BY DR J PATRICK GREENE

## CUSTOMER CARE AND STAFF TRAINING

During the 1990s the concept of customer care has gained widespread, although not universal, acceptance in museums throughout the world. While numerous museums have embraced the idea that members of the public have rights and expectations that should be addressed, there are still many institutions that give the impression that visitors are an unwelcome distraction. The Museum of Science and Industry in Manchester identified customer care as a priority within three years of its first-phase opening in 1983. There was an opportunity to innovate in the rapidly-growing museum, developing in five large, historic, industrial buildings. Indeed, a culture of change was seen to be an essential characteristic of the organisation if it was to avoid the pitfalls of stagnation and departmentalisation that can afflict any institution, and to which museums seem to be particularly prone (Greene, 1994a). The antidote had three ingredients – the identification of corporate objectives with plans for their implementation; good communication throughout the organisation and beyond it; and training available to everyone connected with the museum such as staff, trustees and volunteers.

Corporate planning takes place on an annual basis, with contributions to the process from throughout the museum. The objectives for the year and for the longer term are communicated to all staff prior to the yearly assessment of training needs. Every member of staff has a personal development plan in which the needs of the individual and the organisation are addressed. The training plan is designed to meet needs across the organisation, with a target of providing 95 per cent coverage. There is an opportunity to identify particular priorities that are common to the organisation as a whole. One of these is customer care. An essential element in the development of the museum's customer care policy (Greene, 1994b) was the acceptance that every member of staff and volunteer contributes to the way in which the museum presents itself to its users, and also a consideration of 'who' customers are – for example, conference clients and internal customers. It follows that every person's performance can benefit from training in this area, not just those who work in front-of-house posts.

The communication of the fundamental importance of customer care is essential if the benefits of policies and training are to be realised. In a relatively small organisation (96 full-time posts, 24 part-time and 60 volunteers each week) it is possible for communication to be achieved effectively through a team-briefing system, newsletters and staff meetings, supplemented by less formal methods in an organisation that encourages an open style of management. People working at the museum realise that for the museum to achieve the goals embodied in its mission statement requires a wholehearted commitment to anticipating and meeting the needs of a wide variety of users. Furthermore, it is also recognised that the interests and requirements of people can change rapidly, so it is necessary to monitor the response of the public, to evaluate projects in advance, and to be prepared to modify or change from existing practice and preconceptions. Increasingly, it is those organisations which succeed in adopting a customer focus that flourish; museums rely on the support of large numbers of customers to fulfil their mission and survive financially. These truths can be readily understood by staff, volunteers and board members.

The extent to which a museum has succeeded in achieving quality corporate planning, communications and training should be tested by scrutiny by an external body. In the UK, the Investors in People (IIP) scheme was launched by the government to encourage high standards in these areas, and is open to any type of organisation. The Museum of Science and Industry in Manchester was the first museum to be recognised under the IIP scheme, and subsequently gained a Charter Mark through the Citizen's Charter Initiative to encourage customer care in publicly-funded bodies. Both IIP and Charter Mark status are subject to review every three years. No organisation can afford to be complacent, for it is possible for high standards achieved in one year to be quickly eroded by lack of continuing commitment. Without the demonstrable support and involvement of board members, the director and senior managers, customer care will be regarded as merely peripheral.

**References**

J P Greene, 'Museums for the year 2000: a case for continuous revolution' in G Kavanagh (ed.) *Museum Provision and Professionalism*, London: Routledge, 1994a.
J P Greene, 'Creating a climate for customer care' in S Runyard (ed.) *The Museum Marketing Handbook*, London: HMSO, 1994b, pp 124–7.

*The Museum of Science & Industry in Manchester, 1995.*
*Photograph by Jean Horsfall, courtesy of the Museum of Science & Industry. AE 20 25A*

## 2.3.4.3 Performance reviews

Performance reviews of all staff should be directed toward evaluation of both effectiveness and efficiency in the employee's accomplishment of museum functions, in relation to the museum's goals and objectives. The priority and weight given to various factors should be adjusted annually according to current goals and objectives. The employee should complete a self-evaluation as part of the performance review, and all review records should be held in confidence. The review should include both quantitative ratings and qualitative comments, and should be linked to consideration of promotion and annual salary increments. The review should be carried out in consultation with the employee's immediate supervisor and with one more senior officer. The file on previous reviews, especially that of the previous year, should be re-read by the employee and supervisors participating in the review before each year's consultation.

## 2.3.4.4 The role of unions

In this realistic context of museums as relatively low-paid employment centres where professional recruitment and evaluation procedures, and especially training and development opportunities, can compensate somewhat for the low level of remuneration, trade unions may be seen as supportive forces in the workplace. In general, their pressure for higher pay can only benefit the profession, and they can be a powerful force for employment equity and improved training and development opportunities.

Unfortunately, trade union membership is too often confined to the security staff, where misguided, confrontational policies on both the union and management sides can lead to the imposition of civil service or equivalent procedures that can result in inefficient operations. One government line department museum in Europe, for example, must contend with extended lunch hours and breaks that necessitate doubling the number of warders (security guards) which would otherwise be required for its operation – this results in the regular closure of galleries to visitors. On the other hand, Case Study 2.2 by Mike Leber, Principal Museums Officer of the Salford Museum Service, demonstrates that unions can be co-operative in redefining posts and improving the service to the public.

Another difficulty often encountered, both for the museums and their unions, is the proliferation of multiple unions within one institution. The necessity to conclude separate *collective bargaining agreements* with several unions, often on different schedules, can challenge even the most dedicated personnel department – not to mention the complexities of multiple *grievance procedures*. If the union certification legislation in the museum's jurisdiction provides for separate unionisation for warders, clerks and technicians, for example, the museum may wish to encourage co-operation both among and with its unions to minimise the potentially harmful effects of more or less perpetual negotiations through co-ordination of agreement schedules and grievance procedures.

Unionised or not, museum personnel are sometimes concerned about the role of volunteers if these museum supporters appear to be supplanting staff positions. It is important to ensure that volunteer recruitment aims to facilitate tasks that supplement those that the paid workforce can undertake. For instance, if the education department is mandated to train volunteer docents, interaction between the professional trainers and the volunteers should not be a problem; but if the volunteers are replacing former paid educators, there will almost certainly be strife. Section 2.4 addresses the role of volunteers.

# Creating New Opportunities for Front-line Staff at the Salford Museum Service

BY MIKE LEBER

The transition of role from the traditional museum attendant to the front-line museum assistant began more than ten years ago in the Salford Museum Service, and is an ongoing process. Its origins lie in a genuine desire to improve visitor service and to increase job fulfilment.

It was necessary, firstly, to demolish the barrier between 'white collar' professional staff and 'blue collar' attendant manual workers. All staff employed in the museum section came under the same conditions of service.

This was followed by an honest appraisal and recognition that front-line staff had a key role in museum development and a vested interest in the success of the service. No false promises were made, particularly on pay (although significant progress has been made). The emphasis is placed on personal development, the exploitation of neglected skills, greater flexibility and enhanced job satisfaction.

While there was a clear aim to develop skills, it was also conceded that the pace of change would vary on an individual basis. Some attendants were incapable of making the switch, but these were gradually replaced. Others lacked confidence or required constant reassurance. However, most were willing – indeed demanded – to be given the opportunity to contribute.

Museum assistants have taken on a host of roles, from guiding groups to giving 'costumed' talks, from active involvement in workshops and activities to organising functions, from leading on merchandising matters to hanging exhibitions. In so doing, they have created and fulfilled vital new service provision and contributed to income generation. The importance of their contribution is recognised at all levels of the organisation and, as a result, they play an active part in developing the service.

It would be foolish to suppose that all this has been achieved without encountering problems. One acute area of difficulty has been in training, which, in general, has lagged behind the needs of more progressive museums. Thus conventional attendant training is ignored, and reliance is placed on identifying good practice, in-house training, workplace skills and personal development. In addition, there are regular in-depth sessions on front-line work.

This aside, there have not been, to date, any industrial disputes or the frantic waving of job descriptions. The service is still evolving the concept, but can already boast a highly committed workforce – flexible, responsive, involved, responsible and valued – a transition which has been achieved through creative management and the support and enthusiasm of the staff involved.

*Salford Museum attendant providing a hands-on demonstration to a school party.*

# 2.4 | The Role of Volunteers

Volunteers are vital to the life of many museums, especially those operated by non-profitmaking or charitable organisations. Some museum workers believe that volunteers are not cost-effective, because they require too much staff time for training and evaluation. This can be the case if the volunteer programme is not well organised and controlled. If properly constituted, however, a volunteer workforce can simultaneously link the museum to its community and provide invaluable support to the museum.

Museums in the start-up stage of development are frequently governed by volunteers (the board), managed by a volunteer director and operated by volunteers. This is a particularly challenging situation, in which there are distinct roles and a hierarchy, but all are equally unpaid. It becomes even more challenging when the museum begins to raise enough funds to hire paid staff. In all stages of museum development and in all sizes of museums, it is important to be aware of the distinct roles and responsibilities of volunteers:

- Board members are volunteers who are engaged in governance.
- A volunteer director is engaged in management.
- Task volunteers are engaged in unpaid staff positions.

This section is concerned with this latter category of volunteers, who play numerous roles in museums, including:

- DOCENTS, the most commonly encountered volunteer role, who enable the museum to provide guided tours of its collection to school parties and other groups;
- HOSTS, whose duties range from general visitor reception to making special events possible by providing food services or refreshments;
- RETAIL SALES CLERKS, who allow smaller institutions to run museum shops that can contribute significantly to museum revenue;
- RESEARCH ASSISTANTS, who undertake systematic research tasks for which staff time would otherwise not be available;
- LIBRARY ASSISTANTS, who undertake time-consuming sorting and shelving in museum libraries;
- DATA ENTRY CLERKS, who assist the registrar with the conversion of manual to automated catalogue entries;
- RESTORATION TECHNICIANS, who often work enthusiastically in transport museums, but require careful professional supervision.

Museums that utilise volunteers in these or other roles should address them as workers who are paid not with wages, but with other rewards – of *individual development*, and of *social recognition*. The organisation of volunteers must ensure that both of these rewards are attainable.

The first reward, individual development, indicates that volunteers should also be part of the museum's training and development strategy. A volunteer co-ordinator is essential. The volunteer co-ordinator (who may be paid or voluntary) should maintain a roster on which the training needs and development aspirations of each volunteer are recorded, and the museum should undertake to assist the volunteer in this development – not financially, but through providing training opportunities.

The second reward, social recognition, should be provided by the museum both on an ongoing, day-to-day basis and by means of annual or seasonal social occasions which the senior staff and board members of the institution attend, in order to present certificates or similar printed recognition of services rendered by the volunteers. The museum that understands the importance of volunteers will ensure that its senior staff and board members participate fully in such a recognition meeting, and that virtually all volunteers are recognised for their contribution.

Recruitment of volunteers should be undertaken with the same care as recruitment of staff. Volunteer posts should be advertised, with job descriptions and the qualifications required listed, and those interested should fill out a volunteer application form. A *volunteer manual* that links the museum's mission and mandate to the museum's volunteer policy and to practical details pertaining to the daily work of volunteers (such as provision for out-of-pocket expenses) should be made available to those expressing an interest. For museums with membership programmes, it is important to insist that only members can volunteer, and that any volunteer committee must be part of the membership organisation.

Interviews of potential volunteers should aim to determine the volunteer's interests, abilities and training needs, as well as communicating the museum's requirements. References should be taken and checked, and health and criminal records investigated, following the same personnel procedures as for any prospective employee. Less promising candidates should be politely declined in a letter thanking them for their interest. Some may be redirected to volunteering for tasks other than the post for which they applied.

Aspiring volunteers should then be offered a *volunteer agreement* (sometimes called a 'volunteer contract', although it cannot be legally binding), which should match the needs of the museum to the volunteer's circumstances, committing them to work on particular days and at certain times for a specified period. To ensure fulfilment of this contract, the volunteer should be enrolled in the appropriate training programme, provided by the museum's education department or other qualified staff; this course should include examinations, both theoretical and practical in nature, and it should be anticipated that some would-be volunteers will fail. Those who pass should be evaluated regularly, and further training and development should be planned. A trial engagement (three to six months), the length of notice required in case of the volunteer's resignation, and the museum's provisions in case of unsatisfactory performance should all be set out in the volunteer agreement.

Long experience with volunteers has shown that such a programme can be effective in recruiting, training and maintaining a volunteer contingent with *esprit de corps* and commitment to the institution, constantly developing their own abilities, and gaining the rewards of social recognition as well. Far from resisting such procedures, volunteers welcome the diligence with which their efforts are treated, and respond with a higher quality of work and dependable attendance. With such a programme, the privilege of volunteering may proudly be added to the benefits of museum membership, and the museum will flourish with the full support of an active volunteer base.

# 3

# HOW

## Methods of Museum Management

We are now ready to proceed to the methods of managing a museum. This long chapter answers the often challenging question, 'How?'

The triangle of museum functions described in Chapters 1 and 2 shows the management of assets and the direction of public programmes as two divergent sides of the triangle, held together – hopefully in creative tension – by administration. Leadership to impart movement to the entire triangle, giving it the direction towards accomplishment of the museum's mission, is the responsibility of the museum's chief executive officer, usually the director. This chapter therefore begins with the role of the executive within museum management (3.1).

# 3.1 | The Executive Role

The director's role includes planning, policy formulation, approving procedures and developing and maintaining relations with other institutions. It will be noted that most of these management functions are shared with the board of trustees. That is why it is often said that an effective director spends 50 per cent of his or her time working with the board. This section reviews each of these executive roles. How they are implemented will influence all aspects of museum operations and, in effect, create the museum's *corporate culture*.

## 3.1.1 PLANNING

The director is responsible for the disposition of a wide range of resources – collections, buildings, people and funds. Planning is the primary means of determining how these resources should be deployed.

A CORPORATE PLAN (sometimes called a 'business plan' or a 'strategic plan') is the most general level of planning, drafted with the purpose of organising all aspects of a museum's activities into a co-ordinated direction, articulated as goals to be achieved in the planning period. The mission, mandate and current objectives and goals, as described in Chapter 1, should be identified in the corporate plan and detailed for each museum division, along with a financial plan, including a budget and fund raising targets if necessary, to achieve the objectives and goals during the planning period. If the plan is an update, progress on objectives and goals identified in previous plans should be reviewed. In addition to their value for internal management of the institution, corporate plans are very often used as supporting documents for funding or grant applications.

Since long-range planning is a role shared by board and management, corporate plans are generally prepared by a committee made up of management and trustees led by the director, and often assisted by consultants. It is important that all those who are expected to participate in the implementation of the corporate plan are consulted in its preparation and view the resultant plan as their own because it takes their concerns and ideas into account. Clearly, all ideas will not be included in the final document, but the planning process should clarify why certain goals and objectives took priority over others, and the director should be prepared to explain and discuss these matters frankly with staff, volunteers and trustees. Corporate plans that are imposed from outside or above without this consultation are often resisted (if not merely shelved), whereas when long-range or strategic plans are formulated through consensus, there is the potential to elicit the wholehearted co-operation of all.

*Performance indicators* (PIs) may be included in a corporate plan. Performance indicators may include statistics, ratios, costs or other ways of measuring the museum's or the museum workers' progress in achieving the goals and objectives of the organisation, as established by the corporate plan. Performance indicators can provide an objective and quantitative measure of some aspects of a programme that may contribute to its evaluation. Cost per visitor or revenue per visitor are common examples, but others may be much more refined. They must be used with caution, however, since they usually do not account for the quality of the visitor's experience. Robert Bud, writing in the *Museums Journal* ('Measuring a Museum's Output', *Museums Journal*, vol. 91, no. 1, January 1991, pp 29–31), compared them to a can opener: not very interesting in themselves, but valuable in opening up matters for you to consider.

STRATEGIC PLAN describes both a type of plan and the planning process to arrive at that plan. This planning process involves determining the best future for an organisation by studying its situation in a changing environment through the use of both external and internal consultation and research. *External* consultation – including interviews with cultural, political and business leaders or other members of the community, 'workshop' meetings with people who support or use the museum such as donors, funders, teachers, and frequent visitors, and focus groups with those who do not use the museum – helps planners understand the museum's public role, how it serves the community, where it fails, and how it can be improved. *Internal* consultation includes interviews and workshops with staff, volunteers, members and trustees and helps in assessing the institution's strengths and weaknesses in relation to the museum's mission, and the opportunities and threats facing it. 'Retreats' are extended meetings at which trustees and senior staff withdraw for a day or more to:

- consider long-range directions and key issues and challenges, both within the institution and in its global environment;

- review the mission statement, and revise it if necessary;

- identify a relatively small number of strategic directions (usually no more than three to five) that can then be translated into institutional goals (as defined in section 1.2.).

The specific objectives (described in sub-section 1.3.4) for each division or department, along with the budget and timetable, are developed by management and staff. The strategic plan as a whole is finalised by the board. It will then be implemented by the entire institution, and progress should be evaluated annually to ensure that the organisation stays on target, or that the plan is amended.

The strategic plan usually covers a period of three to five years, and may be the 'ignition' for other planning activities, such as a master plan if some major capital development is foreseen.

A MASTER PLAN is more long-term (ten to twenty years) and more detailed than a strategic plan, and focuses on the museum's resource requirements of space, facilities, personnel and funding and the means of fulfilling them. It should include the following elements:

- *institutional plan*, addressing both the museum's governance structure and its relations with its entire institutional context (government, educational institutions, other museums, private sector, tourism, etc.), as well as the museum's mission, mandate and statement of purpose;

- *market analysis*, which may comprise the results of visitor surveys as well as demographic and sociographic analyses of the community – resident, school and tourist – with the aim of identifying the museum's target markets;

- *collection analysis*, projecting growth as well as describing the present dimensions and directions for the museum's collecting activities, including current and desired levels of density of display and storage of the collections, and issues of collection management and care;

- *public programme plan*, projecting the activities that the museum wishes to undertake, or describing those it has been undertaking, ranging from exhibitions through interpretation of its collection to education, publications, extension services, outreach and such public amenities as toilets, shops or catering, in relation to the museum's target markets;

- *marketing strategy*, dedicated to attracting those target markets to the museum, not merely through advertising but through customer services and activities that will meet the museum's objectives and motivate visitors to return;

- *staffing plan*, projecting requirements for personnel in order to operate the desired level of public programmes with the collection resource identified;

- *accommodations plan*, deducing the space and facilities required for the collections in store and on display, for the public programmes and amenities, and for support facilities and work spaces for staff;

- *capital cost projection*, forecasting the amount needed to upgrade or build the space required, to provide furnishings and equipment, or to build the planned exhibits;

- *attendance, revenue and expense projections*, forecasting all sources of income and categories of expenditure, with a view to identifying the need for subsidy or other fundraising;

- *funding strategy*, to meet both capital and operating fund requirements from public, private and self-generated sources;

- *implementation schedule*, designed to move the museum from its present situation to the one outlined in the master plan.

The interconnectedness of the components outlined in this description demonstrates the benefits of completing the entire master plan. However, when no major capital development programme is foreseen, it may be useful to undertake only some of the component parts – for example, a collection development strategy or an institutional plan – for sectors that are considered to be weak relative to the museum's mission and goals, and need to be improved.

For proposed new museums, relocations or expansions, a FEASIBILITY STUDY would cover the same ground as the master plan, except that it should conclude with a statement of the project's feasibility. This must be based on a set of assumptions about the quality and size of the proposed institution, its location, marketing, management, freedom from debt, and so on. Feasibility of museums is not the same as feasibility of a private sector project, where profit is the criterion; for public museums, it is usually a question of establishing the level of annual subsidy, grant aid or other fundraising that would be required beyond the potential for self generated revenues, and a judgement as to the likelihood of such annual financial support.

Plans developed as a method of managing specific activities – such as exhibition plans (3.3.1), education plans (3.3.3) and marketing plans (3.3.6) – are the shared responsibility of management and staff (not of management and board) and will therefore be considered later in this chapter.

## 3.1.2  POLICIES

While plans are a method of management directed primarily towards future accomplishment, POLICIES are instrumental to regulating both the fulfilment of present museum functions and the achievement of a desired future condition at the requisite level of quality. Policies are formulated in order to ensure standards of quality and public accountability in the accomplishment of museum functions, and are therefore a shared responsibility of management and board, in which management, through the director, is responsible for policy formulation and for presentation of policy options to the board, and the trustees are responsible for ensuring that the policies are consistent with the museum's mission and goals and that the institution has the resources needed to implement them.

The precise number of museum policies varies, as do the terms used to describe them. Among the policies required by most museums are:

- *collection policy* (sometimes called 'collection management policy'), including acquisition, de-accessioning and loan policies;
- *conservation policy*, which may be included in a collection management policy;
- *documentation policy*, another which may be part of the collection policy;
- *education policy*;
- *exhibition policy*;
- *personnel policy*;
- *public access policy*, including policy on access for the disabled;
- *interpretation policy*, which may include publications and media;
- *research policy*, which should also include policy on intellectual property;
- *security policy*;
- *visitor services or customer care policy*.

Policies should identify the museum's goals in relation to each of these functions, and should establish the level of quality to which the museum is committed in the implementation of its policies and plans. Since policies relate to specific functions, they should be drafted by the senior staff responsible – for instance, the chief of security should be asked to draft the security policy – with the director serving as editor and participating in any revision required to align the policy with the museum's plans.

Policies should be recommended by the director to the board. They should not express professional standards that are unrealistic in terms of the museum's budget, space, technology or staff limitations, but should project attainable levels of excellence in each function, given the museum's mission and resources. They should be comprehensive, relating to all implications of the fulfilment of that function.

Once approved by the trustees, policy implementation becomes a staff responsibility, delegated to the respective managers for each policy area. However, trustees retain responsibility for monitoring the policies, so the director should report regularly to the board on their implementation, with recommendations for policy changes, if required, in order to ensure that no museum functions are neglected, and that policies are more than wishful thinking. Since many museums find that they need about ten to twelve major policies, it is convenient to review and report on one policy per month: thus a board that meets monthly may consider a different policy document and a report on its implementation, along with any recommendations for changes, at each meeting – collection policy in January, exhibition policy in February, security policy in March, and so on – ensuring that, through the year, all policies have been considered, reviewed and changed, if necessary. In this way, the board retains an energetic role in the governance of museum functions, and policies remain relevant and implementable.

### 3.1.3   PROCEDURES

A museum's PROCEDURES are its established ways of doing things. Many museum functions must be discharged in a systematic way – such as documentation of a new accession, or security measures. The *procedures manual* is the main means of codifying and communicating the systematic means of conducting museum functions and related tasks.

Like policies, procedures are related to museum functions, but they are more specific and more quantified, because they are linked to the attainment of objectives for those functions, whereas policies are related to goals. Procedures manuals record the steps in an activity recommended by the museum in order to realise the level of quality stipulated in its policies. The subject matter of procedures manuals may range from welcoming and ticketing procedures through documentation forms and condition reporting to security routines and – particularly important – should include an *emergency procedures manual*.

One area where procedures manuals should be used with special caution is in customer service. It is important to remember that each visitor is an individual, and that the service required by that individual visitor may or may not have been anticipated in the visitor service or customer care manual. Staff serving the visitors – including security guards or warders – should be reminded regularly that service to the individual visitor, as long as it is within the guidelines of the museum's policies, may override the strictures of a procedures manual.

Curatorial research, exhibition planning and design are examples of other areas where procedures manuals may not be appropriate. Even here, however, there may be certain segments of the work that can best be accomplished by following a set routine which will most often obtain the level of quality desired. Library practices, for example, may benefit from being the subject of a procedures manual.

Procedures manuals should be prepared by the responsible museum officer, who may find that many manuals are required to provide guidance for all the activities which occur in their department. Procedures manuals are often simply a point-form listing of steps that any employee, including a new recruit, should follow in carrying out a specific activity; but they should always link those steps to the quality level articulated in the relevant policy. They should be consistent with that policy, and should be reviewed and approved by the director, who should ensure that they will result in implementation of the policy. Whenever the policy is changed, therefore, the procedures manual should be updated. The relationship between plans, policies and procedures as methods of management is summarised in Table 3.1.

*Table 3.1    Methods of Management*

| Management Method | Relevant to | Time reference | Drafted by | Approval by |
|---|---|---|---|---|
| *Plans* | Mission & goals & objectives | Future | Director & management | Trustees |
| *Policies* | Functions & goals | Present & future | Director & management | Trustees |
| *Procedures* | Functions & objectives | Immediate & present | Staff | Director |

## 3.1.4    RELATIONS WITH OTHER INSTITUTIONS

The most inspired plans, excellent policies and impeccable procedures may not avail if the museum is not functioning effectively in its institutional context. Museums are not isolated institutions, but in almost all cases exist within a network of related agencies, both public and private. The other institutions that impinge on museums usually include:

- levels of government and government agencies (3.1.4.1)
- other museums and museum associations (3.1.4.2)

- educational institutions (3.1.4.3)

- specialist societies and foundations (3.1.4.4)

- the tourist industry (3.1.4.5)

- the private sector (3.1.4.6)


### 3.1.4.1   LEVELS OF GOVERNMENT AND GOVERNMENT AGENCIES

Museums are inherently 'political' institutions: history museums communicate the meaning of our past, art museums present works of art that often comment on the meaning or values of our personal and social lives, and science museums interpret what we think we know about the world around us. Museums are intensively involved in communicating values and ideologies about the meaning of their collections. These ideologies are usually implicit, but they can become explicit very quickly in the case of a temporary exhibition on a politically sensitive subject – or one that suddenly becomes sensitive because of the content of the exhibition.

In addition, museums are often funded by, or form part of, a government service. Whether they are government line departments or independent, non-profitmaking associations, museums are often dependent on government funding programmes and policies, including many complex tax policies.

Museum management must be concerned with the museum's position in relation to city, county, state or provincial and national government – not only to ministries or departments responsible for culture and heritage, but also those concerned with tourism, education and taxes; if the museum's mandate touches on science, defence, transportation or agriculture, these government departments may become important as well. In many jurisdictions, the ministry or department administering employment grants is among the most important to the museum. Managing the museum's relationship with government is a major responsibility of the museum's director and trustees.

In some jurisdictions one national, state or provincial museum has been assigned responsibility for the administration of the general museums service, or the distribution of grant aid to other museums. This often leads to perceived conflict-of-interest problems, at least in the eyes of the other museums, so that it is usually preferable to establish a separate administration for grants, and often for other centralised services as well. These museum-centred government line departments, or quasi-governmental agencies responsible for museums, have in many instances developed a high level of professionalism in assisting museums. Government agencies like the Museums and Galleries Commission in the UK have established accreditation or registration programmes that have been instrumental in encouraging or requiring museum trustees to ensure that their institutions meet professional standards. The Canadian Heritage Information Network and the Canadian Conservation Institute are government agencies that have established internationally recognised standards. Independent organisations – such as the UK Museums Documentation Association, and, in the USA, the Getty Conservation Institute and the

Museum Computer Network – are actively involved in research and setting standards. Museums in historic buildings may also be concerned to meet standards established by their own or other countries' national trusts or parks administrations.

In recent years many governments faced with fiscal restraints have moved to make museums more self-reliant in obtaining funds. Museums that were formerly 'free' to the public may find admission charges necessary. Others may be obliged to develop their shops, catering or rentals, and may need to seek increasing numbers of donors or sponsorships in the private sector. Managing such transitions is often challenging, and can be much more effective if the museum maintains a positive relationship with government, for in many cases government can provide important help of a non-monetary nature, such as providing buildings, or grounds and maintenance staff.

Another long-term concern is the government's attitude towards museum expansion. Growing collections constantly generate the need for more space. Politicians and government officials may view such tendencies with alarm, especially in times of fiscal restraint; yet in periods of high unemployment, especially in regions with chronic employment problems, the responsible development of museums or historic sites as cultural tourist attractions may be a politically expedient and meaningful initiative that can be launched with government support. In some places, such as Glasgow, museums have become part of a government programme to change the image as well as the economic basis of a community.

### 3.1.4.2 OTHER MUSEUMS AND MUSEUM ASSOCIATIONS

Museums are not directly competitive in the sense that private sector attractions sometimes are. Because a very high proportion of museum visitors also visit similar or related museums in the same area or elsewhere, museums do not compete with each other, but can stimulate greater interest and activity among all their visitors, even when they have related or overlapping mandates in the same market.

Thus museums have everything to gain by co-operation with other museums: this may involve *partnerships* with similar museums, or *pairing* for marketing purposes with entirely dissimilar ones, in order to reach a wider audience. A military or transportation museum, for instance, might find advantages in forming a marketing partnership with a decorative arts museum nearby, so that both might widen their market by offering a mutual discount on each other's entry fees.

Sharing exhibitions, either on an individual basis or via area organisations such as a regional museums' association, is a longstanding means of co-operation among museums. More recently, the possibility of sharing collections has been actively pursued by two American foundations that facilitate long-term loans from the stores of major art museums to regional museums. In England, the National Gallery loans pictures to regional museums, and the Tate Gallery has established branches at Liverpool, St Ives and Norwich to make its collections more accessible. International examples of collection sharing, such as the Guggenheim Museum's project to establish a branch in Bilbao, have yet to be proven effective at the time of writing.

Projects to provide equipment or training in conservation, documentation, display techniques or other specialised skills to museums in developing countries in return for the loan of exhibitions drawn from their collections have proven most fruitful. The Asian Art Museum of San Francisco, for example, provided assistance in conservation to the museum professionals of Mongolia in return for their outstanding 1995 loan exhibition of Mongolian artefacts.

Many museums and museum professionals relate to their colleague institutions through museum associations. At regional, state, provincial and national levels, these have been instrumental in the development of the profession, in English-speaking countries especially. Their conferences, seminars and publications are among the most important means of training and professional development for their members, both as institutions and as individuals. Some, like the American Association of Museums, have established accreditation or registration programmes that have succeeded in raising professional standards for both institutions and individuals.

The International Council of Museums (ICOM) is the world-wide equivalent. In some countries, the national chapter of ICOM plays a similar role to that of museum associations elsewhere. For others, the specialised international committees of ICOM, such as the International Council on Conservation (ICC) or the International Association of Transportation and Communications Museums (IATM), are vital links with fellow professionals or institutions with related concerns. The triennial conferences of ICOM, the annual meetings of its international committees, its journal, *Museums International*, and the many newsletters of its committees are, for many, the very lifeblood of the profession. ICOM's ethical standards and guidelines help to support professional practices in many countries.

The influence of ICOM has been restricted in some countries by the practice of appointing only a few representatives to attend conferences, instead of encouraging membership throughout the profession. Democratising ICOM membership, and encouraging widespread participation in its committees through its publications, is of long-term importance in the development of the museum profession in these countries.

### 3.1.4.3 Educational institutions

Educational services are usually an important part of a museum's institutional role – sometimes in the view of government, and almost always in fulfilling its own sense of mission. The museum's relationship with universities, colleges and schools at all levels is therefore another important dimension of its institutional context that requires adroit management. The possibilities may range from cross-appointments of professors for museum research or curatorial duties to signing a contract with the local school board to provide a certain number of tours to school parties for a fixed level of reimbursement throughout the school year. Some museums have found it advantageous to propose a 'time-share' agreement with schools, whereby the museum is open every morning, for instance, only to school groups for their educational use. Museums can also participate in teacher training programmes, with teachers in training receiving course credits for well-prepared school tours of exhibitions.

In establishing relationships with educational institutions, the museum director or education officer should remember that the museum can be an excellent venue for *informal* learning, while schools and universities usually provide the best setting for *formal* education. Retaining this distinction of roles usually helps to ensure that each institution does what it can do best, without attempting to supplant the other.

### 3.1.4.4  Specialist societies and foundations

Museum research programmes, such as field archaeology activities, are sometimes rooted in their relationships with universities. Others may be developed with special interest groups, such as an entomological society or a local historical association. Public programmes may be developed with a broad range of groups, from local Scout troops to cultural or linguistic minority associations. Committed museum managers should continually explore the museum's potential to extend its services by working closely with community organisations of all kinds.

In some cases such co-operation may have important fundraising implications. This is especially true of working with funding foundations that have special interests. Some of these, like the Getty Foundation or the Gulbenkian Foundation, have programmes that are focused exclusively on museums, whereas others have broader educational or research objectives that the museum can meet. Museum managers constantly need to be aware of the prospects for working with national or international foundations of relevance to them.

### 3.1.4.5  The tourist industry

As museums are obliged to become more self-reliant, many are taking a greater interest in tourism. With international tourism emerging at the turn of the century as the world's biggest industry, and with cultural tourism increasingly recognised as a dynamic sector of that industry, museums must take full advantage of their prominent roles as tourist attractions. Even relatively small museums can play a part in extending visitors' length of stay in a region of otherwise limited appeal, and the director should communicate to political and business leaders the significance of the museum's tourism role.

Co-operation between museums and the tourism industry is therefore of vital importance to both. In general, staff in cultural institutions, including museums, have had limited understanding of – or even sympathy for – their tourist markets, and they often barely tolerate tourism operators. These operators, in turn, are often unaware of the realities facing the museums and other cultural attractions on which they are dependent for their livelihood. Wherever possible, museums should take the lead in bridging this gap, learning to work with tourism operators to mutual advantage.

Tourism has many motivations – visiting family or friends, sports, business or shopping – but cultural tourism is among the strongest of them, and can easily be combined with any or all of the others. Thus it is important for museums to seek ways to include themselves in the tourist industry – a discounted museum ticket or a special offer at the museum shop provided at a hotel check-in can be beneficial for everyone, including the tourist!

*Renewable tourism* is an important concept that is being developed in many of the more responsible tourist attraction centres. It stems from the recognition that tourism can be destructive of the very resource that attracts it – as perhaps most tellingly demonstrated at the world's great historical or archaeological sites. The imposition of special taxes on hotels, restaurants or other businesses benefiting from tourism, passing on the revenue directly to those responsible for the preservation of the heritage, is one way that tourism and the cultural or heritage sectors can work together to ensure that tourism becomes a truly renewable resource industry.


### 3.1.4.6   THE PRIVATE SECTOR

The tourism industry is only one area within the private sector that is of interest to museum managers today. Museum membership programmes increasingly include *corporate memberships* that encourage companies to join in return for such benefits as free admission for employees, discounts at the museum shop or reduced hire charges for meeting spaces. The company's association with the museum is often acknowledged on a plaque near the entrance.

The private sector can also be important as a source of donations or sponsorships. Museums seeking such support need to develop a *sponsorship policy* in order to ensure that their standards of scholarship and objectivity are not compromised by the sponsors' interests. This has proven important, for example, among science centres with commercial sponsors for exhibitions affecting consumer preferences, such as exhibits on food or health choices. If such a policy is clearly articulated and understood by all from the beginning, sponsorships can allow the staging of exhibitions and fund publications or other programmes that could not otherwise be attempted.

Sponsorships need not be on a grand scale. One public art gallery in western Canada, for instance, has had success in developing an exhibition sponsorship programme to appeal to small, local firms. Each company is offered a range of exhibitions each year for a modest fee, and becomes accustomed to choosing and taking an active interest in shows that appeal to its management, with representatives attending the exhibition opening to receive public acknowledgement of the company's assistance and an opportunity to meet the artists.

Working with the private sector can be challenging for trustees and museum professionals, who must ensure that the public interest continues to be served. It can also offer the museum new opportunities to become directly involved in the economic development of its community. If the local economic development priority is to provide jobs in the telecommunications industry, for example, the regional history museum might contribute by staging an exhibition on the history of communications in the area, while the local science centre would present educational and interactive exhibits on the principles of telecommunications, both sponsored by the industry. The Science Museum in London has devised an excellent example of this kind of programming on a national scale, with a decade-long series of exhibitions on new and old materials used in manufacturing, sponsored by the British steel industry. Disciplined by appropriate policies, museums can find ways to serve the public interest in collaboration with the private sector.

## 3.1.5    MEETINGS, MEETINGS, MEETINGS

'Is this meeting necessary?' The director of a large museum confessed that there were at least thirteen meetings *per week* that she was supposed to attend, from annual general meetings through monthly board meetings and staff meetings to meetings of task forces and a seemingly endless round of internal and external committees. Needless to say, she had developed the habit of delegation. But were all those meetings really necessary?

Looking around a meeting room of a dozen staff members or trustees assembled for two hours, it is possible to calculate not only the *direct cost* of the meeting to the museum in person-hours, but also the *opportunity cost*, as its participants are prevented from performing other functions while attending the meeting. The impact of voice mail and computerised bulletin boards may already be weakening the tyranny of the meeting over corporate life, as we all become more accustomed to asynchronous methods of communication: in the 21st century we may well look back on the previous era as one dominated by face-to-face meetings, whereas in the future it may be possible to limit the number of such occasions to those situations where person-to-person communication and collegiality of the group are essential.

However, since they can enable people to work together to achieve institutional goals, meetings often *are* necessary, and it is management's job to ensure that meetings accomplish this, by utilising such simple tools as an *agenda* and *minutes*.

All participants in the meeting should be invited to contribute to the agenda in advance of the meeting. One director is known to have cancelled all further meetings when he realised that only he was setting the agendas, and that all participants were deferring decisionmaking to him. The purpose of a meeting is to share viewpoints, make decisions, and to gain collegial commitment to common purposes; this collegiality should begin with the agenda, and should continue throughout a truly participatory process of discussion.

In order to prevent such discussion from becoming dilatory – and again recognising the considerable opportunity cost represented by the meeting – the agenda should be *timed*, and the chair must keep the meeting on schedule. Time allocations should be checked with all participants at the outset, and adjusted during the course of the meeting only by majority consent.

*Minutes* should be kept, preferably by someone who serves only that role in the meeting, with requirements for action indicated in the margin. If these action lists all point to the same person, it is evident that the meeting was not necessary, but a reconsideration of work loads may be! Minutes should be distributed within forty-eight hours of the meeting, with another forty-eight allowed for corrections, so that the actions arising from the meeting may be implemented quickly, and so that agreements reached may become the basis for future action. Minuting should be understood to be a planning and management tool, not a passive function. Reading the minutes at or prior to the next meeting will then point to the fundamental issues to be resolved.

## 3.1.6   COMMUNICATION

The meeting is an important communication method among those concerned with the museum. In general, the museum manager must continually address both *formal* and *informal* means of communication.

### 3.1.6.1   FORMAL COMMUNICATION

There are three degrees of FORMAL COMMUNICATION among those concerned with the management of a museum:

- notification
- consultation
- delegation

Whenever a decision is taken, the museum manager must determine who needs to be *notified* of the decision. For example, the decision to extend the duration of an exhibition, or simply to open the museum for an evening event, will almost certainly require notification of the security staff, and possibly of the catering, ticketing and shop staff as well. Failure to notify all those involved of decisions affecting them *promptly* is one of the cardinal sins in museum administration, and one of the most common complaints of those who have to live with the consequences. Notification should not be casual, but should be controlled formally within the museum management system by means of official notification memoranda that must be dated, timed and signed by the relevant museum officer.

*Consultation* is a higher degree of formal communication, because it involves the opportunity costs of a meeting or some form of written input from those consulted. In considering a possible decision, the museum manager must determine whether notification of that decision would be sufficient, or whether it requires consultation with those affected before it can be taken. If consultation is thought to be worthwhile, the manager must *truly* consult – he or she must listen and take on board the ideas of those consulted. Another management deficiency is to create the appearance of consultation when all that was really intended was notification. This adds the injury of wasting time to the insult of not listening to people's views, and leads to cynicism among staff, which is unhelpful on those occasions when management really *does* want to consult them.

The value to the institution of the decision under consideration should be proportionate to the person-hours devoted to consultation. A major decision, such as introducing admission charges where there have been none before, may require months of careful consideration in consultative meetings, whereas a decision to add a new line of stock to the shop may be accomplished by consultation with the relevant curator and the retail manager in half an hour. In either case, the consultation should not be casual, but should be announced in advance and consciously undertaken by all concerned.

*Delegation* is perhaps the most important formal means of communication, since it is most directly connected with accomplishing the museum's functions. Like the other formal means of communication, it should not be casual; delegation should be an explicit process. Vague, informal delegation is the root of many of the communication problems that afflict museum workers. Both delegators and 'delegatees' should insist that the act of delegation is recorded, with the extent and limitations of the delegated responsibility clearly set out.

### 3.1.6.2  INFORMAL COMMUNICATION

Careful notification, consultation and delegation may be of little use unless the corporate culture of the museum also encourages a healthy climate of INFORMAL COMMUNICATION. This involves an awareness of the art of *creative listening*, which starts with an understanding that listening is an active, rather than a passive, endeavour. Personnel at all levels, including trustees and volunteers, should be encouraged to understand that listening to each other is a creative task, and that it is useful to 'check back' with each other by saying, in effect, 'What I hear you saying is...' Only when the original speaker confirms that what has been heard is what they said can we be sure that effective communication has occurred.

Even more important for an effective management culture is attention to *motivation*. Proper notification, consultation and delegation, even in a climate of responsible listening, are not enough: the museum manager should also determine whether all those concerned with a policy or procedure have been sufficiently motivated to carry it out. Respect for each of the individuals concerned, as well as linking particular actions or procedures to the long-term goals of the institution, is essential to motivating those of good will to undertake the desired activities wholeheartedly.

Above all, there must be sufficient motivation for individual *creativity*. In particular, it is vital to respect the need for creativity among curators and others concerned with developing exhibitions, education programmes, publications, media and special events, as well as those concerned with marketing them. Plans, policies and procedures must *facilitate* creativity, not stifle it. The effective museum manager should ensure that the corporate culture of communications in the museum is one that *welcomes* the original idea, and that seeks to determine how it can be achieved, rather than why it can't be realised. This criterion of encouraging creativity is ultimately the most important measure of museum management.

*Effective museum management respects and sustains creative solutions to the museum's problems, and creative responses to the museum's opportunities, among trustees, staff and volunteers.*

# 3.2 | Collection Management

Collections are the defining attribute of museums. Their management is at the heart of any museum's operations. Adding to them judiciously is the most fruitful way in which a museum can grow. Documenting them fully and caring for them well is, in the long run, the fundamental criterion of a well-managed museum, since the ability of the museum to provide meaningful experiences for the public today and in the future depends on its care for its collections and the information about them.

This section begins with a consideration of the role of the curator or keeper (3.2.1), reviews the components of collection policy (3.2.2) and the steps towards forming a collection development strategy (3.2.3), before addressing the issues of collection care – documentation (3.2.4) and conservation (3.2.5).

## 3.2.1 ROLE OF THE CURATOR

Despite the centrality of collections, the position of curator (sometimes called 'keeper' in the UK) has been somewhat besieged in recent years. This was originally due to the reorganisation of museums, from curator-led departments to the more functional administration outlined in Chapter 2. This tendency has been intensified by the increasing emphasis on public programmes and visitor services, and by the realisation that exhibitions and other museum activities require input from many other professional disciplines as well as curators.

Yet, with a greater emphasis on visitor-centred exhibitions and other public programmes and services, the curator's role need not be, and should not be, marginalised. On the contrary, the role of the curator in the 21st century should be integral to the success of the museum in achieving its public mission.

One of the difficulties with the role of the curator has been limited comprehension of its primary qualification and activity – CONNOISSEURSHIP. The intimate knowledge of a collection – whether of molluscs or Monets or mummies – is rooted in an ability to see, to make distinctions, and above all, to make judgements about objects. This is connoisseurship, and it is as essential to a science, military or transportation museum as it is to an art or philatelic collection. A scholar, however academically qualified, is not a curator; the curator is not simply a researcher, and is not focused on written evidence as many academics are, but roots his or her knowledge in the works of art, artefacts, specimens or archival documents of that discipline.

The qualified curator brings such connoisseurship to the task of adding to the collection. Curatorial acquisition is a creative response to opportunity, disciplined by the necessities of the market place, the museum's acquisition budget, and the shape of the collection that the curator has, in most cases, inherited from predecessors. Curatorial success in acquisitions requires inspiration, dedication, patience, strategy and a knowledge of sources that is both extensive and detailed.

To sustain their abilities, curators need time for RESEARCH. They need to research potential acquisitions, proposed exhibition subjects, and the knowledge base for publications or media productions that the museum wishes to undertake. Research may be carried out in the curator's office, in the museum library, through fieldwork or through visits to other museums and private collections abroad. The most common complaint among curators of all kinds is the lack of time for consistent pursuit of research objectives.

Research underpins all museum programmes. Without adequate and accurate research, public programmes can be misleading at best, dead wrong at worst. Poorly researched acquisitions can litter the collection with irrelevant or unimportant examples – or worse, with copies or fakes. The most sophisticated, high-technology multimedia programmes depend on the quality and extent of the museum's research – some of them literally transposing the collection database into a publicly accessible format.

Since their responsibilities continually draw their attention to the museum's need for research, curators have devised various ways of finding time to undertake it.

- One strategy is to focus his or her attention on a relatively narrow or even esoteric research programme, often unrelated to the museum's programmes, in some cases even unrelated to the collection. With this approach, the curator plays a minimal role in the public functions of the museum, in some cases publishing results of his or her research in academic journals unrelated to the museum's publications programme.

- The opposite strategy deeply involves the curator in the museum's public programmes, but as a result the curator is dragged from one research topic to another, usually in support of the exhibition programme. For these curators it is difficult to find time for research on acquisitions, and their research work may become cursory, constantly moving from one exhibition topic to another.

Neither of these extremes is desirable, or necessary. The solution of an enlightened museum management is to support long-term curatorial research by establishing a *research policy* and to encourage the development of *research plans*:

- A *research policy* should establish the museum's commitment to research, and to providing the personnel, time, library access, travel budget and other resources needed for it (although it may make some of these resources – such as travel for fieldwork – contingent on the researcher securing grants to pay for them). It should address not only curatorial research, but research by other staff members – conservators, education officers and others – and should outline the museum's policy towards outside researchers using museum facilities, whether they are visiting scholars studying the collection or secondary school students writing an essay. The policy should articulate the museum's position on copyright and intellectual property, usually making a distinction between the results of research undertaken on museum time and personal research which some museum staff may undertake independently. Most important, the research policy should insist that all museum-sponsored research, even if theoretical, should ultimately relate to museum collections or programmes, and must form part of the execution of a research plan.

- *Research plans* should be prepared by all museum staff members (not only curators) who wish to undertake museum-sponsored research. The plan should indicate the relationship of the projected research to museum collection documentation or public programmes, and should include a time estimate for its accomplishment. Plans should be prepared annually, and time estimates should be stated, usually in months or years. Research plans should be drafted by the researcher, reviewed by the deputy director for that division, and approved by the museum's chief executive officer (usually the director).

The value of having a research policy and plans in place is that the museum management can then consider changes in research direction with due regard to the long-term implications of altering its research time commitments. If, for example, the director decides that a new exhibition must be organised for next year, and therefore advises a curator to undertake the necessary research, that curator should respond with reference to his or her research plan, observing what effect the change in research direction will have on the objectives and timing of the formerly agreed research plan; a decision can then be made as to whether this alteration is in the long-term interests of the museum. On the other hand, if a curator suggests a research plan that is not meaningfully related to the museum's collection documentation or public programming needs, but perhaps reflects his or her personal interests, the deputy director of collections management or the director can work with him or her to redirect the research so that it is of benefit to the institution.

Given the centrality of curatorial research to all other museum operations, it is extremely important to establish a sound research policy and a system of research plans as the basis for the curatorial role in both collections management and public programming activities. Neglect of this area (which is lamentably common) results in the worst kind of inefficiency for the museum – waste of one of the museum's most precious human resources, the expertise of its personnel. With policy and plans in place, however, it becomes possible for curators to play a responsible and creative role in all aspects of the museum's operations, and to make the fruits of their connoisseurship fully available to the institution.

In view of the importance of collection development, many museum trusts and boards appoint an *acquisitions committee* from among their members. Such a committee, which should meet with the relevant curator, is useful as a means of channelling trustees' efforts towards encouraging donations or bequests to the collection in accordance with the museum's collection development strategy. Since acquisitions lead to increased operating costs, and ultimately to space and facilities requirements, the acquisitions committee should also function as a committee of approval for major acquisitions, defined as accessions above a certain monetary value. Collections committees with broader powers are not recommended, however, since they inevitably become involved in day-to-day museum operations that should be delegated to the curatorial staff.

## 3.2.2 COLLECTION POLICY

The museum's chief instrument of collection management should be its COLLECTION POLICY (sometimes called a collection management policy). A collection policy should include:

- a declaration of the museum's commitment to maintaining the collection as a public trust, for which it will provide conscientious care indefinitely;

- a definition of the range and limits of the collection, related to the museum's mission and mandate; the policy usually establishes both beginning and end dates (if it is a historical collection), the geographical range (if relevant) and the materials (e.g. ceramics or glass) to be collected;

- a qualitative statement of the objective of the collection – an art collection may try to restrict its collection to *outstanding* examples, whereas a natural science collection may aspire to be *comprehensive* or *systematic*, while a history museum's collection may aim to be a *representative* sample of a particular period. Some historical collections are centred on exceptional items related to great events or individuals, whereas others focus on objects typical of their time and place. The collection of a museum in a heritage building may be restricted to objects that were *actually* used in the building, or may extend to objects of the *type* used there. The policy may also determine whether artefacts must have been *made* in a particular district or era, or merely *used* in that place or period, or both. Natural history collections that aspire to be systematic must further specify whether they will include merely one example of each species, whether they include definitive type specimens, or whether they aim to include an example of each stage of development of each species;

- the *criteria* for inclusion in the collection – these go beyond the foregoing general statements of the collection's range and quality, to identify such particular requirements as size, demonstrated authenticity, an established provenance, the legal issue of clear title, and either display condition or a condition which the museum has the resources to restore and maintain. Monetary value levels which would require acquisitions committee approval should be specified. Criteria may also distinguish between objects for different parts of the collection – for example, original documents, tapes and other media related to the subject matter of the museum may belong in the museum's *archives*, but material in print or other media that is collected only because it provides information about the rest of the collection will be found in the museum *library*;

- approved *acquisition methods*, which may include gifts, bequests, purchases, fieldwork, deposits from other museums, and acceptance of acquisitions from government programmes or agencies (like the UK's National Heritage Memorial Fund) responsible for cultural property protection;

- a policy on *ownership* of the collection, including acquisition procedures for donations (gift agreements) and purchases (receipt requirements). Collection policies usually forbid gifts 'with strings attached', and require that donations must be transferred without restrictions on the museum's use of the acquisition. The museum's policy with regard to tax deductions for donations should be articulated in this document;

- the *ethical commitments* of the museum and its trustees with regard to acquisitions, such as the museum's subscription to international conventions or national laws or treaties, including policy regarding objects from indigenous cultures, and policy regarding the repatriation or restitution of objects to their origins. Ethical guidelines adopted by the trustees regarding potential conflicts of interest with their own or staff personal collecting activities (as discussed in subsection 2.2.3) may also be included;

- a statement of the purposes for which objects may be collected, leading to a classification by purpose, usually including: a *display collection* acquired for exhibition and interpretation purposes; a *study collection* acquired for purposes of comparative or analytical research (such as archaeological shards from a museum dig, or zoological specimens in spirit jars), and a *reserve collection*, which consists of objects pending assignment to either of the first two classifications, duplicate or secondary examples assigned to hands-on educational programmes, or objects pending de-accessioning. The display collection and study collection are to be preserved indefinitely, whereas some of the items in the reserve collection may not be. Some museums acquire a *contemporary collection* of the potential artefacts of tomorrow (while they are still inexpensive and plentiful), and hold these items in reserve for a period of years (say, twenty), after which they may either be transferred to the display or study collections, or de-accessioned. The reserve collection may also house unwanted objects that the museum is sometimes obliged to accept, at least temporarily, as part of a donation that includes other objects needed for the display or study collections; if possible, the donor should be persuaded to give only the desired pieces, but when faced with an 'all or nothing' offer, it is convenient to assign the unwanted objects to the reserve collection (as long as this is explained to the donor and recorded in the gift agreement), so that the museum need not make the commitment of long-term preservation of unsuitable material;

- the museum's policy on *de-accessioning*, as a means of collection management. Although some would resist the inclusion of a de-accessioning policy in a collection policy, it is far better to have a sound policy in place, rather than pretending that the museum will never need to dispose of unwanted artefacts. Certain objects – or the entire display and study collections – can be declared exempt from de-accessioning in perpetuity, with de-accessioning restricted to items in the reserve collection alone. Further, the policy should make it clear that, in general, the museum collects objects only for their indefinite preservation, and therefore that de-accessioning is to be regarded as an aberration. Both the International Council of Museums and many countries' museum associations have published suitably cautious statements on de-accessioning. The 1990 ICOM Code of Ethics says: 'there must always be a strong presumption against the disposal of specimens to which a museum has assumed formal title';

Criteria for consideration for de-accessioning should be listed, including: objects that do not fit the museum's mandate; objects that have been found to be spurious or have been acquired illegally or unethically; objects due for repatriation or restitution to their origins; duplicates that are inferior to more recently acquired examples, or objects in a condition that is not cost-effective to restore. The steps to be taken in the event of de-accessioning should be spelled out – specifying that only curators can initiate de-accessioning, that the process must be fully documented, with the reasons for de-accessioning according to this policy fully recorded, and that any information about the de-accessioned object must be retained. Approval procedures for de-accessioning should always involve the director, and may also require the attention of the trustees.

Acceptable options for disposition of the de-accessioned items should be indicated, with alternatives listed as a sequence of 'first refusals', with the aim of keeping the object in the public domain, if possible within the country, state, province, county or municipality; destruction of objects should be carried out only by curators in the presence of the director, and recorded; in the event of sale, any revenues from the disposition of de-accessioned objects must be used only for new acquisitions – never for running costs.

- the museum's policy on *loans*, distinguishing between long-term loans or *deposits* of items from other museums or collections, and short-term loans (both incoming and outgoing) for temporary exhibitions. The clause on long-term loans is usually written to persuade prospective long-term lenders to become donors instead, and may even forbid long-term loans from individuals entirely, while admitting the possibility of deposits from other collections or museums (which will be restricted by their own collection policies, and therefore can only deposit objects on long-term loan). For short-term, outgoing loans, it is usual to identify the approvals required (such as registrar and curator for most, but director or even trustees for some objects, with still others never to be loaned), to specify that the museum will lend objects only to institutions able to provide an equivalent level of environmental and security protection and insurance, and to require condition reports at each packing and unpacking point. The policy may also specify that couriers must accompany certain loans to supervise their installation and demounting;

- the museum's policy on *appraisals*, which will usually protect curators from being requested to give monetary evaluations, especially if tax deductions for potential donations are involved. Sometimes, curators may appraise items up to a certain market value, with items of higher value being referred elsewhere.

Many collection policies for smaller museums go still further, adding *documentation*, *conservation*, *security* and *insurance* provisions. In a larger museum, these may be addressed in separate policies, drafted and monitored by the responsible departments.

The collection policy should be a public document, which the curator may invoke when necessary in the museum's dealings with prospective donors or vendors. It is most useful as a means to resist would-be long-term lenders, 'all or nothing' donors, or well-meaning trustees whose proffered donations or bequests do not fit the museum's mandate. It should also be used within the museum as an organisational principle – so that all objects are assigned to display, study or reserve collections, for example.

## 3.2.3 COLLECTION DEVELOPMENT STRATEGY

Collections absorb two-thirds of a museum's operating budget and generate major long-range space and facilities requirements that eventually require capital fundraising campaigns (Lord, Lord and Nicks, *The Cost of Collecting*, HMSO 1989). The development of a museum's collections is therefore a central concern for the management of the institution. The collection development strategy addresses this concern.

The collection development strategy, to be drafted by the curator in consultation with the registrar and the conservator (possibly with the assistance of a professional museum planner) for approval by the director and the trustees, should begin with a QUALITATIVE ANALYSIS of the collection. An AESTHETIC EVALUATION is crucial in the case of an art collection, but a qualitative collection analysis will also consider the scope and range of the collection, its international, national or regional significance, its outstanding pieces, its representative or systematic character, and its uniqueness. The qualitative analysis should also address the potential for enhancement of the collection through acquisition – which may be limited by sheer availability, the museum's acquisition budget and other factors.

The collection development strategy should then proceed to a QUANTITATIVE ANALYSIS that includes:

- the present *number of objects* in the collection as a whole and in all relevant categories, such as collection department, artefact type, historical period, materials (important for planning conservation needs of organic, inorganic and mixed materials), the percentage registered and catalogued, and according to the museum's classification by use – display, study and reserve collections;

- the history of the growth of the collection in number of objects (not merely accession numbers) from as early in the museum's history as possible, again in relation to the same categories, and with both annual averages and the most recent *collection growth rate* computed, not in percentages (as is often erroneously advised), but in actual numbers of objects accessioned;

- the current *display/storage ratio* (by collection department, if applicable), and the curator's recommendation of a more acceptable proportion if the present ratio is not satisfactory;

- current *storage densities* – objects per square metre or square metres per object – by object type or materials, together with the registrar's and conservator's recommendation of a more acceptable density if the present stores are too crowded;

- current *display densities* – objects per square metre or square metres per object – in the permanent collection exhibition galleries, linked to an identification of the dominant display mode in that gallery (aesthetic, thematic, environmental, systematic, interactive or hands-on, as described in subsection 3.4.1).

A DESIGN YEAR needs to be determined – the year by which the collection development strategy should be fulfilled – usually about twenty or twenty-five years in the future, since projections beyond those limits are likely to be highly speculative. Any factors anticipated to affect collection growth between now and the design year should be noted – an anticipated bequest, hiring an additional curator or opening a new curatorial department, for instance – and their effect on the present collection growth rate should be quantified. Many curators find such projections difficult, but past growth rates are likely to be indicative of future averages, with whatever qualifications may result from developments that can be anticipated and gauged with reference to past experience. The longer the record of growth, the more it usually reveals patterns that can help us predict the future when correctly interpreted. Thus adjusted, the growth rate (again computed in actual numbers of objects, not as a percentage) may be projected to the design year, for the collection as a whole and for each collection department and material type.

The next variables to be determined are the target display/storage ratio and densities. In order to project these, the director and curators, in consultation with the conservators and exhibitions officers, must decide on the most suitable and stimulating *display modes*. The *aesthetic* presentation of an art collection requires a relatively low density – paintings and sculpture in a gallery need adequate viewing distance for visitors – whereas a *thematic* presentation, linking objects contextually and interpreting groups of them together, is likely to be more dense, and *environmental* exhibits (such as a furnished period room) will have even more objects per square metre. A *systematic* display mode, such as a visible storage or study storage gallery, provides the highest display densities, usually only about one-third less than the closed storage density for similar material. Since the size of museum objects and the nature of museum displays varies so widely, each museum must determine its own density variables, and may then undertake to increase public access to its collections by including at least some display modes of higher density (such as visible storage for suitable collections). Total display space may be distributed by percentage – so much gallery space for aesthetic displays, so much for thematic, and so on.

The collection development strategy may now project the museum's space and facilities needs up to the design year, with respect to the agreed growth rate, display/storage ratio and display modes. It should also be possible to project the number of objects that will be in the collection as a whole, how many will be in storage, and how many on display in each mode. The object is not to get such projections exactly right, but rather to see the implications of proceeding with collection development at the present or projected pace. If the results of the strategy are acceptable within the museum's present resources or anticipated capacity for growth, they may stand as the basis for a master plan; if not, it may be necessary to adjust expectations – either in the rate of acquisitions, or in the intended plans for display.

Since many museums are currently concerned to increase public access to the collections, it may not be advisable to restrict plans for display; quite the opposite: it may however be possible to enhance public intellectual access through the use of contemporary technology – video discs, CD-ROM applications or multimedia terminals – instead of relying solely on the provision of additional exhibition gallery space. Even so, the collection development strategy may serve to project collection development limits for curators.

These restraints should not be viewed as inviolable laws, but only as useful *guidelines*, on the basis of which the museum can plan its space and facilities development, and project future capital and operating fund requirements. The collection development strategy should refer back to the qualitative analysis with which it began, and translate these guidelines into *priorities* for collection development. Curators should be encouraged to adhere to agreed *qualitative priorities* within the *quantitative guidelines* established by the strategy.

Yet the museum must remain open to opportunity. Specific departments may be allowed, or even encouraged, to exceed the guidelines when significant collection development opportunities crop up. The purpose of a collection development strategy is not to inhibit such creative growth, but to ensure that decisions about the museum's acquisitions programme are made in an informed and deliberate manner, so that the institution can continue to provide for its collections in a professional way.

## 3.2.4 INFORMATION MANAGEMENT

Information has been defined as 'reduction of uncertainty'. For a museum, uncertainty about the meaning, status or significance of objects in its collection amounts to the loss of their value, since the museum must be certain enough of their meaning to display, publish or in other ways communicate that meaning to the public. Retention and management of information is thus a central concern of all museums.

In most British museums, the documentation of information about the museum's collection has traditionally been a curatorial function. In the USA, the position of *registrar* has evolved to specialise in managing the documentation base, even though the information usually originates with curators. In recent years, a number of major British museums have found it advisable to appoint a registrar; the change reflects the growing scope and complexity of both documentation and information management in museums. In this section, therefore, we assume that a registrar has been appointed, understanding that in museums without this position, curators or curatorial assistants may be undertaking these tasks.

Given its commitment to the public dissemination of information about its collection, the management of that information is in many ways just as important to the museum as the management of the collections themselves. Furthermore, the *documentation* of an object in the collection is of limited utility unless it can be related to the *location* of that object. The documentation of museum collections therefore means more than their mere registration or cataloguing; it also means management of the location and movement of all objects in the collections. Hence, the registrar should be responsible for the museum stores, and for loans and their insurance, and must be involved in all exhibition planning, in addition to the management of information about the collection through the compilation of records and the provision of access to them.

Some would go even further, and suggest that museums are essentially about the distribution of information. While the primacy of the object in the museum is indisputable, the conversion of formerly manual records to computers, the digitisation of data (including imaging), the provision of both staff and public access to the data, the possibilities of relating the database to other information systems within the museum, and the proliferation of databases as a means of sharing information within a museum and among institutions all point to the growing need for a more integrated approach to INFORMATION MANAGEMENT, of which documentation of the collection is only one important aspect.

Examples of the information that museums manage and the officers directly responsible for it are given in Table 3.2. This list indicates the need for information planning and the advantages to be gained from its integration across departments and divisions. For instance, the media officer may need to convert the catalogue entries for a group of objects into a visitor-friendly database for a visible storage exhibition. When one considers, in addition to the officers responsible for them, the multiple *users* of these information systems – from curators' research of the collection catalogue to providing public access for interactive and multimedia programmes – the need for information management to co-ordinate the many persons involved becomes apparent. It is also obvious that project teams are required to co-ordinate information management, with the registrar playing a leading role on the teams, while focusing on documentation.

Table 3.2   Information Management

| Information Resource | Officer Responsible |
| --- | --- |
| Registration of acquisitions | Registrar |
| Collection catalogue | Registrar |
| Collection management records | Registrar |
| Photographic negative and digitisation files | Photographer |
| Museum library catalogue | Librarian |
| Archives | Archivist |
| Condition reports and treatment records | Chief conservator |
| Building systems records | Operations manager |
| Ticketing records | Visitor services manager |
| Membership records | Membership manager |
| Fundraising and development records | Development officer |
| Current accounts and financial records | Finance officer |
| Exhibition development schedules | Exhibition officer |
| School party visits | Education officer |
| Digital publishing files | Publications manager |
| Interactive and multimedia programmes | Media officer |
| Computerised show controls | Media Officer |
| Evaluation records | Evaluation officer |
| Personnel records | Personnel manager |
| Volunteer recruitment and evaluation records | Volunteer co-ordinator |
| Office automation | Chief clerk |
| Inter-office communication | Chief clerk |

The possibilities for inter-institutional co-operation through the Internet point to still greater opportunities for sharing information *between* as well as *within* museums. The 1995 *Report of the Commission on the Future of the Smithsonian Institution* calls on that museum complex to become 'the leader in establishing such a world-wide computer linkage'. Museums around the world are already eagerly participating in the establishment of such connections, particularly in connecting with the public by establishing 'sites' on the World Wide Web.

All of these somewhat bewildering developments have a constant impact on the task of the museum registrar, who may only recently have converted a card catalogue and a registration book to a computer database – or may only be preparing to do so! Museums, at whatever stage of automation, need a sound information policy and an information system plan.

The museum's INFORMATION POLICY should address issues of intellectual property, compliance with the Data Protection Act or equivalent regulations, and the museum management's orientation to participation in databases or other dissemination of museum information, particularly images. The *digitisation* of information, including imagery, is changing the way that we understand the concept of 'reproduction' or 'replication'. The practical questions of encouraging open access to at least some parts of a museum's database, and how to control such access (if control is either possible or desirable), are subject to much debate at present. Certainly, there is an opportunity to broaden public access, but there are also risks of misuse of imagery, questions of copyright and potential for revenue, now or in the future. Contemporary art museums, where living artists may claim an interest in the information or the images, face a particularly acute challenge.

The information policy should assert the museum's commitment to documenting its collection accurately and comprehensively, retaining all pertinent information in an accessible format indefinitely, and providing public access as appropriate. Certain information – prices and insurance values, for instance – should be kept confidential, but visitor access to most other information – and non-visitor access via a video disc, CD-ROM or the Internet – can now be provided, not only to scholars, but to the general interested public. The nature of knowledge about the collections – no longer the preserve of curators and registrars, but accessible to all – and the nature of publication or dissemination of that knowledge, are changing rapidly, and policies may very well have to be adjusted as technology, legislation and the international flow of information evolve.

Having drawn up, at least for the present, a satisfactory information policy, the museum should be able to develop an INFORMATION SYSTEM PLAN, possibly with the help of specialists in this field. Planning for an information system is most efficient after conclusion of a corporate plan, master plan or strategic planning exercise that has identified all museum functions and priorities. The information system plan begins with a list of all information-related functions (like the list above, but prioritised), and then determines which components can be efficiently integrated in the near future, ensuring, as far as possible, the necessary compatibility of systems so that further links can be forged later. An *information model* may be devised, showing in graphic form the current tasks and consequent information flow, and desired improvements in these patterns. It should then be possible, with some specialist consultant assistance, to list *functional requirements* of the information system, and to use these as guidelines in preparing specifications for both hardware and software. Costs – in terms of training and development as well as money – must also be computed, and the plan may have to be adjusted to realistic parameters, although the potential for sponsorship by computer hardware or software companies should not be forgotten.

With both information policy and an information system plan in place, the registrar may need to upgrade the DOCUMENTATION PROCEDURES MANUALS to ensure that they are compatible with the entire system. Procedures manuals are usually important for both registration and cataloguing. In addition to the steps involved in making a satisfactory record of a new accession, these manuals must provide very explicit instructions for the cataloguers and data entry clerks who will be using them. The steps in the *registration procedures manual* should include at least:

- *entry* of identification, source and history in a secure and permanent file;
- *numbering* of both object and record;
- *acknowledgement* of the source of the acquisition;
- *formal transfer of title* by gift agreement form or receipt;
- inclusion of the object in the museum's *insurance* cover;
- an initial *condition report* by the conservator;
- the initial *location record* for the object.

Although a wide variety of registration systems have been employed throughout the museum world – forty-five different ones were found to be in use within the museum when the Victoria and Albert Museum commenced automation of its records a few years ago – most museums today register acquisitions by means of what is called the *three-part numbering system*. It comprises:

- a three-digit number referring to the year of accession – 997, for example;
- a full stop and a number referring to the number of the acquisition in the present year – so that 997.13 refers to the thirteenth accession made in 1997;
- another full stop and a number referring to the object within that accession – so that 997.13.4 refers to the fourth object donated by the source of the thirteenth accession of 1997;
- if necessary, a lower-case letter designating part of an object, so that 997.13.4a might refer to a teapot, while 997.13.4b might refer to its lid.

Such a numbering system that does not rely on specific object categories can be applied to collections of all kinds. Some collections may need to correlate it with other conventions. There is an international registration system for stamps, for example, and archaeological collections may need to correlate finds with the universal geographical site reference system. Many natural history collections find it preferable both to document and to organise their holdings by genus and species, while coins are classified by country, ruler, material, denomination and date. Others may have inherited an historic system that remains viable – although any system must be flexible enough to allow for change, as the conceptual bases of classifications of objects of all kinds are continually evolving. It has not proved useful to base a documentation system on the periods of art history, for example, since the very basis for the period classifications is questioned and revised from time to time by the discipline itself.

Number labels may be attached to very small objects, or ones where all surfaces are of aesthetic importance, by means of tags. Unbleached cotton labels may be discreetly sewn into costumes. For most other objects, numbers may be applied on the base, or in a similarly inconspicuous place, in varnished drawing ink on an acetone base coat; conservators recommend that the base coat should include a 20% Paraloid B72 solution, and that the work area where numbers are applied must have adequate ventilation for the safety of those working there. The registration procedures manual should detail the numbering process, and recommend suitable, standardised procedures for locating numbers on the types of objects in the museum's collection.

The documentation procedures manuals should also refer to the museum's *location tracking* method. This should be initiated at registration with the *entry documentation*, and maintained for each acquisition throughout its retention in the museum, regardless of when or whether it is subsequently catalogued. The manual must specify who is allowed to move objects in the collection, and what procedures they must follow, to ensure that others will be able to find the objects subsequently. All storage and display locations should be codified for easy reference. In the event of loans, the manual should provide an approved *exit documentation* procedure, which must be checked by security officers as well as collection management personnel.

Maintaining a sound location tracking practice is essential for the success of a collection *inventory*, which is vital to security as well as to collection management. Government line department museums may be expected to meet auditors' requirements for maintaining an inventory of their collections, but all museums should undertake inventories in regular rotation, with every object, even in large collections, being checked at least once every few years.

*Cataloguing* is a more extensive recording process than registration, and many museums that keep up to date with their registrations have a backlog in cataloguing. While registration records a limited number of data fields – name and function of the object, its source and provenance, place and date of its origin, its materials and a brief description, for instance – the museum catalogue aims to record a full sense of its significance in relation to other objects in the collection, in other collections and in the world at large. While the registrar and data entry clerks may be able to register an object with input from the curator, the catalogue entry should be primarily a curatorial concern. It should include references to relevant literature and reproductions – much of which may be standardised for groups of similar objects. Developing a comprehensive catalogue of a collection is a museum's major responsibility, and it should not be postponed indefinitely due to deadlines of temporary exhibitions or opportunities to add even more acquisitions.

The *automation* of collection records often throws a spotlight on hitherto little-known lacunae in the museum's catalogue. Early endeavours to transfer records to computers attempted to collate complete catalogues, trying to record comprehensive information about a necessarily restricted number of objects; experience has shown that entry of only a few key data fields from the registration records for a large number of objects is far more efficient and effective, as long as the system allows further information to be added in future. In this way, the registration records and the eventual, complete catalogue can be integrated in one automated system.

The *nomenclature* used to record museum objects has become an important subject in itself, particularly as computer word and field search programs facilitate access for everyone, from curators to visiting scholars and schoolchildren. Standardising terminology internationally, not only for technical terms but for colour references, for example, will assist global access to the world's growing collections database. Some disciplines, such as the natural sciences, have inherited conventions such as the genus and species classifications, whereas others are still in the process of development. In the UK the *Social History and Industrial Classification*, published by the University of Sheffield in 1983, may be helpful for collections of that kind, while in the United States, *The Revised Nomenclature for Museum Cataloguing*, published by the American Association for State and Local History in Nashville, Tennessee in 1988 (based on the earlier edition by Chenhall) is almost universally employed for historical collections of artefacts. However, some Australian museums have found it necessary to develop their own standard guide for their historical collections.

Many software programs specifically designed for museum registrars are now available. Some museums that chose their systems ten to fifteen years ago have had difficulty in acquiring imaging capability, or providing public access, and have had to convert to other systems or upgrade. Waiting for the ideal software is not a solution, however; instead, the registrar or curators, often with specialist consultant advice, should undertake systematic development of an information system plan to ensure that all possible specifications have been considered, and should then either make a commitment to the best system on offer, or even develop a program unique to the museum's needs, but compatible with as broad a range of applications as possible. The capacity of some computer programs to accommodate non-alphabetic languages may also be important – for Asian art and archaeology collections, for example.

Data entry to transfer manual records to computer software programs is labour-intensive. One major British museum reports that trained workers there can input only seven 1,000-character records per hour from cards or book entries. Such data entry almost always involves reconfiguring the original record into the format required by the computer program.

Digitised *imaging* is another important step in the upgrading of museum records. In some cases, this may require re-photographing an entire collection. However, the benefits for both the museum's documentation system and interpretation of the collection to the museum public are usually sufficient to justify such an undertaking.

Public access to documentation is a growing field of applications. Visible storage has been made far more attractive, since a simplified keyboard or touch-screen monitor can provide interested visitors with access to catalogue information about the objects on view. The amount of information which can be made available to the visitor about a collection in this way is far greater than could be communicated via a label and museum graphics in a contextual or aesthetic exhibition. Multimedia applications can animate such catalogue data, and can add to its appeal to visitors at all levels of familiarity with the subject matter. Video discs and CD-ROM applications make it possible for users to browse through such information at home, and the Internet could facilitate even wider public access.

The future is bright, if a little uncertain, for museum documentation and information systems. This is an area where museums have already changed extensively and rapidly in recent years, and where the pace of change may be expected to continue. Information systems provide an exciting interface between the museum's knowledge base and its users. 'Virtual exhibitions' are now being planned and presented. The potential for users to access data and imagery from home is growing rapidly. The very nature of the museum as a public institution is being transformed. Yet the desire to see 'the real thing' grows apace. Museum managers will have to keep abreast of the possibilities – and the pitfalls – as the digital information age unfolds.

# Increasing Access to Collections:
# The MicroGallery at the National Gallery, London

BY ERIKA LANGMUIR

The MicroGallery, which opened in 1991, is a computer information room located in the Sainsbury Wing of the National Gallery and intended for the general visitor. The concept of such a public information room to supplement guided tours and the lecture programme was mooted within the gallery as long ago as 1944. An early version was introduced in 1980, when a reading room was provided where visitors could consult gallery publications. Plans were then made to set up a mechanised slide display with accompanying texts. Shortly after, the possibility of digitising images revolutionised the whole concept. Dr Christopher Brown, Curator of Dutch and Flemish Paintings, Secretary of the Trustees' Sponsorship Committee, and subsequently Chief Curator, obtained seed money to develop a prototype, and later found sponsorship for the entire project from the American Express Foundation.

The seed money was used, in the first instance, to appoint a Project Leader, Martin Ellis, who was responsible for the choice of hardware, and who put together a team, based on Cognitive Applications Ltd, to work on the software and editorial aspects of what was then a pioneering enterprise. With the participation of Dr Allan Graham, then Keeper and Curator of the Spanish and Later Italian Paintings, the Head of Education, Dr Erika Langmuir, and two young art historian consultants, Christopher Baker and Tom Henry, the team developed a program illustrating and providing information on every painting in the gallery. Originally based on the entries in the gallery's *Illustrated General Catalogue* and on the painting labels provided by the curators, this much-expanded, specially-written program consists of four indexes through which information can be accessed. A traditional *Artists' A–Z* gives access to individual biographical entries, with small 'thumbnail' images of each of the artist's works held in the collection. The *Historical Atlas* considers the paintings according to when and where they were produced – each short article is illustrated with contemporary maps and 'thumbnail' images of all relevant works. The most innovative index is that of *Picture Types*, which branches out from simple categorisation by genres into many subdivisions. This is a primarily visual index, which enables visitors to search through 'thumbnail' images for a painting remembered only by sight, or to pursue a particular theme. Finally, the *General Reference* index provides definitions of arcane terms, or refers users to specific subject matter.

Whatever the point of entry into the system, the touch screen enables users to access a large image of an individual painting, with accompanying text; in the case of a significant proportion of works, these articles run to several screen 'pages', with details, comparative illustrations, animated sequences, and so on. At every stage, text and image were subjected to curatorial approval and revision.

With complete cross-referencing, an intuitively easy-to-grasp user interface, rapid response, an unintimidating screen layout mimicking the 'neutral' look of an illustrated book, and the facility to print out a personal tour of works in the collection, the MicroGallery is, to date, the largest and most widely used system of its kind.

The success of this information system within the gallery was confirmed when, in 1993, it was published as a CD-ROM, the *Microsoft Art Gallery*. Users throughout the world have found it an absorbing and rewarding aid in 'learning to look at paintings' — more than fulfilling its creators' original aims.

*Visitors in the MicroGallery in the Sainsbury Wing of the National Gallery, courtesy of The National Gallery. M 1353-2*

### 3.2.5 MANAGING TO PRESERVE THE COLLECTION

Preservation of a museum collection entails the indefinite provision of security (considered as an aspect of accommodations management in subsection 3.4.2.3), and CONSERVATION, the subject of this subsection. A complete museum conservation programme should comprise:

- preventive conservation (3.2.5.1)

- investigation and treatment (3.2.5.2)

- restoration (3.2.5.3)

- conservation research (3.2.5.4)

In addition, the preparation and installation of museum objects for exhibitions – the work of the museum's *preparators* – should be closely integrated with that of the *conservators*.

#### 3.2.5.1 PREVENTIVE CONSERVATION

The aim of the CONSERVATOR is to preserve the museum object, and to retard any change in its original qualities as long as possible. This must be accomplished in the context of a public museum, which wishes to make the object visible to the public. Thus the conservator's ideal storage medium of a black box with unvarying temperature and humidity and no light must be compromised to meet the needs of the visitors, and of staff who wish to study the object from time to time. A CONSERVATION POLICY should establish the long-term, qualitative standards for this endeavour, particularly with regard to preventive conservation measures.

Over the past few decades, conservators have increasingly shifted their emphasis from treatment of objects to concentrate on the prevention of deterioration by maintaining conditions as conducive as possible to the long-term survival of the museum object. PREVENTIVE CONSERVATION is the applied science of providing an environment that minimises the object's deterioration in the public museum context. It focuses on the following key environmental factors:

- temperature and relative humidity

- air filtration

- light

- pests

- handling

- emergency procedures

TEMPERATURE AND RELATIVE HUMIDITY: These two climatic factors are closely inter-related; relative humidity is the ratio, expressed as a percentage, of the absolute humidity of sampled air to that of air saturated with water at the same temperature. Organic materials respond to fluctuations in temperature and relative humidity, especially the latter. Continued fluctuation results in a weakening of the organic material. Textiles, paper, leather and wood are among the objects commonly found in museum collections that are particularly susceptible to such deterioration, which can present special difficulties in objects made up of mixed organic and inorganic materials. If RH is too high for too long, mildew and mould are additional hazards, along with corrosion of metals.

As noted in subsection 3.4.2.1, the standard for environmental conditions for many museum collections of organic or mixed materials in temperate zones is usually a diurnal constant of 50% RH $\pm$ 3% all year round at 20–21°C, $\pm$ 0.5°C in winter, modulated upwards by 0.5°C per month to 21–24°C in summer. For new buildings constructed to withstand such conditions, especially in a temperate maritime climate, this standard need not present a major problem; for historic buildings, or other structures not built to sustain such a standard, especially in continental climates, 55% RH is likely to be the best that can be maintained, or it may be necessary to adjust humidity from 55% in summer to 40% in winter by three monthly 5% steps in RH settings each spring and autumn. If engineers still find such limits constrictive, or the museum finds their maintenance too expensive, allowance can be made for wider variations for, say, 5–10% of operating hours during a year, with the standard maintained for the rest of the year. Metal and unbound paper collections require a lower RH, around 40%, while collections that have originated in the tropics have higher hygroscopic capacity, and may require 65% RH. Recent energy-saving measures, in UK museums in particular, have led to some recommendations for more relaxed requirements.

Once the standards are agreed, it is the conservators' responsibility to monitor these environmental conditions closely – traditionally with psychrometers or hygrothermographs, although computerisation of building management systems now provides digital means of recording RH and temperature. Monitors should be positioned to record conditions at all levels in galleries and stores, and in major display cases. Simultaneous records should be kept of outside climate conditions, and of internal spaces that do not benefit from the museum's heating, ventilating and air conditioning controls designed to maintain this collection environment. Zones that do not normally contain collections may be maintained at human comfort levels for the benefit of those who work in or use them.

The climate controls are usually maintained by a ducted air handling system that provides heated or cooled, humidified or dehumidified air as required. Unmodified replacement air is normally kept to a minimum, and building engineers must provide not only insulation, but also a vapour barrier of 0.04–0.08 perms to prevent water vapour from dampening the insulation, and an air barrier to stop air from leaking into the fabric of the building from the interior. Fenestration, if present at all, should be triple-glazed, with panes at least 1.3 cm apart, and skylights, if present, may be buffered with an area that provides a 'half-way' zone between the exterior climate and that in the galleries or stores. Section 3.4 indicates some of the architectural challenges that arise from the climate control requirements of preventive conservation.

AIR FILTRATION: Dust and air pollution are other environmental factors affecting the condition of artefacts, especially in the industrial or high-traffic areas where many museums are located. Fortunately, these can be controlled with an appropriate system of filters – ideally a 25–30% efficiency pre-filter (according to the American Society of Heating, Refrigeration and Air-conditioning Engineers' Dust Spot Efficiency Test section of ASHRAE test 52-76), followed by a medium 40–85% efficiency filter, and a 90–95% after-filter. This bank of filters should be positioned so that both outside and re-circulated internal air pass through it. (Electronic air filters should not be used, because the ozone they generate can be harmful to the collection.) For gaseous pollutants, the standard test is to place polished metal 'coupons' around the museum for long periods, and then to analyse any corrosion products that form on them. Activated-charcoal filters are recommended to eliminate or reduce air pollution.

LIGHT: Deterioration of colour due to natural or artificial light is another concern of conservators. Providing dimmer capability to turn light levels down to 50 lux is essential for exhibitions of works on paper, drawings and watercolours, feathers and other light-sensitive organic materials. A level of 150–200 lux is usually recommended for oil or acrylic paintings and other moderately sensitive objects, while items such as ceramics, glass, stone and most metal artefacts are not particularly light-sensitive, and can therefore sustain 300 lux, resulting in a *contrast ratio* of 6:1 from the most brightly to the most dimly illuminated object on display.

The prime concern is the duration of exposure, with conservators recommending withdrawal of light-sensitive items as necessary to keep lux-hours down; *rotation* of objects on display should accordingly be planned into all exhibitions containing works on paper, and the number of hours of light exposure should be carefully controlled. Standards ranging from a maximum of 120,000 lux-hours per year to less than 60,000 lux-hours have been proposed for highly-sensitive 50-lux items.

Ultra-violet light is another concern, with standards recently dropped to <10μW per lumen from the previous level of 75, due to technical improvements in the UV filters built into fluorescent light tubes or made available as film or laminations for window glass. The choice of fluorescent tubes and incandescent lamps – and now the availability of fibre optics – provides the conservator, the curator and the exhibit designer with a wide range of illumination possibilities, and although many aesthetic factors (such as a colour rendering index minimum of 85) may be considered, the preventive conservation requirements of lux and UV control must be paramount.

PESTS: Rodents and insect pests are among the enemies of the conservator. Good housekeeping is the best defence against them. Poisons and chemical treatments are also of value, but their use must take into account any effects they may have on the object. *Fumigation* of new accessions used to be widespread in museums, and is still used in some areas, but in many locations it has been found to be highly problematic due to risks to staff and the consequent need for licensing of operators in many jurisdictions. Current experiments with the use of nitrous oxide appear to be promising as a less noxious way of eliminating insect pests. Anoxic chambers are taking the place of the former fumigation chambers on museum plans. Another non-toxic method has been devised in which artefacts are placed in a chamber that heats them to 52°C, but keeps relative humidity of the object and the environment constant.

Handling: The preventive conservator should be concerned with the training of all museum personnel who will be allowed to handle artefacts. They should develop procedures manuals that prescribe safe practices for handling, movement and installation. The use of unbleached cotton gloves, for example, should be prescribed for all artefacts except for a small class of items where it is not advisable (such as intricately carved lacquer, for example, where the cotton could catch in the carved detail); handling and installation techniques designed to sustain support for the object at all times should be tailored to the needs of each collection and the materials in it. Dusting or cleaning procedures must be detailed, along with instructions on who is to undertake such work at what level. Requirements for museum vehicles, vans and dollies should also be specified in the manual, ensuring that padding is provided where necessary to protect works of art, artefacts, specimens or archival materials in transit.

Emergency procedures: Conservators should confer closely with the chief of security to ensure that the effects of emergency procedures on the collection are fully considered. For example, conservators should ensure that the appropriate type of sprinkler system is installed, and that procedures in the event of sprinkler discharge are well understood by those whose actions will affect the collection. Fire, flood, earthquake, hurricane or tornado may equally be the conservators' concern. The chief conservator should certainly be a member of the emergency action team. An emergency procedures manual is mandatory, and there should be regular (but unpredictable) drills for staff to prepare for emergencies.

### 3.2.5.2 Investigation and treatment

Although preventive conservation has become an increasing concern, the investigation and treatment of museum objects with a view to preserving them is still an important part of the work of any museum conservation department. The CONSERVATION STUDIO is the usual locus of this work, unless the objects in the collection are too large to be moved there.

Investigation and treatment may range from a *condition report* (mandatory if the object is to be loaned or taken from store to be displayed) through routine cleaning to extensive investigation and non-destructive tests of objects in order to determine the treatments needed to conserve them, followed by treatments which are sometimes prolonged. This work can be extremely varied, ranging from re-lining a painting on a 'hot table' to preserving waterlogged wood by soaking it in tubs of polyethylene glycol over many months or years. Conservation laboratory equipment to undertake such investigation and treatment is highly specialised, and is constantly subject to technological upgrade, so that equipment budget allocations are a recurrent concern. In larger museums, specialised laboratories may be required for conservation of paper, paintings, metals, archaeological materials, waterlogged wood or other types of objects or materials in the collection.

Planning and management of this investigation and treatment is a challenging task of assigning priorities and attempting to maintain them, usually in the context of pressing demands for temporary exhibitions or loans that the museum wishes to make. A CONSERVATION TREATMENT PLAN should be drafted by the chief conservator, and requests for variations from it should be considered in consultation with the deputy director for collection management and the director or curators, so that the museum can balance the pressure of exhibition and loan needs with its long-term concern for the treatment needs of its collection.

The materials used in some conservation treatment processes may be potentially harmful to those using them. The laboratories must therefore be furnished with exhaust devices to eliminate harmful chemicals from the atmosphere, and the museum's first aid centre, including eyewash and shower facilities, should be adjacent to the laboratories in the event of splashes or other accidents.

### 3.2.5.3   RESTORATION

While conservation treatment focuses on the preservation of the object, or at least on retarding its deterioration, the restoration of museum objects aims at returning them to a previous condition – either an original state, or some other condition that is preferred, usually for purposes of display. This activity needs to be controlled by both a RESTORATION POLICY and a carefully considered RESTORATION PROCEDURES MANUAL.

The museum's restoration policy should clarify its philosophical intent in restoring objects. It should make clear that lacunae in the original object must generally remain visible (by painting them with a neutral colour, for instance), rather than attempting to conceal or repair them as if they were originally intact. This policy is extremely important in retaining both the integrity of the collection and the trust of the visitor, who will recognise that the museum has taken pains in restoring the object to allow him or her to distinguish what is original from what has been fabricated in the conservator's laboratory.

There are exceptions and qualifications, however. The policy may appear to be straightforward enough if the object is a prehistoric pot being reassembled, with unpainted areas indicating where the museum has supplied material to hold the shards together. But if a relatively small area of a painting is being restored, the purpose is usually to match the original artist's intention and hue as closely as possible; areas of the canvas will be left untouched only if they are so large that it has been decided to let the visitor see where the original artist's work is no longer visible. The policy may become even more contentious where machinery is being restored, or if a recovered shipwreck is to be prepared for display; the museum's intent to communicate clearly to the visitor what is original and what is not must be applied responsibly but imaginatively in each instance.

One important principle common to most conservation treatment and restoration policies is to *do nothing that is irremediable*. This entails written and photographic documentation of treatments in detail, and prior investigation of how to remove or undo treatments if this should become necessary in future.

Restoration policy and procedures manuals are particularly important in institutions where volunteers participate in restoration work – as commonly encountered in transportation and military museums, or in agricultural museums and heritage villages. The well-meaning intentions of such volunteers are sometimes directed toward 'restoring' vehicles or machinery to a 'band-box' finish never present in the original. The restoration procedures manual should require them to proceed with work only under professional supervision, following a step-by-step plan written by the responsible curator or conservator. Documentation of each step in the restoration process, by means of photographic and written reports, is also of the utmost importance where volunteers are involved.

### 3.2.5.4 Conservation research

The job descriptions provided in the Appendix include both conservators and conservation scientists. The latter employees, if a museum is large enough to employ them, should focus exclusively on conservation research. However, conservators may also find it valuable to include research as part of their job descriptions.

In the discussion of research plans (see subsection 3.2.1), it is noted that they are needed for conservators and others in the museum who carry out research, as well as curators. Conservators or conservation scientists should therefore be asked to draft such plans, with indication of likely time requirements for each project. As with curators, these research plans may be useful when the inevitable pressure to respond to an exhibition schedule or new acquisitions leads the director or the chief conservator to consider redirecting their efforts. The plan will allow all concerned to note the effects of such a redirection, and to decide collectively if the interests of the museum are best served by the change.

Conservation research is a particularly important aspect of museum operations, whether it is directed at the testing of new materials proposed for display, at contemporary conservation and restoration techniques, or at investigation of the materials and methods of manufacture of the artefacts or works of art in the collection. Museum management should aim to ensure that conservators have the time, space, facilities and equipment to undertake such research, and that the results of their inquiries are published and disseminated to other museums and collectors.

Such research needs to be planned carefully, however, in consultation with those in academic institutions or in other museums who may be working on related pursuits. Museum conservators need to participate fully in international conferences and subscribe to all relevant journals in order to ensure that they keep abreast of contemporary developments, and do not set out to 're-invent the wheel'. Participation in the computerised International Conservation Network and the International Conservation Committee (ICC) of the International Council on Museums (ICOM) are two important ways for museum conservation scientists to keep abreast, and to communicate their results to others.

### 3.2.5.5    EXHIBIT PREPARATION

PREPARATORS are often one of the more under-rated professional groups in the museum. Yet their work in preparing museum objects for display or loan, and installing, dismounting and returning them to stores brings together both the conservation and public aspects of the museum, in specific relation to the collection. They should be encouraged to work closely with the conservators, especially in ensuring that all support materials used in display or storage are tested beforehand or are known to be safe. Preparators working in museums in areas prone to earthquakes have a special concern to devise ways to exhibit and store works of art or artefacts in such a way as to minimise any potential damage from a quake on or near the museum site.

# 3.3 | Public Programme Management

Public programmes encompass all those activities that increase public access to and involvement with the collections: they enrich the visitor's experience, enhance enjoyment and understanding, attract new audiences and encourage return visits. As museums prepare for the 21st century, two qualities characterise the successful management of public programmes: visitor-responsiveness and creativity.

VISITOR-RESPONSIVENESS refers to the simple fact that museum programmes are for people. Unlike educational institutions which offer courses as part of degree studies or accreditation, museums offer programmes that respond to people's interest in self-directed learning, or 'life-long learning'. From the scholarly symposium to the Saturday afternoon treasure hunt to the World Wide Web site, museum programmes respond to the interests of the public.

Does this mean that museum programmes are designed by survey? No, they are designed by professionals who are steeped in the museum's mission and who also understand the interests and needs of the public. Continual evaluation, including surveys, is the only way to ensure that programmes are visitor-responsive (rather than staff-responsive) in their content, quality, format and method of delivery.

CREATIVITY is the 'wow' factor. It is the inspiration of a docent, the juxtaposition of two paintings never before seen in the same gallery, the new meaning an object theatre display gives to artefacts of everyday life, the wonder of electricity when the visitor creates an arc of light, the magic of being in the presence of museum objects that are beautifully displayed, the enthusiasm of information desk staff. Museum managers who nurture creativity in staff and respect the creativity of visitors will best be able to facilitate creative public programming.

This section explains how to manage public programmes and activities under the following headings:

- Exhibitions (3.3.1)
- Interpretation (3.3.2)
- Education (3.3.3)
- Extension and Outreach (3.3.4)
- Publications (3.3.5)
- Marketing (3.3.6)
- Visitor Services (3.3.7)

## 3.3.1  EXHIBITIONS

Exhibitions are the museum's main forum for interacting with the public. Indeed, the success or failure of a museum is most often judged by the public in terms of its exhibition programme. The exhibition policy and the exhibition development process are two important tools for managing a successful exhibition programme – and museum managers need to use both of them.

### 3.3.1.1  EXHIBITION POLICY

The EXHIBITION POLICY, which is formulated by the museum leadership, is the principal management tool for establishing:

- the objectives of the exhibition programme
- the philosophy of presentation
- the number, frequency, size and scope of temporary exhibitions

It is equally important for the staff and the museum's supporters to understand the *objectives of the exhibition programme* – for example, the particular balance between scholarship and visitor attraction, the emphasis on exhibitions of local, regional, national and international significance, and the degree to which the museum endeavours to increase public access to its collections through rotation and special exhibitions.

The *philosophy of presentation* defines the ways in which the museum will use the medium of the exhibition to communicate with the public. Today, there are many choices of exhibition philosophy, and some museums take advantage of all of them, while others focus on a single approach, and still others take one approach for the permanent collection and use temporary exhibitions as an opportunity to experiment with various philosophies of presentation. We briefly describe six of these here:

CONTEMPLATIVE: In this mode of presentation, museum specimens, artefacts or works of art are presented in an aesthetic mode which enhances the affective experience. This approach is most common in art galleries, but it is used to good effect in many other types of museums to evoke a sense of wonder or awe as, for example, in the dramatic display of a piece of moon rock in a science museum.

THEMATIC: Graphic and other interpretive devices place museum objects in a broader social, historical, cultural or scientific context. Sometimes referred to as didactic displays, they are generally used in history and science museums of all types.

ENVIRONMENTAL: Room settings or large-scale exhibits are used to recreate or evoke the atmosphere of time and place in which museum objects were used or developed – from the Court of Catherine the Great as featured in the 1995 'Treasures of the Czars' exhibition to the 'Challenger Space Centres' located in many American science museums.

SYSTEMATIC: The comprehensive display of museum objects to demonstrate type variations was the dominant form of museum exhibition in the Victorian period. Today there is a renewed interest in the 'visible storage' mode of exhibition which allows for the systematic display of collections with extensive information on flip card files or computer terminals, such as in the new Glass Gallery of the Victoria and Albert Museum in London (see Case Study 3.9) and the permanent collection galleries of the University of British Columbia Museum of Anthropology in Vancouver.

INTERACTIVE: This mode of display involves the visitor in dialogue with the exhibition. Touch-screen computers utilising multimedia technologies have been particularly effective in helping visitors explore scientific theories, such as in the Dinosaur Galleries at the Natural History Museums in London and New York, and to guide themselves through entire art collections in the MicroGalleries at the National Galleries in London and Washington, DC (see Case Study 3.1).

HANDS-ON EXHIBITS: These encourage visitors to learn through physical experience. Once the preserve of science and children's museums, now many types of museums provide 'touch tables' and other forms of access to study collections where visitors of all ages may feel the weight of an ancient bronze and touch the different glazes of Japanese ceramics. Duplicates, secondary examples or replicas are used.

Underlying the contemporary approach to museum exhibition is a fundamental shift from the idea of the museum as representing absolute authority in its field to the idea that the museum presents and interprets facts which are frequently contradictory and reflect the ideas of many experts from which not only the curator but also the visitor may choose. The Tate Gallery in London continually re-interprets its collections by annually re-installing the galleries, changing pictures and themes. Its new audio-guide reinforces this approach by featuring a number of keepers describing their approach to the installation of specific galleries – thus allowing visitors to experience the intellectual excitement of museum institutions where different perspectives lead to the creation of new ideas about art (see Case Study 3.4).

Another fundamental shift is from the museum as a closed institution to an open one that invites both the specialist and broad publics to contribute their knowledge and information. This has the greatest impact on exhibition planning procedures, but there is also an impact on the exhibition floor. At the Art Gallery of Ontario in Toronto, for example, visitors are invited to record in words and sketches their feelings and ideas on the Group of Seven Gallery, and these are regularly added to the interactive computer terminals which are discreetly located in the gallery, so that visitors may experience the responses of other visitors to the works of this famous group of Canadian artists, as well as those of the curators and educators who planned the gallery.

The exhibition policy should set out guidelines on issues of authority and openness for museum staff in addressing these complex matters during the exhibition development and design process.

The *number, duration, frequency, size* and *scope* of temporary exhibitions is cause for continual debate. Determining a number of changing exhibitions that is neither too many for curators and exhibit staff nor too few for the public is very difficult. It is equally daunting to determine how many exhibitions the market will bear in the face of curatorial enthusiasm to create more exhibitions. The duration of travelling shows is often too short to be effectively marketed, and some museums would do better to show fewer exhibitions for longer periods, but market them better. Size and scope are more controversial, with partisans on both sides of the 'blockbuster argument': those who insist that blockbuster exhibitions present great opportunities, both for scholarship and audience development, and those who see these large, high-profile exhibitions as obstructing the museum's real mission. Geographic scope can also be an issue when a beloved local exhibition (the science fair or the artists' society) is replaced by an exhibition from elsewhere.

The role of the exhibition policy is to provide general guidance on these issues, so that the museum's exhibition schedule is consistent with its mission and with the objectives of the exhibition programme. The policy should consider the different types of exhibitions and set a range for the frequency and scope of each type, including:

- rotation of displays of sensitive objects for conservation reasons;

- small feature exhibitions to provide public access to new acquisitions, current research or to collections in store; there is a trend towards 'one-object' exhibitions, in which the museum provides a great breadth and depth of information about the making and meaning of a single important item from its collection;

- major thematic exhibitions from the museum's collection, possibly supplemented by borrowed works, which may be designed to travel or to be exhibited at one museum;

- loan exhibitions of various sizes, originated by another museum, by a museum consortium, a private sector organisation or government agency;

- large, high-profile exhibitions which are so spectacular that they attract a huge attendance (in the hundreds of thousands) – 'blockbusters'; while fine art and archaeological treasures blockbusters are most prevalent, there are also major exhibitions like 'The Science of Sport', organised by a consortium of US science centres, the touring dinosaur animatronic shows and the loan to zoos of rare animals like the giant pandas; small and medium-sized museums can participate in the local or regional blockbuster by producing exhibitions that focus on their particular aspect of the subject.

The simple two-year chart in Table 3.3 is a useful tool for ensuring that the exhibition policy maintains an appropriate balance between these many possibilities. The left-hand column indicates whether the exhibition is primarily local, regional, national or international in scope. The various types of exhibitions appear across the top.

*Table 3.3   Guideline for Two-year Museum Exhibition Schedule*

| Scope | Rotate | Small | Theme | Loan |
|---|---|---|---|---|
| Local | | 3 | 2 | |
| Regional | 4 | 3 | 2 | 2 |
| National | | | | 2 |
| International | | | | 1 |

The example in Table 3.3 is for a museum with a strong regional history mission and mandate. The policy guideline seeks to mount nineteen exhibitions over a two-year period. About one-quarter would be small exhibitions that rotate the collection of textiles and works on paper. Six small exhibitions would focus on new acquisitions and items of local and regional importance from the collection. Over two years the museum would mount four thematic exhibitions, two on local and two on regional subjects. The museum would borrow five exhibitions over two years, three of them national or international, providing the community with a 'window on the world'.

At the end of this period, staff should evaluate the effectiveness of the programme, and the director should recommend changes to the board, if a new balance or focus is needed at the policy level.

It is worth noting that the board's role is not to debate the exhibition programme, but to debate and formulate policy on programme objectives, the philosophy of presentation and the guidelines for the exhibition schedule, and then to provide oversight to ensure that the director and staff are fulfilling the institution's exhibition policy.

### 3.3.1.2   ORGANISATION OF THE EXHIBITION DEVELOPMENT PROCESS

An exhibition is a medium of communication, and it is the museum's main means of communicating with the public. To communicate effectively requires all the resources of the museum – and increasingly, resources from outside as well. The exhibition development process sums up the procedures that the museum has established over time to co-ordinate all these resources so that exhibitions open on time, within budget and to the agreed level of quality.

### 3.3.1.2.1   The exhibition committee

While the director is the ultimate decision maker on the exhibition programme, many museums establish an exhibition committee, comprising curators and senior managers, that meets periodically to review exhibition proposals and concepts and to formulate the exhibition programme and budget.

### 3.3.1.2.2   Exhibition project teams

Each exhibition is the project of a specific project or task force team that combines the talents of all those responsible for the many aspects of an exhibition project. Each team should include representatives of the following functions in the museum:

- **Collection Management**
  - curatorial
  - conservation
  - documentation
- **Public Programmes**
  - exhibitions
  - design
  - education
  - publications
  - marketing
- **Administration**
  - finance
  - development
  - security
  - visitor services

The idea of project teams is that they are project-oriented and non-hierarchical (see subsection 2.3.2.3); therefore, in selecting personnel to serve on a particular committee, department heads should take account of the knowledge and ability of the staff member, rather than their position or title. Where outside contractors are involved – for example, in design or marketing – they should also be represented on the team and attend meetings.

The director should have final approval of the composition of the project team and should appoint the chair or co-ordinator. Although the relevant curator might be the obvious choice to chair an exhibition project team, in many cases the exhibition department representative, educator or conservator is a suitable choice. The director delegates penultimate decision-making on the budget and schedule to the project team, and the team chair or co-ordinator reports back to the director or the senior management exhibition committee.

The team may begin by meeting monthly, and should receive regular reports from all participants so that security concerns, for example, are not left to the last minute. The project team is the forum for staff ideas and creativity – all staff should feel able to present ideas and suggestions on the exhibition to the project team. The frequency of meetings should increase as opening day nears. Crediting the members of the team on exhibition literature and signage is a good way to inspire dedication to an outstanding result.

The challenges experienced by exhibition project teams are legendary: the members are required not only to bring their professional expertise to the table, but to be skilled in working cross-functionally under great time and budget pressures. The team co-ordinator needs to be both a skilled facilitator and a gifted project manager. These are not necessarily the same abilities required to achieve a PhD in Art History, nor to be a talented designer. Some museums, recognising that staff need new skills to develop effective teamwork, are implementing special training programmes. The American Association of Museums has developed a programme called 'Vision 2000' that can assist museums to build effective teamwork in their organisations.

### 3.3.1.2.3   Advisory committees

In order to bring outside resources into the exhibition development process, many museums establish exhibition advisory committees. These may be advisory committees of academics, collectors and scholars, whose knowledge and networks will enhance the quality of the exhibition and facilitate loans; or they may be more community-based advisory committees, who bring a 'stakeholder' perspective to the exhibition, helping to ensure that it responds to community interests and sensitivities. The results can be far-reaching: from high levels of attendance by communities who had not previously visited the museum to long-term involvement as members, volunteers, trustees and donors. The key to successful advisory committees is the director's personal commitment and involvement, and to be prepared not just to listen, but to implement suggestions or to explain why not, and to achieve consensus concerning other solutions.

# Exhibition Advisory Committees:
# Inviting the Community to the Core

BY DR ROBERT P BERGMAN

At the Cleveland Museum of Art we convene exhibition advisory committees in connection with many major special exhibitions. I began this practice at the Walters Art Gallery in Baltimore in 1985. The principle behind these initiatives is simple: inspiring profound relationships with people in the community is most effectively fostered by involving them in core aspects of the operation. The exhibition programmes at these museums – visible, varied and embedded in an array of activities and programmes appealing to many different interests – are perfect vehicles for such profound community involvement.

Some exhibitions have natural affinity groups. Often, but not always, the affinities are based on national (Hungarians for a show coming from Budapest), racial/ethnic (African-Americans for an African art show), collector (jewellery and precious object fanciers for a Fabergé show), religious (Catholics for a show coming from the Vatican) or other identities. Inevitably, these natural affinity groups form the majority of a typical committee, but the committees are by no means monolithic. Around this core, others interested in the exhibition – trustees and a sprinkling of those just interested in the museum or in the civic good – are convened to form a committee of twenty-five to fifty members. The chair can be a staff member, a trustee, a museum supporter or a new community face identified specifically for the purpose of heading the committee.

The committees generally meet three times. The first meeting might occur four to six months before the show's opening. At the meeting, the curator presents an overview of the exhibition, its aims and content. Educators indicate the general scope and direction of programming. Development staff describe the show's financial support. Public relations, marketing and special events staff describe plans in their areas for the project's promotion and for opening events. Throughout the meeting, we ask for suggestions and advice and for help with specific tasks, such as clarifying aspects of the installation and its interpretive apparatus, finding programme participants and identifying mailing lists, fundraising prospects, even caterers for the opening. We don't necessarily accept all the advice we receive, but we do listen hard, we listen sincerely, and we listen with an eye towards improving our public communication. Might misunderstandings and disagreements occur? Absolutely. Could someone walk out in a huff when their suggestion hasn't been accepted? Maybe, but I've yet to see it happen. A second meeting is usually scheduled about a month before the exhibition opens, during which progress on plans is reviewed. The final meeting is held a few days before the opening. This is a particularly fascinating one for committee members, since we invite them in to see the installation in its final stages of preparation and to share in the excitement of last-minute preparations.

When you invite the community in to participate at this level, it can sometimes be uncomfortable. But in my experience, an outspoken and even contentious committee is not necessarily a bad one. On the contrary, such groups provide for our initiatives the kind of commitment and passion about our work that the organisers share, but that we often fail to find in our audiences. Exhibition advisory committees bring the community to the core of the museum. Committee alumni extend the museum family in a particularly meaningful fashion.

*Children's classes at the Cleveland Museum of Art create projects inspired by the Baroque paintings. Photograph by Gregory M Donley, courtesy of the Cleveland Museum of Art.*

### 3.3.1.3    STAGES IN THE EXHIBITION PROCESS

Where do exhibition ideas come from? The director's leadership, curatorial research and suggestions of the education staff are among the most frequent sources. If the museum is developing its guards or warders as museum attendants (see Case Study 2.2), a suggestion box in the attendants' changing room is a good source, since the attendants have the best opportunity to observe public interest, or lack of it. A visitor suggestion box, asking for exhibition suggestions, is also a good idea.

Just how the exhibition evolves from the idea stage to opening day will differ from museum to museum, depending on the size of the institution, the balance between in-house production and contract services, and the institution's culture. Below, we define some basic steps that are used by many museums.

### 3.3.1.3.1    Concept stage

At this stage, the exhibition idea has received some tentative approval from the museum leadership and is developed by its proponents into a concept that articulates:

- exhibition objectives;
- the scholarly significance of the exhibition;
- the interest to visitors;
- what the exhibition will look like (in words) and the amount of gallery space required;
- the art works or artefacts to be used from the museum's collections, those to be borrowed, and the likely availability of these;
- the costs involved;
- potential sources of funding and support;
- the likely time requirement.

### 3.3.1.3.2    Interpretive plan

Once the museum leadership has approved the exhibition concept and it has been added to the museum exhibition schedule and budget, the exhibition project team is formed and starts work. The first step is to write the interpretive plan which is the exhibition brief. This is an extraordinarily important document, which will guide the exhibition development process right through to opening.

Many large museums will have specialist 'interpretive planners' on their staff. Experienced interpretive planners may be contracted as outside consultants, with the exhibition concept serving as their terms of reference. Alternatively, a museum might consider training some curatorial or public programmes staff in interpretive planning.

The interpretive plan or exhibition brief articulates:

- the objectives of the exhibition
- the visitor experience of the exhibition
- component-by-component description of the exhibition, which lists:
  - the communication objectives of each component
  - the potential means of communication to achieve these objectives
  - diagrams of visitor flow patterns
  - concept sketches to give an idea of the 'feel' of the exhibition

The plan will be reviewed several times until the entire project team and the director are in full agreement. Once the interpretive plan is formally approved by the director, each member of the exhibition project team can carry through his or her areas of specialisation: the design, selection of artefacts and preparation of label text, the marketing plan, the security arrangements, the tasks of preparing museum objects for display, loan arrangements, and so on. If the museum has in-house exhibition designers, the interpretive plan may simply go to them for design; if not, it will become the Design Brief for tendering exhibition design. This tender may be for design only, or may be a 'design-build' tender.

### 3.3.1.3.3   Schematic design

'Schematic design' refers to the period in which designers are drawing up the design of the exhibition to fulfil the interpretive plan. This is usually a combination of floorplans and three-dimensional views (often called 'presentation drawings') of each exhibit component. Again, there will be several reviews until the designers (whether in-house or outside contractors) develop a suitable solution. These drawings are especially useful for development and marketing.

The more accurate the interpretive plan, the less time it will take for the team to develop an appropriate schematic design and to agree on it. This is an important factor in staying within the exhibition budget – design is expensive, but the exhibits that result from the design will be even more costly. This is equally the 'sketch stage' for all the specialists on the team – for example, the educator will draft an education programme so that he or she can make sure that the design takes account of where the large numbers of schoolchildren will need to gather or sit in the galleries, and security will look at the floorplans to establish potential surveillance issues *before* design is finalised. The marketing plan will produce clearer ideas of the numbers of visitors that can be expected, and the visitor services staff will now be able to plan the special exhibition shop and to address queuing and special ticketing arrangements, if necessary. Depending on the size of the project, schematic design can take from three months to a year, and the schematic design must be formally approved by the team and the director before design development can start.

### 3.3.1.3.4　Design development

This is the stage in which detailed design takes place. Each exhibit component is designed, with a view to eventual transmission to a fabricator. The drawings carry specifications regarding colour, materials and dimensions. Every member of the project team should be involved in the review and approval of the design so that it goes to the director with the input and agreement of representatives of each of the museum's functions.

The exhibition text and any audio-visual scripts will be developed towards the end of this stage. As will be discussed in subsection 3.3.2.2, there are many approaches to the preparation of text and labels. For a special exhibition, the text is usually generated by the curator, and it is then applied to the exhibition by the interpretive planner: the educator reviews and edits the text from the visitors' perspective, and publications staff carry out final editing from a stylistic point of view. The graphic designers (either in-house or contractors) provide a design for the text and graphics that conforms to the 'levels' of interpretation indicated by the communication objectives in the interpretive plan. The curator must also work with the interpretive planner and the producers of any shows or multimedia interactives on the scripts for these components at this time. Depending on the size and complexity of the exhibition, design development takes from three months to a year.

### 3.3.1.3.5　Formative evaluation

This term means, quite simply, evaluation while the exhibition is taking shape. At various points in the process, the director and exhibition committee or the advisory committees will provide input into the development of the exhibition, which the project team will take on board. Formative evaluation is initiated and organised by the project team to make sure that the exhibition works from the user's perspective. One member of the team (usually from marketing, or education, or the museum's evaluation specialist, if it has one on its staff) will organise some outside groups of likely users (such as members, teachers, or visitors selected at random) to 'walk through' the plans and the text to identify any problems or pitfalls. If it is a major exhibition or a re-installation of the permanent galleries, the museum may prefer to employ an outside evaluator.

### 3.3.1.3.6　Construction and installation

The final, approved design and text package can then go into production. Few museums have all the required construction capabilities in-house, so many aspects of construction will be put out for tender to outside contractors. The contractor selection process should be managed according to the museum's procurement policies by the museum's purchasing department, in close consultation with the exhibition department. However, the museum must not be tied to accepting the lowest or *any* bid – museum exhibitions are labour-intensive and customised, and frequently a low bid may indicate a lack of experience with the level of quality the museum is seeking.

Once the construction and installation process has commenced, the primary role of the project team is quality control and keeping within the budget and schedule. The exhibition department has the expertise to play the leadership role in this, but all members of the team should participate in the oversight role to ensure that all museum requirements in the brief are fulfilled. Because of the special security requirements of working in a museum environment, there need to be clear policies and guidelines for all outside contractors: the British Museums Association has published an excellent guideline for museums to use: 'Museums Association guidelines on security when using outside contractors', *Museum Yearbook*, 1995/96 (London: Museums Association, 1995, pp 35–6).

During this period, project team meetings are an important forum for connecting the entire museum to the exhibition and ensuring that plans are co-ordinated for education activities, special events, publicity, fundraising and visitor services.

### 3.3.1.3.7   Near opening day

The construction should be completed, the dust removed and the contractors off the site in good time for the installation of artefacts. Prior to final approval of construction and installation, the team chair, the head of exhibitions and the head of contracting should tour the exhibition and draw up a 'snag list' of deficiencies that the contractor must correct. Some negotiation will ensue regarding which deficiencies fall under the contract and which are client changes, but all problems identified on the snag list must be resolved. The stage is set for the installation of artefacts, audio-visual elements and final text. In an ideal world, there should be time for pre-testing with sample visitors, and final adjustments; then: the opening.

### 3.3.1.3.8   Evaluation

The exhausted project team still has one more job to do: evaluating the exhibition process. It is crucial, both for the museum and the field as a whole, to look back on the exhibition project to identify aspects of the process that worked well and why, and changes to the process that will improve success in the future.

A 'summative evaluation' of the visitor experience of the exhibition should be conducted by the museum's evaluation specialist or by an outside contractor. This type of visitor evaluation is most effective if it goes back to the original interpretive plan to evaluate whether or not the exhibition actually communicated what it planned to communicate. The evaluation should be submitted to the director and to the exhibition department, which should be developing an exhibition procedures manual based on the cumulative experience of the museum's many exhibition project teams. This type of manual should be a vital document that facilitates the creativity of future exhibition project teams.

# Exhibition Teams at the Field Museum of Natural History, Chicago

BY JANET KAMIEN

The development, design and production method established at the Field Museum, Chicago, between 1985 and 1995 resulted in the creation of 135,000 square feet (12,540 square metres) of new, dynamic exhibition brought in at an average of US$250 per square foot ($2,700 per square metre). Although both in-house and outside scientific expertise were essential to this effort, the teams were formed around individuals (principal developers) whose main focus was the learner, rather than the material to be learned. This individual became, in essence, the project director, and individuals representing all other areas of expertise worked in support of the educational vision supplied by the principal developer, within the confines of scientific accuracy.

The research involved in this type of approach is both traditional and non-traditional. The usual effort of investigating the latest scientific ideas on a subject and isolating the collection objects to be used in support of these ideas is joined by intensive visitor research designed to identify visitors' interests, baseline knowledge and misconceptions, and by more informal investigation and testing of methods that may be successful in getting the ideas across to the public. The questions that the team may pose to themselves during the development process include not only enquiries about the best vehicle and/or metaphor to elucidate an idea (i.e. a label, a film, a specimen, an interactive device), but how best to test the idea's soundness before it is produced and the money is irrevocably spent.

The basic skills needed within each team include expertise in budget and schedule design and management, team facilitation, visitor research, subject matter, label-writing, editing, design and production, cost estimating, educational theory, three-dimensional design, and production management. Although it does not matter much how these areas of expertise are spread across the team, it is imperative that they be brought together into a working whole that has a universally understood mission, schedule and budget, and timely decision-making process. This kind of clarification is a primary task of the principal developer.

The total budget, opening date, location and size are the parameters given to each team at the outset, and these do not vary during the process. In addition, there is a mandate to save a minimum of 10% of the production budget in a contingency line and 10% in a revisions line to be spent on mistakes and improvements after the exhibit opens. In general, preliminary budgets create envelopes of about 10% of the total for shell work, 50% for production, 5% for contingency, 5% for revisions and 30% for all the development, design and consulting tasks. These disciplines create a coherent environment in which the creative work may take place.

*The Field Museum of Natural History, Chicago, 1994.*
*Photograph by James Balodimas, courtesy of the Field Museum of Natural History. GN-87244.33c*

## 3.3.2 INTERPRETATION

'Interpretation' is the term used to describe the ways that the museum *communicates* with the public about its collections and research activities. The term 'interpretation' is somewhat misleading, because it suggests that the 'language' of museum objects is somehow 'foreign' and needs to be 'translated' – which is essentially one-way communication, whereas museums in the 21st century should be concerned with two-way communication between the museum and the public. However, 'interpretation' is the term generally used by the museum profession, and includes:

- orientation (3.3.2.1)

- labels and text (3.3.2.2)

- provision of information (3.3.2.3)

As with other programme areas, the museum should formulate a policy to express its philosophy of interpretation or communication. For example, there are some art museums that have a philosophy of 'letting works of art speak for themselves', and they therefore provide a minimum of labels in their galleries; others adopt a contrary approach, because their philosophy is 'the more the visitor understands, the more the visitor will gain from the works of art', and there are many approaches which fall along the continuum between these two philosophies. Indeed, some museums may have certain galleries devoted to an 'art for art's sake' approach and others that are heavily interpreted. Among science and industry museums, some have a philosophy of 'every exhibit must be hands-on in some way', while others prefer a more contextual approach, with objects in cases and extensive graphic explanations – very hands-off. Again, there are many possible variants along this continuum. The interpretation policy provides a helpful framework for staff who are responsible for the museum's many forms of interpretation.

### 3.3.2.1 ORIENTATION

Visitor orientation is of two types, and museums tend to undervalue both of them:

- PHYSICAL ORIENTATION: informing visitors about where they are, the visitor services available and in what languages, what there is to see and do, and how to find it;

- INTELLECTUAL ORIENTATION: clarifying what the museum is about and the many ways to explore it, so that visitors are able to make informed choices about their visit. For example, should they follow the prescribed visitor route, or is there a quick highlights tour? Is there a special family gallery? Is there a resource centre for visitors who prefer to cover fewer subject areas in more depth?

Visitor studies and common sense indicate that visitors who spend most of their time lost, looking for the toilets, or who are not sure what is on offer in the various galleries, do not gain as much from the exhibits as those who know their way around. There is evidence that being lost increases the 'I don't belong here' feeling and discourages repeat visits. Informing visitors at the outset about services such as cloakrooms, rest areas, restaurants, shops, toilets, baby changing areas, first aid posts, use of wheelchairs and push-chairs, and the roles of guards and information desk staff helps first-time visitors especially to feel at ease.

The quality of orientation also has an impact on the museum's revenue stream. If visitors are not aware at the beginning of the visit that there is a pleasant cafe, they may not make time to visit it. If they do not understand the full range of the museum's exhibits and programmes, they may leave mistakenly thinking 'We've done that', rather than 'There's so much more to see and do, we must come back.'

Once museum management and staff grasp the importance of orientation to the quality of the visitor experience, visitor orientation can be addressed:

- If there is not enough room in the lobby, consider whether posters or banners outside the building could begin to communicate the museum's philosophy and what is inside.

- Use all possible means to communicate the visitor's choices, such as information signs, interactive kiosks, the information desk, pamphlets and floor maps.

- Develop a consistent wayfinding system, starting outside and with directional signing throughout the museum's public spaces, and link signing with print and audio-visual materials.

- Train all front-line staff in the importance of helping visitors to find their way, encourage staff to report back to management on the problems they learn from visitors – then do something to solve the problems.

### 3.3.2.2  Labels and text

'Labels are the footsoldiers in the museum wars' is how one curator recently described the central role of labelling in a staff workshop facilitated by one of the authors. And 'wars' may be an apt description of the label-writing process in many museums. As with exhibition development (see subsection 3.3.1), each museum develops its own procedure for writing label and panel text. The museum's philosophy of interpretation will govern:

- the names or themes of galleries;

- the size of label or text panel;

- the type of information to be provided (date, artist/inventor, provenance, accession number, gift, description, uses, etc.);

- the tone (is it authoritative, Socratic, objective?);

- the style (every-day language or technical terms?).

The museum's label-writing procedure establishes:

- the word limits;

- type size and colour;
- placement;
- writing and approval procedures.

The label text process generally starts with the curator responsible for a particular gallery or exhibit. Next, the education department reviews it from the visitor's perspective, and the publications department edits for style. The curator gives final approval to the text, while the director's office is usually the court of last resort.

Some museums designate one person to be responsible for interpretation. The Tate Gallery has appointed a Curator of Interpretation who is a member of the Department of Communication, where he has been very effective in working with both curators and educators to produce a wide range of interpretive materials, including labels, wall texts, broadsheets, gallery guides and the new TateInform audio-guide system.

# New Displays at the Tate Gallery, and the Role of Interpretation

BY SIMON WILSON

By the late 1980s only about one-fifth of the Tate Gallery's collection could be shown at a time. In response to this situation, Nicholas Serota, when he took over as Director in 1988, instituted a policy of annual re-displays of the permanent collection, together with a radical change in layout, creating a continuous, broadly chronological sweep of displays from the early 16th to the late 20th century, where before there had been two parallel sequences of historic British and International modern art. These annual changes were branded as New Displays, and the Tate was fortunate in finding in British Petroleum (BP) a major and faithful sponsor for them. As well as bringing work out of store, New Displays enabled curators to create thematic displays, breaking away from traditional chronological and canonical art historical concepts.

Intrinsic to New Displays was a fresh (for the Tate, at least) approach to interpretation: for the first time, each room was provided with a title as well as its number, and a wall text of some 200 words giving an account of its contents. Each work was provided with a 'caption' (our term) of 112 words.

It has to be said that both the change in display policy and the introduction of texts aroused considerable opposition from some collection curators. As Head of Education at the Tate in the 1980s, I had unsuccessfully urged the adoption of wall texts and captions, finally going public at the 1987 London Conference of the Association of Art Historians in a paper entitled 'Curators . . . and the Myth of the Self-Evident Art Work'. It was with the arrival a year later of a director with a new vision, and the determination to carry it through, that texts and captions became possible, and even then, at first, only some works were captioned. All now are, and the Tate is now unthinkable without these brief notes for the public, which, as our 1994 Visitor Audit revealed, have been greatly appreciated. It is notable, too, that the audit also revealed a public demand for even more information about the collection. This has in part been satisfied by the introduction of TateInform, a hand-held audio-guide which permits the visitor to gain access to commentary on any work in the gallery carrying an Inform number on its label.

Wall texts, captions and audio-guides complement an extensive existing apparatus of interpretation for adult audiences, developed at the Tate since the early 1970s, comprising daily tours provided by volunteer guides (docents), daily gallery lectures, regular documentary and artists' film and video programmes, specialist lecture series, a range of seminars, conferences and short courses, a writer in residence and a range of publications of various kinds. Schools and young people have their own equally extensive programmes.

Since 1993, responsibility for all the above has been divided between the Tate Education Department and a new Interpretation Section located in the Communications Department, which in turn is part of the Directorate of Public and Regional Services. So far, the section consists of one person, the author, who is principally responsible for creating or editing all written or audio material about the collection that is produced for the general public – everything that is not a specialist exhibition or collection catalogue. The Interpretation Section provides advice to curators on communicating with a non-specialist audience, and results in a more collaborative approach to providing information for visitors. On the creative side, the Interpretation Section is responsible for written guides to the gallery's major loan exhibitions and for the 'book' of the Tate, its *Illustrated Companion*. It is also responsible for overseeing and training the volunteer guides. The Interpretation Section also provides an interface with the public and the media, and the Tate's role as a museum of contemporary art in particular has caused this aspect to take on some importance, especially in relation to the often hysterical response of the British media and public to some of the more extreme manifestations of the contemporary art scene when these appear within the state-sponsored walls of the Tate.

*Tate Gallery exterior.*
*Photograph by Gill Selby, courtesy of the Tate Gallery, London.*

## 3.3.2.3 PROVISION OF INFORMATION

We are living in an 'information age', and for museums, this means that visitors have an insatiable desire for more information, as every visitor survey will demonstrate. Information provision may include:

- THE INFORMATION DESK: This is the front line for information. The staff and volunteers should be prepared to respond to questions ranging from where to catch the bus to where a specific painting is to be found. The Art Institute of Chicago has placed information desks throughout the museum, as well as at the entrances.

- INFORMATION STAFF: These may have a roving brief, as at the Tate Gallery in Liverpool, where 'zone guides' are prepared to answer visitors' questions and engage in discussion. At Glasgow's museums and galleries, warders have been trained and their positions upgraded to provide visitors with information.

- INFORMATION CENTRES: These are being developed in many museums to provide visitors with a range and depth of information convenient to the galleries. For example, the MicroGalleries at the National Galleries of Art in London and Washington offer the visitor the opportunity to explore the entire collection on CD-ROM and to plan a personal visitor route (see Case Study 3.1). A study room on each floor of the Seattle Art Museum encourages the visitor to explore the collection on CD-ROM, consult catalogues and to explore the study collection.

- THE LIBRARY: This may be fully accessible to the public, or open at certain times or by appointment.

- COMPUTERS AND MULTIMEDIA TERMINALS: These are being installed in or near galleries to provide contextual information, access to some card catalogue data on objects, or simulation exercises and games to explain processes, concepts and principles.

- AUDIO-GUIDES: In the past, these were used primarily in tour format for special exhibitions; they are now being developed for permanent collections. This is a result of new digital technologies which make it possible for the visitor to 'browse' and select those pictures, objects or displays of interest to him or her, rather than conforming to a particular route. Another benefit of this technology is that visitors do not have to bend or stoop to read labels, nor do they have to continually move back and forth between the label and the exhibit – thus reducing both visitor fatigue and crowding in front of popular exhibits. The National Gallery in London was the first to make information accessible about every picture on the main gallery floor. The Tate Gallery in London and the Museum of Modern Art in San Francisco decided to provide an introduction to each gallery, and information on selected works of art. The content and tone of each of these audio-guides is quite different, reflecting the galleries' different philosophies of interpretation.

- TOURS, LECTURES AND DEMONSTRATIONS: Because of their personal quality, these continue to be the preferred means of communication for many visitors and museum interpreters. Most museums offer a range of tours and lectures conducted by inspired volunteers, museum staff or special lecturers. In history, science and children's museums, there may be demonstrators (sometimes costumed) and interpreters on hand to explain the exhibits.

## 3.3.2.4 LANGUAGES

The languages in which interpretation will be available and provision for the sight- and hearing-impaired are important considerations in the interpretation policy.

In a globalised world, museums must cater for the main languages spoken in the community – whether official or unofficial – and for the main tourist languages. Where there are two official languages – as in Wales or in Ontario, Canada – provincial and national museums provide all interpretation in both languages, including signs, labels, publications and guided tours. In regions and communities that are culturally diverse but where there is only one official language, the museum should provide leaflets, guidebooks, information paddles and directional signs in the main minority languages. Label text may be made available on broadsheets in many languages, as well as in large print size for the sight-impaired. Directional signs and floorplans in minority languages are particularly important for reasons of public safety. The museum should ensure that at least one member of the information and interpretation staff who is able to communicate in the main languages spoken in the community is on duty at all times.

Tourism, and particularly cultural tourism, is growing so rapidly that museums which attract, or hope to attract, a high proportion of tourist visitors should provide services in the four or five main tourist languages, including Japanese. The main orientation and directional signs and information leaflets should be prominently displayed in these languages, with translations of label text, guidebooks and catalogues available for sale in the shop and for consultation at information desks and in study and rest areas.

Guided tours should be available in various languages and for special needs groups, including the sight-impaired. The new digital audio-guides described in subsection 3.3.2.3 can easily be adjusted to meet the needs of the hearing-impaired, and can be made available in numerous languages. Offering guided tours, particularly in Asian languages, can be instrumental in increasing foreign tourist visitation.

## 3.3.2.5 INTERPRETATION MANAGEMENT

Centralised management of the museum's interpretation services is rarely found in museums. Information desks are usually managed by visitor services or communication department staff, while tours and lectures are organised by the education department, and the library forms its own department; meanwhile, label-writing, audio-guide and multimedia production are undertaken by many different departments in different museums, including curatorial. Should there be one interpretation department, in the public programmes division, or is there a virtue in having a multiplicity of departments providing information and interpretation? Since every department communicates with the public, it makes most sense to create an interdepartmental interpretation (or communication) project team that implements museum policy and co-ordinates the growing number of communication initiatives that will – as long as the museum staff are visitor-responsive and creative – keep emerging everywhere.

# Improving the Visitor Experience at the Tate Gallery, London

By Damien Whitmore

The Tate Gallery houses the national collection of British Art from the 16th century to the present day, including the Turner Bequest and the national collection of international painting and sculpture. The Tate has three galleries: in London, founded in 1897, in Liverpool, built in 1987, and at St Ives, opened in 1993. Each year, the gallery rotates and re-hangs the display of its permanent collection in a programme called New Displays (see Case Study 3.4). To complement this, the Tate hosts three major exhibitions annually, as well as a series of displays dedicated to a single artist, theme or historical period. Admission to the Tate Gallery in London and Liverpool is free. There is, however, a small entrance charge to the Tate Gallery at St Ives. In the year 2000, the Tate Gallery in London will divide into the Tate Gallery of Modern Art at a new site at Bankside and the Tate Gallery of British Art at the present site at Millbank.

The Communications Department at the Tate Gallery is the focus for the gallery's relationship with its visitors. The department manages press relations, design and print production, advertising, promotions, information provision in the gallery and interpretation. The Tate is one of the few galleries in the world to have the post of Curator of Interpretation based in a marketing department.

## INTEGRATED MARKETING AT THE TATE GALLERY

During the past decade, marketing in museums and galleries has focused on external communications. Increasingly sophisticated methods of attracting visitors have been employed, and large budgets have been channelled into public relations, advertising, design and promotional activities. During the past three years, the Tate has benefited from a new corporate identity created by Pentagram Design, the appointment of advertising agency and public relations consultants, new publicity materials, collaborations with broadcasting and a host of promotional collaborations with organisations ranging from department stores to airlines. The gallery has even published its own magazine – *tate: the art magazine*. Visitor figures are currently at an all-time high, so clearly, some of these activities are working.

However, recent visitor surveys have revealed that up to 40 per cent of the Tate's visitors come to the gallery because of a recommendation made by a friend or relative. Word of mouth is a vital marketing tool which can bring in over a third of the gallery's audience. It is for this reason that the Tate integrates external communications and visitor services within one department, and why a number of innovations in both these areas have been introduced.

## EXTERNAL COMMUNICATIONS

The most visible of these innovations was the creation of a corporate identity for the Tate Gallery. This enables the organisation to communicate with one voice and provides a tangible means of bringing together its many varied activities. The identity was created by David Hillman at Pentagram Design, and is now in full operation throughout the three galleries. The identity is made up of a main logo and two specified typefaces for each gallery. The typefaces were deliberately chosen to provide strong, clear headlines and elegant, readable body copy, as well as to reflect the particular style of each gallery. At Millbank, for example, the identity has to embrace a diverse range of activities and art from different periods. Franklin Gothic and Jansen Antiqua typefaces were chosen, as both work well with historic and contemporary images, and both, while traditional, can at the same time serve as assertive, modern typefaces. The benefits of having a unified identity are numerous: all print represents the gallery in an appropriate way to a high standard; each item of print promotes the gallery, as well as communicating its individual message; successive pieces of print all reinforce each other – they are not fighting afresh for recognition and impact, and finally, the identity allows the gallery to maintain a single, high standard of design, across all departments, and for many different uses.

*tate: the art magazine* was launched in September 1993 and is produced by Aspen Publishing. *tate* has an international perspective which emerges from a close relationship with the gallery. However, it is an independent publication with its own voice and vision. The magazine explores issues in art, design, architecture and electronic media from around the world, as well as addressing ideas and debates within contemporary cultural affairs. The magazine has a circulation of over 30,000, which includes Friends of the Tate Gallery, visitors, international subscribers and general readers.

The gallery employs a range of *external consultants* to enhance and develop its external communications activities. As well as Pentagram Design and Wordsearch, the Tate employs an advertising agency, a political lobbying company and a press consultancy. The press consultancy has been particularly successful, bringing to the gallery a more proactive approach to press work and a substantial increase in the amount and range of media coverage for the gallery. The advantages of using external consultants are numerous: they are able to bring fresh ideas into the organisation; they are not bound by internal, organisational bureaucracy;

they are task-oriented, so their energies are focused on one project; they are well motivated, because they are working on a short-term contract; they are aware of developments in other organisations, and they bring this knowledge and experience to other projects.

## VISITOR SERVICES

In order to assess the effectiveness of the gallery's services for visitors and understand more about the visitor experience, the Tate commissioned a qualitative visitor audit during 1993. A number of quantitative studies had already been commissioned, so there was a great deal of information about visitor profile, effectiveness of advertising, and seasonal attendance. The Visitor Audit, however, explored the visitor's attitude to the gallery and the quality of their experience.

A consultancy (Lord Cultural Resources Planning & Management Ltd.) was appointed to manage the project, and a cross-departmental team made up of representatives from curatorial departments, education, exhibitions, warder staff, membership and front-of-house staff was established to co-ordinate the work and offer different perspectives on the project. The consultants developed a research design which included gallery observations, in-depth personal interviews, tracking and focus-group discussions. The research itself focused on the *provision of information*, including printed material, the information desks, information staff and interpretation (which included wall texts, captions and broadsheets); *orientation*, which covered signing and visitor flow, and *access*, which looked at facilities for disabled visitors and visitors with children, as well as seating and the general 'feel' of the gallery.

The Visitor Audit produced a number of surprising findings. The most startling fact was that visitors were either unaware of, or didn't understand, the New Displays concept. Also, most visitors, rather than following a prescribed route through the gallery, prefer to browse through rooms in random order. Many found the signing system inadequate, and others wanted more communication with gallery staff. The consultants assembled a list of twenty-five recommendations in a detailed report.

Following discussion with colleagues in the gallery, a number of recommendations were implemented. The most visible and interesting of these focused on improving means of explaining New Displays to visitors, increasing interpretational resources for the collection and developing the role of front-of-house staff in visitor services.

EXPLAINING NEW DISPLAYS: It was generally agreed that the gallery should define the New Displays concept before visitors came to the gallery. An advertising agency was appointed to create a series of advertisements for the press and London Underground which both promoted and explained New Displays. On banners and hoardings outside the gallery, the slogan 'New works, new ideas, every year' appeared under the heading 'New Displays'. In the gallery itself, a range of New Displays banners were produced, and all directional signs carried a reference to New Displays. Most importantly, in each room, below every explanatory wall text, the following information appeared:

> 'With New Displays, every room in the gallery changes. Each year, new acquisitions and works from the stores join established masterpieces to explore new themes. New Displays has been sponsored by British Petroleum since 1990.'

Recent visitor research has shown that over 43 per cent of Tate visitors now understand the concept of New Displays (MORI, October 1995).

IMPROVING INTERPRETATIONAL RESOURCES: In January 1994, the Tate introduced TateInform, a personal audio-guide to New Displays. TateInform allows visitors to gain access to audio information when they wish, and not as part of a fixed tour. The visitor audit revealed that most visitors prefer to browse through the gallery, but still want information about individual rooms or works of art. Commentaries about works on display were provided by artists, writers and Tate curators, and can be rewound, fast-forwarded and cleared as the visitor wishes. After an initial commentary, the visitor can key in another number for additional information, although this facility of layered information is available only for certain works of art. TateInform systems were introduced for New Displays and for the Turner Collection.

TRAINING FOR FRONT-OF-HOUSE STAFF: At the beginning of 1995, a training scheme was introduced for all front-of-house staff working in the gallery. This includes warders, information staff, shop staff, cafe and restaurant staff, guides and volunteers. The training, which lasts six months, covers two areas: *learning about the Tate and its related activities*, so that staff are able to give clear and accurate information about the gallery, and *communications skills*, so that staff are able to communicate with and relate to visitors in a friendly and welcoming manner.

Each of those initiatives, and other activities which emerged from the recommendations from the Visitor Audit, will be reviewed in Visitor Audit Phase 2, which is being conducted during 1996/97. Information from this second phase of the audit will be vital in planning visitor services in the new Tate Gallery of Modern Art and Tate Gallery of British Art.

### 3.3.3 EDUCATION

Museums are redefining their role as public educational institutions: the museum's education department is its principal advocate and source of expertise for this role. So, when you enter the Education Department of the Cleveland Museum of Art, you read their Mission Statement, which is screen-printed on the wall:

> *'The Education Department staff serves as a catalyst between the works of art in the Museum's collection and visitors, young and old, from the Cleveland community and beyond. A passion for and understanding of art objects – as embodiments of aesthetic quality and of culture/history – is core to achieving this mission.*
> *Through programs and teaching, the Education Department staff strives to foster non-elitist perceptions of art and the Museum, strengthening the Museum's commitment to its community, and making the museum accessible to the widest possible audience.'*

In fulfilling such a mission, it is important for educators to remember that museums work best as *informal*, rather than organised or formal, educational institutions, and that informal education is most successful at *affective* learning, resulting in a change of attitude or interest level, rather than the formal transmission of data.

#### 3.3.3.1 PROVISION FOR SCHOOLS

School parties often constitute from 15 to 25 per cent of museum visitors, introducing many young people to museums and performing a valuable service for school systems. There is an increasing emphasis on relating museum visits to the school curriculum, to learning objectives and educational attainment targets. Museum education officers and education departments are working more and more closely with teachers and curriculum advisers to integrate their programme with the needs of the schools. Some of the tools being developed include:

- ADVISORY COMMITTEES: Museum educators work with teachers' and community advisory committees to ensure that the themes, classes and workshops they present are relevant, up-to-date and meet the children's needs.

- TEACHER RESOURCE CENTRES: Many museums establish centres where teachers can borrow materials to use in the classroom to prepare students for the museum visit and for follow-up activities. The resource centre may also provide training workshops for teachers. Some museum training programmes can lead to vocational qualifications for teachers.

- SECONDMENT TO THE MUSEUM: Staff may be seconded from the school system to facilitate close co-ordination and mutual understanding.

- YOUTH ADVISORY COUNCILS, student volunteers, interns and students on work-study programmes provide invaluable training opportunities and keep the museum in touch with young people.

- THE INTERNET: Connecting museums to the Internet can create a closer relationship between museums and schools. Students can gain access to museum collections and information about them from museum staff from their classroom, and schools may pay a subscription fee that will help to fund the service.

Most museums rely on volunteers to act as guides for school visits and activities so that the staff educators may focus on programme development, training and evaluation to ensure a growing level of quality. While a dedicated corps of volunteers is a tremendous asset for the museum, the challenge is to attract volunteers who are able to respond to the interests of an increasingly diverse population, particularly in urban schools. Many museum education departments are working with community advisory committees to develop strategies to meet this challenge.

To cover the costs of school programmes, museums may contract with school boards or education authorities to receive an annual funding allocation for a specific service. Some museums levy a charge per student which varies with the cost of the programme. Other museums offer school programmes free of charge in recognition of local or central government grants. Many museums are developing partnerships with the private sector to provide free or low-cost school visits, especially for areas where schools and families may not have sufficient means to pay.

### 3.3.3.2 PUBLIC EDUCATIONAL ACTIVITIES

Museums offer informal education or self-directed learning. The goal is *affective* rather than cognitive learning, and programmes should be aimed at changing attitudes or raising levels of interest in the subject matter. This means that organised education programmes need to respond to people's interests and abilities and thus will vary widely, including workshops, courses, lectures, films, concerts, family activities, tours, seminars, symposia and artists in residence. These may be scheduled events – such as a seminar in the auditorium for which a ticket must be booked in advance – or a 'drop-in' event in the gallery. The National Portrait Gallery in London has commissioned a number of play productions based on specific paintings that 'bring them to life' – right in the gallery.

Programmes may be rather unusual, like the highly popular 'sleep-overs' at science museums in the UK and the USA, wherein children participate in an overnight programme of learning activities that includes sleeping in the galleries and having breakfast in the cafe the next morning.

Families with young children are particularly eager to find learning opportunities near home, and this is a segment of the population that is projected to grow into the 21st century. Meeting the needs of this group is especially important because studies show that those who participate in cultural activities with their family as children are more likely to be participants as adults. Museum 'Saturday morning classes' that date from the early part of this century are a good example: they are still going strong in many communities, and are being extended to summer and holiday museum camps.

Today, museum education departments are reaching an even wider family audience through special education galleries with a variety of exhibits and hands-on activities for school groups on weekdays, and families at weekends and during holidays. Successful examples include the Royal Ontario Museum's pioneering Discovery Room in Toronto, the Art Institute of Chicago's Family Education Centre, the Science Museum's Launch Pad in London, and the Information Technology Centre at Sydney's Powerhouse Museum, discussed in Case Study 3.6.

The cost of providing public education activities is often covered by user fees, corporate sponsorship or project grants from government agencies and private foundations.

# The Powerhouse Museum Information Technology Centre, Sydney

BY TERENCE MEASHAM

The Powerhouse Museum, which opened in 1988, is a large building flanking Darling Harbour, just west of Sydney's central business district. The museum is noted for its collection in fields which include space technology, aviation, land transport, steam technology, ceramics and glass (both studio and industrial), textiles, dress and fashion, furniture, philately and numismatics. The two linking factors in all this are design and usage or function.

There is also the question of meaning and significance. Society invests many things with a meaning or significance that may prove to be an extra dimension when considered against the intentions of the original design. And this last point, 'assigned meaning', is perhaps the best link we have to our social history collection and exhibition programmes.

There is also a section of the museum called Experimentations, which is, in effect, a science centre.

In all its activities the museum aspires to be a museum of influence. We therefore give special emphasis to one field which is of acute significance in today's society – information technology (IT).

The Museum, with some 20,000 square metres of exhibition space, has benefited from a series of sponsors far too long to list here, but prominent among them has been IBM. Their principal involvement, since 1988, has been with an exhibition on computing called 'The Information Machine', but in March 1996 IBM and the museum entered into a partnership with a new venture, The Powerhouse Museum Information Technology Centre. What makes the Powerhouse Information Technology Centre very special is that its programmes are carried out in the context of museum displays and structured museum visits and programmes.

The Centre consists of two neighbouring and interconnecting sections, the Classroom and the Applications Room. In a sense, our differentiation between the two is arbitrary, but it recognises that the range of applications on the menu at any one time will be subject to change.

The Classroom is generously equipped with its sponsors' machines of substantial power and sophistication. This allows the acquisition and development of computer skills by students. There is a range of typical programmes which relate to the museum as a whole. Digital cameras, for example, are used to provide imagery derived from objects or designs discovered in the museum. Such images can be incorporated into a variety of statements or presentations: for example, students might prepare video programmes or printed documentation, or a mixture of both, as a basis for discussion. Students can lay out digitised photos and the text of a newsletter describing their museum visit, print it out and take it home. CAD (computer-aided design) software, together with the museum's own CIS (collection information system), is accessible to users, as is the Internet. Overhead projections in the Centre allow group discussion and other group activities.

The adjacent Applications Room provides different computer platforms and deals with different productive technologies. For instance, having designed a textile pattern in the Classroom using CAD, in the Applications Room a student can transform it into a garment design, using a pre-loaded garment template. The Applications Room introduces students to the whole world of CAM (computer-aided manufacturing). One CAM program turns a lathe that cuts a student's CAD design into a cylinder of wax.

The Information Technology Centre's programmes were extensively trialled before their official opening. The trials involved several different school levels: pre-school, primary and secondary. Parties of students were booked in, and all their teachers were interviewed in depth after the event. Also evaluated, as part of the process, was the integration of the Information Technology Centre with our specially-designed museum visit packages written by our Education and Visitor Services (EVS) staff and published by Powerhouse Publishing. It is our EVS staff who organise bookings and programmes, and I'm glad to say that the Information Technology Centre is booked for months ahead.

The museum has published *Connecting to the Future* as a guide to the Powerhouse ITC and a how-to-do-it manual for other museums wishing to establish an IT centre. The booklet is available from the Powerhouse Museum.

*The Powerhouse Museum Information Technology Centre, Sydney. Photograph by Sue Stafford, courtesy of the Powerhouse Museum.*

### 3.3.4 EXTENSION AND OUTREACH

'Extension' refers to the programmes museums offer outside the museum building to their traditional audiences, while 'outreach' refers to museum activities that are designed for new or non-traditional audiences, whether offered in the museum or at another location.

High levels of staff effort are involved in providing both extension and outreach programmes, and the risks inherent in working with unfamiliar audiences or in new places are relatively high. The facilitation and oversight role of management is particularly important in projects of these types, because the impact of failure can be quite devastating to the institution; success requires considerable leadership. The staff working on an extension or outreach project need realistic, measurable objectives, as well as an inspired sense of mission.

For example, offering a popular museum lecture series in a suburban community centre so that the residents of that area would not have to travel to the town centre could extend the museum's activities outside its walls to a traditional high-education, high-income group. This could be a strategically important extension programme if it builds the museum's relationship with that community, resulting in new members and supporters; or it could be a waste of resources if objectives are not met and the museum does not have the capability to develop the programme over time.

Inviting local families to a special 'community celebration evening' at the museum would be an example of outreach, if the local residents have a different demographic profile from that of the majority of the museum visitors. Involving the neighbouring community in the museum is a strategically important outreach goal – but it cannot be accomplished in one night. To be successful, this needs to be planned as one event in a five-year outreach programme that must be developed to meet the needs and expectations of this non-traditional visitor group. One American Children's Museum went so far as to send vans into an underprivileged area to pick up children, bring them to the museum and return them to their communities.

The future of museums depends on extension and outreach programming: taking the museum beyond its walls to community centres, television screens in people's homes, and the Internet, and making museums accessible to those who, for educational, economic or social class reasons, have not yet dared to enter their doors.

### 3.3.5 PUBLICATIONS

The museum's publications programme provides information about the museum collections, services and research to visitors and to an expanded audience of the interested public which may not be able to visit, but may consult the museum's publications in libraries or purchase them in bookshops, from newsagents or by catalogue.

The range of publications includes: exhibition catalogues, guidebooks, catalogues of the collection, children's books and games, teacher packs, leaflets and brochures, postcards, posters and prints. Museums may publish scholarly journals, magazines, membership newsletters and occasional papers.

Museum publishing has entered the multimedia age with considerable imagination and creativity. Many museums have produced videotape recordings of popular selections from their collections and special exhibitions on particular subjects and historical events featuring artefacts and archival materials from their collections. CD-ROM technology has been used to publish the catalogue of the National Gallery, London, as well as its MicroGallery and that of the National Gallery in Washington. Both video and CD-ROM formats are available, for instance, of the Chinese art collection of the Palace Museum in Taipei.

The high cost of high-quality publication has led museums to forge partnerships with the private sector. Whilst some museums have their own imprint, many publish books and catalogues in collaboration with academic publishers; some produce large-circulation magazines in conjunction with commercial magazine publishers. Private sector partners have played an important role in assisting museum CD-ROM publication.

### 3.3.6  MARKETING

Museum marketing is closely connected to audience development, which aims to create a broader visitor base while at the same time building a closer relationship with the museum's regular visitors. Thus marketing is an integral part of the museum's communication with the public. Marketing is closely allied with public programmes, but this function is frequently based in the museum's administration division. Many museums which have highly effective marketing programmes do not have a 'marketing department' at all – the marketing function is part of the communications or development division.

Wherever the marketing function is located on the museum's organisation chart, the management of marketing is important to the entire institution – curators, who care passionately about how an exhibition is promoted and whether the public attends; warders and visitor services staff, who welcome the public through the doors; development staff, who know that an increase in membership and donations accompanies high levels of public awareness; and the finance staff, who see a substantial improvement in the 'bottom line' when attendance increases. This means that the marketing function is best undertaken by an interdepartmental project team (see subsection 2.3.2.3), especially in marketing major exhibitions and special events.

The management of the museum's marketing focuses on:

- identifying the museum's present and potential markets, and communicating effectively with them;
- advocating within the museum the continual improvement of the museum's products and services to meet the needs of these people, so that they will visit the museum and return again;
- increasing attendance and visitor-generated revenues.

Extensive national and international research on cultural participation and museum attendance tells us that from 27 to 35 per cent of the adult population attends museums. The frequency of attendance varies greatly, from those who visit more than ten times as year and are likely to be members and supporters, to those who visit occasionally, and especially as tourists. The typical characteristics of museum visitors are that they have higher education and income than the general population (although education is a far more significant factor than income) and that women attend more frequently than men. The prime age for attendance varies with museum type: for example, science centres and children's museums attract young families, while art galleries appeal to young, single people and adults over forty-five. Attendance tends to decline after the age of sixty, but this is expected to change as the population ages and museums become more attuned to improving facilities for the elderly and disabled.

Within these broad groups of visitors and non-visitors, there are many specific 'market segments' – homogeneous sectors of the population that share common demographic, geographic and behavioural or lifestyle patterns. Through its marketing strategy, the museum can influence their attendance patterns.

- The first step in museum marketing is to understand the museum's existing visitors – the market segments they represent, the frequency of their visits, and their motivation. This may be accomplished by studying daily attendance records, through observation and visitor surveys, which are discussed in subsection 3.3.6.2.

- The next step is to compare this reality with the demographics of the resident market (obtained from census data) and the tourists who visit the area (available from the local tourist board or chamber of commerce) and with visitor survey results for other museums and visitor attractions in the area (which, with luck, will share information), enabling analysts to determine which market segments are under-represented in the museum's visitor base.

- The third stage is particularly challenging: to analyse what it all means, to set marketing priorities around 'target market segments', and to identify marketing strategies that will boost attendance from those market segments. This stage constitutes the 'marketing brief' for tasks ranging from advertising, promotion and public relations to the creation of special programmes. These tasks may be carried out by museum staff – say, in the education department for the creation of programmes, or in the graphics department to create posters – or they may be carried out by outside consultants, including public relations firms and advertising agencies. It is important to note that strategies may aim at developing under-represented markets or, on the contrary, may choose instead to serve current market segments better – and the choice must be made by the museum director, not by marketing personnel alone.

- The fourth stage is implementation of the marketing plan. The role of the marketing manager is effectively to monitor the brief, co-ordinating completion of all the tasks on time, within budget and to agreed levels of quality.

- The final step is evaluation of the results, recording what should be changed, and the production of a manual for future marketing efforts.

### 3.3.6.2 VISITOR RESEARCH

Visitor research collects up-to-date and reliable information about the museum's visitors to enable the museum to:

- improve its performance in its public role;

- focus on meeting public needs and expectations and achieving outcomes related to visitor and public interests;

- demonstrate to current and potential funders and sponsors, whether in the public or private sectors, the degree to which the public is served, and which sectors of the public are using the museum.

In order to meet these objectives, there needs to be a balance between quantitative analysis of demographics and behaviours and qualitative methods that focus on the feelings, attitudes and motivations of visitors. This is particularly important because:

- Museums that thrive in the future will be those that are of real value to the community.

- Visitor data shows that 'word of mouth' is often the most frequently cited motivation for a museum visit; this means that visitor satisfaction is likely to be the most significant generator of attendance.

- Museums have become more dependent on visitor-generated revenue and visitor spending in their gift shops and restaurants, and the potential to convert visitors to museum members and supporters is related to visitor satisfaction with the museum experience.

Attendance counts and visitor surveys are used to create a database of attendance, demographic and lifestyle information, while methods such as in-gallery interviews, observation, workshops and focus groups are used to understand visitor motivations, expectations and the quality of the visitor experience. This type of research is particularly important in addressing the needs of outreach audiences such as minority and low-income groups, because these groups are under-represented in traditional museum surveys, and therefore little is known about their attitudes, expectations and experiences in the museum.

The most effective and efficient approach to visitor research is to develop a comprehensive three- to five-year rolling programme that focuses on quantitative research in some years and qualitative in others. The key is to involve representatives of all departments who work with the public in the audience research project team, to ensure that all the museum's many evaluation activities (whether of education programmes or from visitor comment cards) contribute to the visitor research database. The museum should have an evaluator on its staff (a full-time or part-time position depending on the size of the museum) to design and implement research, or brief outside consultants to do so, to analyse and disseminate the results through the project team and to persuade the museum trustees or governors to take action on recommendations.

### 3.3.6.3 TARGET MARKETS

There are many potential market segments that a museum may seek to attract. Selecting target markets means choosing which of these segments will be the focus of the museum's energy.

The decision on which market segments to target will be based on many factors, from *affordability* (unless the market is saturated, it is less costly and less risky to target larger numbers of the type of people you are already attracting) to *responsibility* (as a public institution, it is important to reach out to the underserved). Five main factors need to be considered in selecting and prioritising target markets:

- the size of the market segment and its growth potential;
- the importance of the market segment to the museum's mission and mandate – this applies particularly to the museum's role as a public educational institution in a culturally and economically diverse society;
- the ability of the market segment to contribute to visitor-generated revenues;
- the contribution of a particular market segment to the tourism or economic development objectives of the area – there is a growing recognition of the central role of museums in attracting high-income 'cultural tourists' and in helping to increase the length of stay and visitor spending of all tourists; communities also value museums because they are symbolic of the area's 'quality of life' factors in attracting new industry and service companies to the area;
- the costs associated with attracting each segment.

These policy decisions should involve senior management and the board on the basis of recommendations from the marketing manager regarding quantitative goals to be met for each market segment in the context of three- to five-year attendance projections.

### 3.3.6.4 MARKETING STRATEGIES

'Marketing strategies' refers to the many ways in which the museum can improve its communication and service with the objective of boosting attendance and visitor spending. The marketing strategy also aims to build a closer relationship with the museum's visitors, leading to repeat visits and increased membership and donations. This is a continual process, in which the manager of the museum's marketing activities must work closely with evaluation, curatorial and programme staff, and development and visitor services, ideally through a project team.

Once the overall marketing strategy has been established, there may be as many as fifty specific marketing strategies to be implemented, for example: new admission prices to appeal to local families; an advertising campaign in collaboration with local hotels to attract summer tourists; evening openings targeted at the 'singles market'; and special seminars to appeal to collectors. Developing the correct strategies requires expertise in museum marketing, and knowledge of what has been successful elsewhere. Museums can benefit greatly from learning about the successes and failures of museums of comparable size and scope – this is called 'comparables analysis', and consists of in-depth interviews with staff in comparable institutions. 'Best practice study' is also helpful – this involves identifying examples of outstanding successes in institutions which may be much larger or smaller than yours, and analysing how their methods could be applied to your museum. In order to avoid taking the wrong lessons from examples or imitating failures that are only apparent successes, both types of research should be facilitated by staff or external consultants who have considerable experience in museum marketing and managing organisational change.

Marketing strategies should be implemented methodically, and should include opportunities for both quantitative and qualitative evaluation.

### 3.3.7 VISITOR SERVICES

Visitor services – including admissions, retail, hire and food services and general visitor care – greatly influence the quality of the visitor experience and communicate the museum's attitude to the public.

These services are often managed by administrative departments, even though the staff, whether full- or part-time, salaried, contract or voluntary, have more personal involvement and communication with visitors than most other staff. They offer a wealth of mostly untapped information about the museum's visitors and their needs, and to do their job well, they need extensive training, monitoring and evaluation.

If museums are to become truly visitor-responsive, they need to redefine the role of front-line staff from 'administrative' to 'visitor services', and create a new working environment that integrates visitor services staff into the museum profession.

#### 3.3.7.1 ADMISSIONS

The first museum staff whom visitors meet are usually security, information or ticketing staff, especially if admission is charged. The admissions desk is a key point for establishing the museum's attitude to the public: the clerk at the ticket counter has the opportunity to 'sell' the museum every time visitors ask questions about admission charges, voluntary charges, surcharges for special exhibitions, group discounts, free admission for members and the various other concessions on offer. To create a positive image for the museum in the face of the crowding, conflicts and complexities that accompany ticket sales takes some training and inspiration, which means that admission staff must be regarded as providers of visitor services, rather than as simply operating a ticketing system. Admissions staff are also in a position to record data about visitors – number in party, time of day, gender distribution and so on – if trained to include this recording as part of their routine.

### 3.3.7.2  VISITOR-RESPONSIVENESS

In addition to their security functions, warders and guards continually respond to visitor needs by providing assistance with wheelchairs and push-chairs, administering first aid, giving directions, answering questions about the museum, and managing the cloakroom. Comment cards usually indicate that visitors have both good and bad experiences with security staff. Many of the bad experiences, such as visitors feeling that they were being followed because of their age or colour, stem from a lack of sensitivity to cultural diversity in the museum, which usually indicates that guards and other front-line staff have received little or no training in this area. As with admissions staff, training of staff can dramatically improve visitor experience.

### 3.3.7.3  RETAIL SERVICES

Museum retailing as a revenue source is discussed in subsection 3.5.2.1.2, but it is also an important visitor service in strengthening the relationship between the visitor and the museum. Visitors value the quality and uniqueness of the products, the personal service provided by shop staff and volunteers, and the sense that in making purchases at the shop, they are helping the museum. The product that the visitor takes home or purchases as a gift should include a small card or label that explains its relationship to the collection and how the purchase helps the museum, in order to extend the museum into the home and serve as a reminder of the visit.

Museum shops can extend their services by:

- opening satellite shops in high streets and shopping centres convenient to high-income, high-education markets;

- placing their 'trademark products' in other museum shops outside their market area;

- selling their products through retail stores;

- catalogue sales on a national or international basis, either through the museum's own mail-order catalogue, or through partnership with other museum catalogues or with complementary, niche-market catalogues;

- World Wide Web site 'shops' on the Internet – it will soon be possible to order products from museum shops by computer.

### 3.3.7.4 Hiring out facilities

Hiring out facilities for special events can bring the museum closer to actual and potential visitors and to potential sponsors and donors. When people hold important family occasions at the museum, from a wedding reception in the courtyard to a child's birthday party in an education classroom, it gives the museum a special place in their lives and introduces their guests to the museum, some of them for the first time. Business, political and professional events, such as conferences and receptions, also extend the museum's relationship with the community. The demand may be so great that some rentals can only be provided as a benefit for the museum's highest corporate membership and support categories. The quality of service in responding to enquiries, in negotiating rental agreements and in the event itself should reflect the visitor service orientation of the museum.

### 3.3.7.5 Food services

The main reason for utilising museum space for a restaurant or cafe is to enhance the visitor experience by providing visitors with rest and refreshment, and a place to socialise or meet friends. High-quality catering can extend the time visitors spend in the galleries, and can encourage repeat visits; poor quality and poor service may have the opposite effect. When food services are contracted out, the museum's standards and requirements should be incorporated into the contract with the caterer.

These standards and requirements can only be developed on the basis of understanding the museum's visitors and their needs, and balancing these with the need to generate revenue (see subsection 3.5.2). For example, young families usually want simple, healthy, inexpensive food, served in an atmosphere where spills and tantrums will not be too embarrassing; older visitors usually prefer a quiet environment with inexpensive refreshment, with table service; there may also be a market for a restaurant with white table cloths and elegant cuisine or a casual cappuccino bar.

The staff who work in the cafe, like those in the shop, have the opportunity to serve visitors and communicate with them personally. It is important that they understand that their job is *serving visitors*, not just serving food. This means providing training, monitoring and evaluation for contractors as well as salaried staff.

### 3.3.7.6 Visitor services as a responsibility of all museum staff

To achieve the goals of visitor-responsiveness, museum management and programme staff need to develop a more intimate relationship with visitors than surveys, reports and comment cards can achieve. It will be difficult to create a visitor service orientation for the museum if management, curators, educators and programmers are not even at work during those times when most visitors are in the building – weekends and holidays. Part of the institutional change required to focus the museum on its public role involves management rethinking its role, which could start with such simple measures as rostering so that all staff work on some weekends.

# Dealing with Prejudice and Discrimination in a Museum Environment

By Marjorie L Schwarzer

'The art of putting up with people may be learned by practising patience on inanimate objects, which, in virtue of some mechanical or general physical necessity oppose a stubborn resistance to our freedom of action.' (Arthur Schopenhauer, *The Wisdom of Life*)

As part of its new facility, Chicago Children's Museum opened an experimental new exhibit, 'Face to Face: Dealing with Prejudice and Discrimination'. Initial visitor response has been overwhelmingly positive and gratifying. Although I am still reeling from the thrill, pageantry and last-minute details of opening both this exhibition and a 57,000 square foot (5,300 square metre) museum, I wanted to record my first impression before the crowds fade away and we enter a post-opening evaluation phase.

Like other museums since the turn of the century, the new Chicago Children's Museum attempts to provide visitors with a sense of beauty and delight. However, responding to social and market demands on the eve of the millennium, it is also designed to be a place for reflection, and more of a catalyst for stimulating social dialogue and active problem-solving. Putting current educational theories – especially those of Howard Gardner and Mihaly Czikenmihaly – into practice, the twelve large-scale, permanent exhibits provide entry points for many learning styles. The exhibits are interdisciplinary, and in addition to prejudice and discrimination, explore such topics as water, recycling, family history and the processes of invention, building and creating art. The entire museum is intellectually and physically challenging to both visitors and staff.

The architectural metaphor for the museum is the town square – or public meeting space – a centre in this large, divided city where visitors may pose powerful questions about how new social paradigms are affecting children and families. One social paradigm we have focused on vigorously is how to reflect Chicago's cultural, economic and racial diversity in a way that is honest, relevant and meaningful to our primary audience – children up to the age of ten and their families.

Three years ago, as we began planning exhibits for the new museum, we commissioned a report to gauge Chicago-area children's questions about, and perceptions of, people who were different from them. Children's museums before us, including Boston's, Houston's and Cleveland's, have developed exhibitions that interpret cultural diversity and awareness to their audiences. After listening directly to the feelings and misconceptions voiced by a cross-section of Chicago children, we decided to develop an exhibition that opens up a dialogue on prejudice and discrimination. Our Exhibition Team worked together on the project for over two years. It consisted of a project manager, designer, preparator, board member, developers and educators. I served as the visitor advocate, school group curriculum developer, and as a researcher on the project. We worked with an advisory team of local child psychologists, community activists and other experts on how racism affects children.

The exhibit's goal is proactive: to provide tools that help children (aged seven to ten) and their families recognise and respond to prejudice and discrimination in and around them. We chose to focus on typical manifestations of prejudice that affect children: stereotyping, name-calling and exclusion. The interactive components are designed to allow visitors to observe and experience how prejudice and discrimination feel, and to make choices about ways to deal with it. Among these nine components — all of which were extensively prototyped — are a simulated school bus on which children hear insults, including racial slurs, that we collected from children in the target age range, and an interactive video about an African-American boy who is excluded from a lunch table in the school cafeteria. The components are followed by activities that present tools children can use when they are confronted with these situations, either as victims or bystanders. Reinforcing information is presented to caregivers in the form of both labels and handouts which they can take home.

Since this exhibit is fairly hard-hitting, the museum sponsored a series of mandatory, all-day, cultural diversity training for all full- and part-time staff. The goal of these sessions was not only to provide a forum for questions about the exhibit, but to open institution-wide dialogue about racial and cultural equality. It is difficult to cross the line between polite on-the-job conversation with one's co-workers and meaningful dialogue about race relations. Like a deep talk with a new friend, the training sessions were at the same time awkward and stimulating; staff reactions were mixed. The Education Department also ran separate training and discussion groups for our youth staff, all of whom are members of low-income 'minorities'. They have, on occasion, experienced incidents of prejudice while working with visitors, and we wanted to prepare them for the issues we would be raising in the exhibit. Anticipating equally mixed reactions from the public, the museum recruited and trained forty volunteers to mediate the exhibit experience for visitors.

Why should we as museum professionals take on these issues? 'Face to Face: Dealing with Prejudice and Discrimination' opened, ironically, just after the O J Simpson verdict. During the first few hours of the exhibition's opening, an African-American family approached me – a white woman – and asked: 'Who thought of this exhibit? Why did you do it?' I responded that I had been a member of the team. 'Can we give you a hug?' they asked, 'It was so brave of you to take this issue on. Thank you so much for doing this.'

**BIBLIOGRAPHY**

Ivan Karp and Steven D Lavine (eds), *Exhibition Cultures: The Poetics and Politics of Museum Display*, Washington, DC: Smithsonian Institution Press, 1991.

Ivan Karp, Christine Mullen Kramer and Steven D Lavine (eds), *Museums and Communities: The Politics of Public Culture*, Washington, DC: Smithsonian Institution Press, 1992.

Peggy McIntosh, 'White Privilege: Unpacking the Invisible Knapsack', *Independent School*, Winter, 1990.

Patricia A Stewart, Aylette Jenness and Joanne Jones-Rizzi, *Opening the Museum: History and Strategies Toward a More Inclusive Institution*, Boston: The Children's Museum, 1993.

*Chicago Children's Museum. 6 R2*

# 3.4 | Accommodations Management

Museum sites may be town-centre complexes, country estates or archaeological ruins. Museum buildings range from contemporary creations by today's leading architects to historic structures on every scale. There is a widespread myth that old buildings make good museums, and another that great architects build great museums. Neither is necessarily true. Planning the development of accommodations for museums and managing them well are the subjects of this section.

## 3.4.1 ACCOMMODATIONS PLANNING

In most cases, museums grow beyond their bounds as a result of one of their essential activities – collecting. Museum buildings are also continuously being expanded or upgraded because of growing audience expectations and technological change: tourists visit, along with local residents, with ever higher expectations of the museum experience, intensified by their acquaintance with the world's leading attractions via television and other media, as well as international travel. Multimedia imaging technologies are only the latest of a series of technological breakthroughs that have affected the nature of the museum experience, as well as the research and knowledge base underlying it.

All of these factors result in a continual process of growth in the number, size and complexity of museums around the world. In fact, museum buildings are among the most complex of building types, and among the most costly. As a result, they are inevitably products of compromise, as budget and technical limitations must be balanced. Yet museum projects around the world, in a distressing number of cases, have not fulfilled the expectations of those responsible for them – buildings that are too small or too large, lifts that open onto corridors with lower ceilings or inadequate turning space, and lost opportunities that could have rewarded visitors with a far richer museum experience are observed around the globe.

The planning of museum buildings, their extension, relocation or renovation, is a process that must be executed carefully in order to ensure that it meets the needs of the museum profession to care for the collection, serves the museum's visitors as creatively as possible and fulfils the requirements of the community. This is the subject of a previous book of ours, with contributions from other specialists around the world, entitled *The Manual of Museum Planning* (London: HMSO, 1991), sponsored by the Museum of Science and Industry, Manchester.

### 3.4.1.1 THE ROLE OF THE ARCHITECT

Accommodations planning for museums is a field in which several disciplines have an interest. Many museum professionals and trustees assume that planning a museum is 'a building problem', and therefore can only be solved by an architect. There is no question that the architect has an important role to play – but the architect does not necessarily know how a museum works. Determining the functional requirements of a museum is best carried out by museum professionals before the architect begins work. Calling in the architect too soon is the most common error in the museum accommodations planning process.

Architects have two favourite phrases that most museum directors and curators who have been involved in museum planning projects will recognise. The first is:

'It's too early.'

This may be said when the museum director or curator attends a meeting at which he or she sees architectural concepts but does not see certain features that, as a museum professional, he or she knows to be vital to a successful museum. When the director or curator asks about these features, the architect assures everyone that these are concept sketches, and that it's too early to go into the kind of detail implied by these questions.

So the museum director or curator waits. Some months or even years later, depending on the timescale of the project, he or she goes to another meeting, at which much more detailed plans are shown by the architect. The museum's requirements are still not in evidence. When he or she repeats these concerns, the museum professional hears the architect's other favourite phrase:

'It's too late.'

The museum's requirements can now be met, the architect assures us, only at considerable expense. The museum requirements should have been stated earlier!

Such a frustrating experience is by no means solely the architect's fault. Very often it is the museum professionals who do not or cannot articulate their needs in ways that the architect can use.

The same is true of exhibit designers, market analysts, management consultants or others who may be consulted in the museum planning process. Each of them can make a useful contribution only to the extent that museum planners make the museum's needs known to them. Taking the time to plan the accommodations before consulting architects, designers or others is the first step towards building, expanding, renovating or relocating a museum successfully. This type of planning is often called *briefing* or *programming*, and its result is termed a *functional brief* (in the UK) or a *functional program* (in the USA).

# The Need for a Functional Brief

BY BARRY LORD

I was invited, with a group of museum professionals, to review three sets of architectural drawings and models for the expansion of a venerable museum in continental Europe. The collection featured medieval and Renaissance oak and other wooden furniture and carvings housed in a 1950s structure with a massive floor-to-ceiling window wall along all of the galleries. With that much glass, environmental controls were quite impossible: the curator told me that on a humid summer afternoon one could hear a concert in the galleries – the squeaking of the joints of the furniture!

The three sets of shortlisted architectural plans and models (for which the museum had paid) all provided a mixture of temporary exhibition galleries, a members' lounge, a pedagogical centre, a restaurant and many other attractions. But what was to be done with the permanent collection? I was advised that the plan was to build all these new facilities, and then to renovate the existing building with whatever funds remained. But this was the only time in twenty years when the museum would have the funds to accomplish any substantial physical improvement, and their money would all be spent by the time they completed the extension, so that nothing would be left for the permanent collection galleries.

When the time came to make comments on the architects' plans, I had to say that I chose none of the three. The architects were all disappointed, but I reassured them that it was not their fault. No one had asked the right questions, so none of the architects could give the right answer. No one had recognised that the museum's highest priority had to be the preservation of its collection, and that this need should have been at the centre of the brief given to the competing architects. I could only recommend that the museum reconsider its brief, before beginning all over again with the architects – which, I understand, was subsequently done.

## 3.4.1.2 FACTORS AFFECTING ACCOMMODATIONS PLANNING

Six areas related to the museum's requirements need to be studied in order to develop a museum facilities plan that can lead towards a successful functional brief:

1 VISITOR ANALYSIS: Both qualitative and quantitative analysis of the museum's present visitors (if the museum is already open) help us to determine visitor needs in the facility.

2 MARKET ANALYSIS: Even more important, it is necessary to analyse the potential market, again both quantitatively and qualitatively, so that the new facility might reach out beyond the present attendance group to serve a broader public. The analysis may aim to identify target markets for a new facility, or the different markets attainable after an expansion, renovation or relocation.

3 COLLECTION ANALYSIS: The heart of the museum is its collection of works of art, artefacts or specimens. A thorough analysis of not only its present size and character, but especially of its anticipated growth – along with decisions about the amount we wish to display, and the ways we wish to display it – are essential. Provisions for adequate security and collection care are also vital considerations.

4 PUBLIC PROGRAMMES EVALUATION: Museums appear to be about objects, but are really about people. What do we plan to do in the museum? For what activities must we provide? The museum's exhibitions, its approach to the interpretation of its collections – with all the technological potential now available – its education programme, its publications and media productions, its extension and outreach programmes and the amenities to be provided to the visitor, including shops and food services, all have important implications for the museum plan. Often neglected but most important – the unseen heart of the museum's public programmes – is scholarly *research* within the museum: staff, space and facilities must be provided for the research activity that is the museum's lifeblood, and the research conducted in the museum must be planned to meet the museum's public programming needs.

5 INSTITUTIONAL CONTEXT: A much neglected but very important sector of museum planning is the determination of the museum's relationship with government, educational institutions, other museums, the tourist industry and potential donors or sponsors in the private sector. Although these issues are more frequently considered in the context of corporate or strategic planning, they are equally important for accommodations planning because the needs that they generate require space and facilities. If, for example, the museum is to become more independent of government, it is likely to require more retail space, food services and function rooms, and their location may need to be improved. If it is to offer programmes in partnership with local schools, additional facilities may need to be designed and built, with input from the schools.

6 INSTITUTIONAL PLAN: Another often neglected area is the most fundamental one – determining or reconsidering the museum's mission, its mandate and its purpose, as well as its mode of governance and the structures through which it is administered. Although these are often thought to be part of a corporate plan rather than an accommodations plan, they directly affect the priorities that must be decided as it becomes apparent that all the space and facilities desired cannot be provided.

These six areas of analysis point to conclusions about the museum's needs for:

- STAFF: How many people will be needed to run these programmes with the museum's collection? Where will they work? Are there sufficient staffrooms and support facilities?

- SPACE: Galleries, storage areas and the public and non-public support spaces need to be listed and associated in terms of the adjacencies required, and grouped in zones that meet engineering requirements and cost considerations.

- FACILITIES: An exhibit plan may form part of the facilities plan, as may facilities and equipment requirements for conservation, documentation and the many other specialised museum activities.

Planning for staff, space and facilities is sometimes approached, especially by engineers, primarily in terms of meeting relevant *building code* requirements for fire protection, health, safety and the needs of the disabled. Compliance with the code is, of course, essential, but accommodations planning should also be seized by museum planners and trustees as an opportunity to fulfil the museum's mission more fully than before – or perhaps even to reconsider that mission.

In particular, museum managers need to consider the fundamental question of the degree of visual *access* that they wish to provide to the public. Again and again, unplanned museum building projects proceed without examination of this basic issue. Many museums exhibit only 5–15 per cent of their collections, and there have been numerous instances of museums concluding capital expansion projects with a *lower* percentage of their collections on display. This would be acceptable if it was intentional; but very often the key questions have not even been asked, such as:

- What is the current display/storage ratio?

- Is it satisfactory?

- If not, what ratio would be acceptable?

- How could we achieve it?

The answers to these questions very often lie in changing the density of objects on display by introducing new methods of display, or increasing the space devoted to certain modes. Possible modes of display include:

- AESTHETIC OR CONTEMPLATIVE DISPLAY, usually found in art museums, typically with the lowest display density (for example, twenty to thirty pictures in a gallery of 150 square metres);

- CONTEXTUAL, THEMATIC OR DIDACTIC DISPLAY, with objects placed in context so that they may be understood, usually allowing a higher density (more objects per square metre) than the aesthetic approach;

- ROOM SETTINGS, grouping objects as they would have been found in their original setting, often allowing an even higher density than contextual display, especially if the collection allows the room to be well furnished;

- VISIBLE STORAGE (sometimes called 'study storage'), in which objects are grouped by type as they would be in storage, except that they are intended for visual inspection and comparison, allowing the highest level of density, and often the highest density of information as well, especially if the objects are keyed to an adjacent computer terminal offering public access to the catalogue information about them.

Considering such options is the first responsibility of the museum gallery accommodations planner. In calculating their effect on the number of objects that can be provided for public viewing, and the space required to do so, museum planners must begin by determining the existing display densities, past and projected collection growth rates, and the museum's policies towards improving visual access and the visitor experience.

Once all possibilities have been considered, the museum's requirements for staff, space and facilities can be translated into monetary needs – anticipated expenditure for both capital and operating costs – and into opportunities for revenue. If the result is beyond the museum's fundraising means, then it may be necessary to reconsider. But at least all the options will now be known, choices can be made with a clear understanding of the opportunities being lost, and priorities can be decided.

# Visible Storage at the Glass Gallery
# at the Victoria and Albert Museum, London

By Hilary Young

The re-display of the Glass Gallery, which opened in 1994, was prompted by a conservation survey carried out in 1990. This revealed that adverse environmental conditions were accelerating the decay of parts of the collection (caused by an inherent instability in the composition of the glass itself), and that this was affecting parts of the collection previously considered immune. The new cases, made by Glasbau Hahn, were therefore built to the highest specifications, enabling the case environment to be controlled and the process of decay to be halted.

It was with the defects of the old gallery – which had been laid out after the war – very much in mind that the new gallery was planned by Ceramics and Glass Section staff working closely with the gallery architect and designer, Penny Richards. The gallery was divided up into two main parts: a study collection accommodated on a glass-and-steel mezzanine inserted into the gallery (with a balustrade commissioned from glass artist Danny Lane), and the main displays on the floor of the gallery. These 'main run' displays were arranged thematically, the story of glass being divided into broad swathes of history – 'Glass in the Ancient World', 'Islamic Glass', 'The Venetian Tradition', and so on. The titles were clearly signposted, both above the cases and on outrider or 'index' cases, each of which bore maps and explanatory texts and housed a single object chosen to act as a visual signpost and to exemplify the contents of the adjacent displays.

Our intention was to get as many of the 8,000 or so pieces of glass in the collection on display (and into sound environmental conditions) as was physically possible. In a single gallery of very limited size, this necessarily entailed a certain density of display – partly made permissible, and in fact encouraged, by the transparency of many of the exhibits – but at the same time we aimed to avoid crowding in the 'main run'. On the mezzanine, however, which was intended from the start as a resource for the specialist rather than the general visitor, some crowding was accepted as inevitable.

The pressure on space made us rethink our approach to labelling. The solution we arrived at was to devote space to texts that explained the thematic groups and historical sequence, rather than giving objects individual labels, which tend to be very wasteful of space, as they repeat information. All objects were assigned a four-digit display reference number, which could be used to cross-refer to brief descriptions and attributions positioned on the bevelled edge of the lowest shelf, and to access longer entries held in a computer database of the collection. Six computer terminals in the gallery hold this database, and five of these also run *The Story of Glass*, a touch-screen-operated, interactive system which the Victoria and Albert Museum's Ceramics and Glass Curators developed with colleagues at the Corning Museum of Glass and a company called The Art of Memory, which designed and programmed the software. This allows visitors to call up information – in the form of still images, text and video clips – on glassworking techniques, individual objects, glassmakers and terminology, and to follow a number of brief introductions to glass history and other short narratives. In keeping with the approach throughout the gallery – in which several different levels of displays and information exist side by side – our intention in planning the touch-screen computer systems was to meet the needs of both the non-specialist visitor and those of a knowledgeable audience.

### FURTHER READING

Oliver Watson, 'Windows on glass', *Museums Journal*, vol. 94, no. 11, November 1994, pp 28–30.

*View of the Glass Gallery at the Victoria and Albert Museum, courtesy of the Trustees of the V&A. 35319*

## 3.4.1.3 Site selection

Site selection is sometimes part of the planning of suitable accommodations. Lists of FACTORS affecting the decision are usually drawn up, including:

- availability
- access
- audience development potential
- cost of acquisition and development, balanced by funding opportunities
- security considerations
- building type (if it is a question of renovation of an existing structure)
- size and layout of site or existing structures
- parking
- visibility
- compatibility of neighbouring facilities
- contribution to local development plans

Each factor should be given both a *value* and a *weight*. The *value* may be quantified on a scale of 1–10, which may be arbitrarily adapted to the conditions of the sites under consideration. For instance, a site with excellent access might rate a 9, while one with poor access would rate a 2 in value. But each factor should also be *weighted* according to its relative importance to the museum. Again, this weighting may be arbitrarily adapted to the specific site inquiry: for one museum, access may be much more important than parking (if all sites are equally well served by public transport, for example), so that access may be given a weight of 9, whereas parking may be given a weight of only 2. For another museum, their weights might be equal. The total rating of each factor is determined by multiplying the value given to each site for each factor by the weight attributed to that factor. The total rating for each site is, of course, the sum of all these weighted values.

The weighting of site selection factors should be carried out in relation to fundamental issues of the museum's mission, its policies and its institutional character. If, for example, it has been a government, corporate or university museum but is now being encouraged to become more self-sufficient, the site selection criteria related to audience development should be very heavily weighted indeed; sometimes a difference of a few hundred metres is crucial in relation to the resultant building's public image, and the museum's ability to function effectively as a public attraction. If funding is possible only for some sites, but is crucial to the enterprise, then that factor must be given heavy weight. On the other hand, a security issue may be so alarming that it outweighs all other factors, so security must be assigned an appropriate weight.

A question frequently asked is whether renovation of an historic building is preferable to a new, purpose-built structure, or vice versa. The answer must always be specific to the particular comparison being made. Renovation is often less expensive, sometimes by as much as a third of the capital cost.

But the governing body of the museum may find itself paying this difference many times over in higher operating costs, while the staff may be regretting the decision to renovate daily, as they try to cope with inadequate spaces, awkward corridors, multiple floor levels and insufficient turning room outside lifts.

Very often the preservation of an historic building for which no other use is feasible may be given as justification for preferring renovated space. This may be praiseworthy from the viewpoint of architectural preservation – and preserving the fabric of the building may indeed be part of the museum's mission – but the justification should be recognised as falling outside the functional requirements of the museum, so that the costs in both capital outlay and operations may also be considered.

### 3.4.1.4 ORGANISING THE ACCOMMODATIONS PLANNING TEAMS

Who is to undertake accommodations planning? The governing body usually establishes a *building committee* to guide the process by establishing and monitoring the policy and budgetary framework for the project. The museum's director must provide leadership. It is essential for the museum to name a *project manager*. He or she may already be on staff – but if so, must be relieved of other duties while assuming the project management role; alternatively, someone with project management skills may be engaged on contract for the life of the capital project only. The museum accommodations planning and briefing process is often facilitated by specialised museum planning consultants (like the authors), who work with all of the above personnel to achieve the optimal result. Even with professional museum planners and an experienced project manager, it is vital to involve all those who will have to provide services to the collection and to the public in the new facility. Museum accommodations planning is very much a team effort.

The most important step in organising the museum's forces to address a capital project is therefore to establish both a MUSEUM PROJECT TEAM and a BUILDING TEAM:

- THE MUSEUM PROJECT TEAM comprises museum personnel who address the various museum functions affected by the capital development – curatorial concerns, conservation, security, revenue generation, and many more. This team should be led by the *museum planner*, whether a professional consultant specialising in this area or an appointed member of the museum staff. The museum project team's task is to ensure that the museum's requirements are clearly stated, and that those requirements are met by the architects, engineers and contractors. The quantity surveyor should also meet with this team, to ensure that the cost implications of their requirements are made clear.

- THE BUILDING TEAM includes the *architect*, *engineers*, *landscape architects* and other technical specialists needed, along with the *contractor* and the *construction manager*. Their task is to answer the requirements of the museum project team with technical drawings and specifications. The quantity surveyor also meets with the building team to estimate cost implications of its designs and specifications; he or she is thus a member of both teams.

It is hoped that the architect's response and that of the rest of the building team will be inspired, and the resultant building will be memorable. But the job of the museum project team is simply that the building should meet the museum's requirements.

The project manager should meet with both of these teams, and from time to time convene a meeting to bring the teams together. The museum's director should attend these meetings, and can then report back to the building committee of the museum's governing body.

### 3.4.1.5   THE FUNCTIONAL BRIEF

The sequence of events in the museum accommodations planning process ought to begin from a corporate plan, which should be agreed or updated as required, in order to place the capital project in context, in relation to the museum's mission, mandate and objectives. Beyond the corporate plan, the project requires the collection analysis and development strategy, public programming plan, market analysis and marketing strategy that together make up a master plan. If it is a new museum, of course, this will be called a feasibility study. (Subsection 3.1.1 describes these preliminary planning steps in more detail.)

With the strategic or corporate plan and master plan as a basis, establishing the institutional goals and the collection, programming and marketing objectives, it is finally possible, preferably with the aid of experienced museum planners, to draft the key document known as a functional brief – a statement of the museum's functional requirements for space and facilities. A functional brief is written in language that the museum's trustees and management can understand (i.e. not in technical language, although highly detailed), and usually includes:

- site characteristics and requirements for access, signage and security;
- building access, egress and circulation patterns for visitors, staff, suppliers and others, and for collections, supplies, rubbish and other objects;
- a list of all spaces in the building, organised by zone (outlined in subsection 3.4.1.8);
- space descriptions – succinct accounts of the purpose of every room, grouped by zone;
- building systems and standards required;
- detailed functional requirements of every room in the building, again grouped by zone.

The analysis of circulation patterns in an existing structure should be carried out in consultation with the building's operations manager and engineers, as well as with the chief of security. It is crucial, for example, for planners to ensure that food supplies can be delivered and rubbish removed without crossing or duplicating collection circulation paths, if at all possible. Similarly, service personnel access to plant rooms for repair and replacement should be made possible without passing through or near collection zones. Provisions should be made for visitors of all kinds, including children, toddlers, the disabled, and very important persons (VIPs), as well as visitors to offices who may arrive when the museum is closed.

The building systems and standards and the detailed functional requirements for every room systematically record the variables for:

- architectural issues – floor, wall and ceiling surfaces, doors, windows, glazing types and insulation levels required;

- atmospheric functions – air conditioning, humidity control, outside air controls, room pressure, heat gain and other environmental control standards including air filtration requirements;

- mechanical specifications – hot and cold water, steam, gas or compressed air requirements, floor drains, exhausts and room controls;

- visual requirements – focal contrast levels, daylight or blackout provisions, views into or out of the room, privacy requirements, light fixtures, direct or indirect lighting recommendations, colour rendering index and colour temperature;

- electrical functions – intercom, telephone, audio, video, cinematic, power and emergency requirements, clocks or other applications, computer needs, power surge protection and other power security functions;

- acoustic functions – ambient sound and speech privacy levels;

- security levels – motion sensors, closed-circuit television surveillance alarms, panic hardware, locks, hinge pins and glass breakage detector requirements;

- fire safety issues – fire ratings for structures, doors and dampers, smoke density and flame spread numbers, fuel contributed levels, fire detectors, extinguishers and sprinklers;

- special functions, such as vibration and load bearing levels, and hazard controls;

- a matrix of all functions related to spaces, grouped into zones of public/non-public and collection/non-collection (four in all) that are most useful for both engineering and costing purposes (see subsection 3.4.1.8).

In addition to listing the requirements for these factors, a good functional brief ensures that the building:

- complies with relevant building codes;

- fulfils the requirements of regulatory authorities (such as the Museums and Galleries Commission in the UK);

- satisfies the expectations of national and international lenders;

- operates as efficiently as possible, given the special requirements of a museum.

The drafting of this functional brief or programme cannot be assigned to architects or engineers. Their expertise does not lie in stating museum requirements. The development of museum planning as a specialised role within the museum profession has been a direct result of this demand for experienced museum professionals who have learned the language of the functional brief. The role of the architects and engineers, as outlined in the following section, is to respond to the functional brief or programme.

## 3.4.1.6 From architectural concept to evaluation

Whereas the functional brief asks questions – sets the requirements – the task of the architects and engineers is to provide answers. Their drawings and specifications may be called a *technical brief* (or *technical programme*), or simply *architectural documentation*. The museum project team and the building team should meet together to resolve issues that arise as the functional brief is translated first into an ARCHITECTURAL CONCEPT, and then into progressive stages of schematic and detailed architectural designs and specifications which constitute the technical brief. Compromise is inevitable – and welcome – but should always be made with due regard to ensuring the optimal achievement of the museum's functional requirements within the limitations of budget, time and technology. Consideration must be given to the usually inverse relationship between capital and operating costs – a saving in the former often leads to an increase in the latter, and vice versa.

The design stage concludes with the production of *tender documents* on which tenders or bids, and consequent contract negotiations, will be opened. The quantity surveyor should have provided estimates at each stage, beginning with very rough order-of-magnitude projections based on the master plan, refining the estimates through the briefing process, and costing each set of designs. The process of inviting tenders or bids will prove how accurate the process has been. It is important to include a review of the competing tenders in terms of their compliance with the functional brief as a prominent part of their evaluation.

The construction of new or renovated museum space proceeds towards *commissioning* (handing over the building to the client), as do most building projects, but it is important that the project manager, the museum project team and/or the museum planners should be able to review the project at various stages of its completion, to ensure that the museum's needs are being met. And the final stage of the process should not be forgotten – EVALUATION of the building's performance, again measured against the requirements of the functional brief.

## 3.4.1.7 Cost of accommodations planning

The cost of accommodations planning is often considered to be high, but this is usually because it has not yet been placed in the perspective of the cost of the capital project as a whole. Most museums are cash-poor, even at the beginning of major capital projects, and are often reluctant to allocate money to planning when it could be used to 'get on with the job'. The entire planning and briefing process usually costs no more than 1 per cent of the total project's value. Even taken together with the cost of reviewing the architects' and engineers' drawings and specifications, total planning costs are likely to reach only 1.5 per cent. The costs should be seen as the initial 1.5 per cent being spent to ensure that the remaining 98.5 per cent is well used. The costs of the contractor's change orders may be much greater if not guided by good planning.

The cost of the entire planning and design phase will vary according to architectural billing practices throughout the world, but is usually only 11–12 per cent of the total project's value. During this phase, making changes is still relatively inexpensive – before we hear 'It's too late!'

## 3.4.1.8 ZONING

Throughout the accommodations planning process, the best way to control costs, as well as to understand the complex spaces found in a museum, and to organise their engineering requirements, is to group the museum's spaces into four zones (A–D):

A  PUBLIC NON-COLLECTION ZONE: spaces like lobbies, theatres, shops and restaurants. These require a high level of finish for the public, but do not require the high security and environmental controls necessary for protection of the collection.

B  PUBLIC COLLECTION ZONE: galleries and any other areas where both the public and the collections (including borrowed collections in temporary exhibitions) may be together. These are the most expensive and demanding areas in the museum, since they combine high levels of finish for the public with museum standards of environmental controls and security for the collection.

C  NON-PUBLIC COLLECTION ZONE: storage, conservation laboratories, curatorial workrooms and other support areas where objects from the collection will be located. This zone requires the same environmental controls and high levels of security required for the public collection zone, but not the high levels of finish necessary for the public zones.

D  NON-PUBLIC NON-COLLECTION ZONE: support areas behind the scenes where collections will not be permitted – such as the plant rooms and the offices. These areas require neither the sophisticated environmental controls and security required for the collection zones nor the high levels of finish necessary for the public zones.

The analysis of the museum's space into these four categories is of immeasurable help to the architect and engineer in planning efficient adjacencies, and to the quantity surveyor in determining where and how to cut costs, if that should prove necessary. It also allows us to establish clearly how efficient the

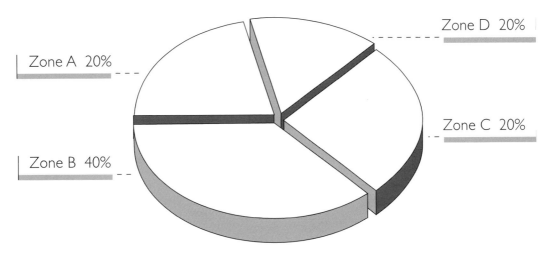

*Figure 3.1    Normative Space Distribution by Zone*

building is, or could be made. The norm is for most museum buildings to include about 60% public space, with about 60% of their space holding collections. About 40% is usually gallery space, and 20% collection support space.

Zoning of the building is also essential in planning to maximise operating efficiency. This is usually a challenging problem in a museum, since its requirements for environmental controls and security may necessitate equipment or facilities or operating schedules that could be cheaper if standards were lower. Proper zoning of spaces allows engineers to work with museum planners to mitigate these effects wherever possible, and at least permits the identification of those factors where cost savings and compromises can or must be made.

## 3.4.2   SITE AND BUILDING OPERATION

The operation of museum sites and buildings involves three functions:

- managing daily operations (3.4.2.1)

- maintenance and repair (3.4.2.2)

- security (3.4.2.3)

### 3.4.2.1   MANAGING DAILY OPERATIONS

Managing the operations of a museum site and building requires the correlation of five major factors, which are usually prioritised as follows:

1   health and safety of visitors, staff and others

2   security and preservation of the collection

3   comfort and convenience of visitors

4   facilitation of staff requirements

5   preservation of the building

If the building is a historic structure, priority 5 is likely to be promoted to priority 3, and visitors and staff will be relegated to priorities 4 and 5 respectively. If the historic building is more important than the collection it contains, priority 5 may even be promoted to priority 2, and the collection may be relegated to priority 3. The operation of a museum site and building may be seen as an art of balancing all these concerns, some of which will be mutually exclusive at times. It is helpful if the operations manager or building engineer makes clear the priorities, not only in general, but with reference to specific directives or practices.

Both *monitoring* and *control* functions are required to manage these five factors. In addition to the operations manager, the conservators and those responsible for public programming should have a say in the standards to be achieved, and should receive regular progress reports. Co-operation between those responsible for building operations, those responsible for the collections and those concerned with visitor services is vital to the smooth functioning of the museum, and may require the intervention of senior staff from time to time to ensure efficient collaboration. Regular meetings, perhaps monthly, are recommended.

The inherent conflict that is often observed between preservation of the collection and preservation of the building should be acknowledged, and the priorities must be clearly understood by all. The collection manager's goal of maintaining a constant relative humidity (RH), in temperate zones usually at 50% $\pm$ 3% at 20–21°C, with as little variation as possible, may present a difficult challenge to the building engineer, especially in historic structures, if the external RH is varying widely, from 90% in mid-summer to 20% in mid-winter, for example. Air barriers to stop conditioned air from entering the structural envelope, and vapour barriers of 4 mm polyethylene with a permeability rating of 0.04–0.08 perms to stop water vapour from dampening the insulation must be carefully designed and installed, stapling both sheets to each stud. Failure to do so can harm the building fabric, and may be signalled by such symptoms of dampness as efflorescence on the museum walls.

Air circulation is a function where the needs of the collection and the public must sometimes conflict. Since it is expensive to condition air in order to prolong the life of the collection, it is foolish to replace that air with large volumes of unconditioned outside air that requires re-conditioning. The outside air dampers should be of fixed-volume design, controlled by a timer to admit the minimum acceptable volume of fresh air during public hours, and to close at other times. Carbon dioxide monitors that allow automatic adjustment of the amount of outside air admitted according to requirements are expensive, but may repay their costs many times over in day-to-day operating efficiencies – given the particular concerns of museums for conditioning the air in their buildings.

Nowhere is the collection–public conflict more apparent than in questions of *fenestration*. People like windows, and architects and many museum professionals believe that skylights are attractive features in a museum gallery, as many of them prefer natural light, especially in art museums. Windows opening directly into galleries are not recommended; in historic structures today, they are usually blocked (in such a way as to ensure that the window blocks are not visible on the historic facade). But skylights over galleries are commonly found, even in new structures. All these openings in the museum wall and ceiling challenge the ability of the best building engineers; some have been heard to say that there is no such thing as a skylight that doesn't leak, only one that hasn't leaked *yet*! Others find that solutions that work in temperate climates, such as the ingenious arrangement of louvres and computerised environmental controls in the area under the skylights above the *Neuepinakothek* galleries in Munich, do not work nearly as well in harsher climates of greater extremes. One very expensive new art museum in a northern climate had to install buckets to collect drips on its carpeted and cathedral-ceilinged skylit gallery floors only a few weeks after it opened.

All fenestration should be triple-glazed, with at least 1.3 cm between panes; laminated glass or plexiglass should be used with an ultra-violet (UV) filtration capability of reducing UV radiation to 10 μW per lumen, and with a polycarbonate outer layer for security. Louvres, operated by hand or automatically though a photocell, are needed to ensure that the sun's rays enter the gallery indirectly, and the area below the skylight may have to be separated from the gallery (with another layer of glass as its floor and the gallery's ceiling) to provide a 'half-way house' in which the difference between the outside and internal environments can be equilibrated to prevent condensation along the edges of the panes.

Museums in tropical climates experience the added problem that most of the professional literature is focused on temperate-zone conditions. We are only now beginning to develop specialised requirements for artefacts or specimens of tropical origin, in recognition of their differing hygroscopic capacity. The surfaces of some fine furniture in one tropical museum were inadvertently sacrificed in the attempt to meet inappropriate temperate conditions. At present, we suggest 65% as the RH base for collections of tropical origin. The Singapore Art Museum, for which we produced the functional brief, aims to provide 65% RH to its own collections, but has the capacity to provide 50% to works of art borrowed from temperate zones, as it did in 1996–97 when it showed an exhibition from New York's Guggenheim Museum.

Recent approaches to operating museum buildings, particularly in the UK, have emphasised energy-saving using lower-technology approaches to control the environment, with the added attraction of cost savings. Conservators allow somewhat greater ranges of fluctuation in conditions affecting the collections. For instance, the engineer may be able to allow a 5–10 per cent variation from the RH standard for about 5 per cent of the museum's annual operating hours. The effect of such reconsideration is limited, however, by the fact that museum buildings must meet not merely the requirements of the institution itself, but also those of potential *lenders*. The need to maintain the highest standards in the temporary exhibition galleries, generally 50% ± 3% RH at 20–21°C 24 hours per day, all year round – or at least to maintain the capacity to achieve these standards when needed to meet the demands of lenders – is the ultimate criterion determining the provision or the upgrading of many museum heating, ventilating and air conditioning systems. And if that capability must be provided for the temporary exhibition gallery, it is often cost-effective to provide it for all the collection zones.

Maintaining the 50% ± 3% RH standard at 20–21°C all year round should not present a major problem in a well-designed new building constructed to comply with this standard, especially in a maritime, temperate climate. In a historic structure, or in any building not constructed to maintain such a standard, it may be difficult or impossible, especially in a continental climate. A 55% RH standard may be the best compromise possible, and even then it may be necessary in a historic structure to adjust the humidity settings by 5% RH each month for three months each spring and autumn, allowing a fluctuation from 40% RH in the winter to 55% in the summer, and a temperature swing by 0.5°C from 21 to 24°C and back during the same period. In any event, metal and unbound archival paper collections require a dryer store, kept closer to 40% RH, if possible. British Standard BS 5454 (1989) for museums and libraries recommends that paper should be stored at a constant temperature within the range of 13–18°C and at a constant Relative Humidity within the range of 55–65%, but with the added provision that little-used paper not bound in volumes should be stored at a Relative Humidity of 40%.

Whatever standards are required by the museum's chief conservator, it is important that those responsible for the building's operation insist that they can and must be attained. Engineers themselves are often resistant, or point to the consequent high cost of building operations, so the museum manager needs to be certain of the conditions required, and to insist on them. Several years ago, a survey of a series of Florida museums found that only one had a perfect record of maintaining the humidity and temperature levels that the managers of all the museums surveyed said they wanted, but did not think they could achieve. The director of the one successful museum observed that the difference was simply his unrelenting quest over a two-year period with his consulting engineers – reinforced by his refusal to pay them until the desired results were obtained!

The control systems and the equipment provided to the museum can be decisive in facilitating achievement of the desired standards. Electronic humidistats with a low drift factor and a short operating span should be used, connected to a direct digital control, computer-operated electronic control system. The control humidistat should be mounted on a wall of the room with the tightest specifications. Ducted electronic electrode disposable-cylinder steam humidifiers are recommended for small to medium-sized museums, although larger institutions may utilise central steam humidification.

*Redundancy* is an important consideration in planning and operating a museum building system. By 'redundancy' here we mean the capability for building systems to continue operating despite malfunction or interruption of the power supply to the regularly operating equipment. This need not mean that the museum must maintain 200 per cent of its heating, ventilating and air conditioning equipment requirements; it may be sufficient to have about 130–140 per cent, since normal usage is likely to require only about 65–70 per cent of capacity at any one time. Redundant power capacity is also important to maintain security, as well as for preventive conservation purposes.

Once the standards for both regular operations and redundancy capacity have been determined and the equipment has been installed, much of the site and building operations schedule can be formalised in procedures manuals. The director should ensure that these manuals and the priorities they set out are consistent with museum policies. Simple procedural errors, such as leaving the front doors of the building open, allowing outside air through a foyer directly into expensively air conditioned galleries, have been observed even in otherwise sophisticated institutions – no one had explained the museum's requirements and the reasons for them to the warders, who opened the doors to enhance visitor comfort.

The loading dock and the shipping and receiving bay are areas where staff procedures sometimes transgress not only museum policy but the reasons why expensive equipment was provided in the first place. One useful way of ensuring that roll-up loading doors are not left open too long is to install interconnected locking mechanisms on two sets of doors – one at the outside vehicular access to the museum, and the other at the interior access from the shipping and receiving bay to the area where crating and uncrating will take place – so that if one door is open the other must be locked. Providing a separate personnel door beside the shipping door is also important, with a security station controlling access to both, preferably with the help of closed-circuit television and a sound system, so that delivery personnel can be identified before either door is opened. Viewing panels 75 mm wide by 450 mm high should be provided at 1.4 m above the floor in all doors through which collections are to move, and doors, corridors and lifts should be at least 2.44 m wide and 3 m high (and preferably 2.5 m by 3.4 m) on the route from the loading dock to the galleries and stores.

Co-operation between security staff and building operations personnel is crucial to ensuring a well-managed museum. Both should be familiar with the policies and procedures of the other, and regular (perhaps weekly) meetings between the chief of security and the operations manager or building engineer may be rewarded by greater efficiencies in operation as well as assured security. It is particularly important that both departments are fully informed well in advance of such events as the delivery of exhibitions or the shipment of collections. The operations manager should also have an arrangement with the registrar to ensure that no artefacts, specimens or works of art enter or leave the building unless authorised by signature.

Computerised *building management systems* (BMS), with screens on which conditions in each room can be observed and printed out if required, have made building operations far more efficient in museums where they have been installed. Certainly, no new museum and no major renovation should be undertaken without including a BMS room. These should incorporate RH readings for each room where they are required, including the internal conditions of display or storage cases, which should be recorded on a chart (not simply as lists of numbers). The traditional conservators' hygrothermographs, with their styluses recording temperature and RH on graph paper drums in the corners of galleries, will be replaced in the 21st century by less cumbersome and more easily monitored instruments integrated into the BMS display.

3.4.2.2  MAINTENANCE AND REPAIR

The cleaning of museum buildings is another area where building operations come into contact with the needs of both collections and the visiting public. Clear lines of demarcation must be drawn between building maintenance and collection care responsibilities, especially if there are open displays or large artefacts or specimens that are easily accessible to cleaners. This is particularly important if cleaning staff are on contract, and so do not report directly to museum management.

Museum concrete should include a hardening agent, and all surfaces should be *sealed*, including those above false ceilings. This is not only to prevent concrete dust from falling, but especially to prevent it from entering the air circulation system. All other surfaces should be painted.

Vacuum cleaners should be central systems vented to the outdoors, or may be portable, high-efficiency particulate air filter systems, which boast a dust capture efficiency of 99.97 per cent. Carpentry workshops and any other dust-producing workrooms should be vented outdoors, and care should be taken in planning the air circulation system to ensure that dusty air from such work stations is not re-circulated.

The correct replacement of air filters is a task that requires a carefully drafted procedures manual. The bank of filters, measured in the US by the American Society of Heating, Refrigerating and Air-Conditioning Engineers' (ASHRAE's) Atmospheric Dust Spot Efficiency Test section of ASHRAE test 52–76 ('Eurovent 45' is the European equivalent), should provide 25–30% pre-filter capacity, 40–85% medium-efficiency filters, and 90–95% after-filters. Activated-charcoal filters are recommended for the filtration of gaseous pollutants. Each filter should be provided with its own manometer to indicate any drop in pressure, and these should be monitored individually, with each filter changed as necessary.

Cleaning materials and techniques should be reviewed and approved by conservators, and maintenance personnel should be included in training sessions to familiarise them with the requirements of the collection. Similarly, public expectations and those of the staff providing visitor services should be made clear, so that performance evaluation of cleaners can be based on compliance with museum policy and specific public needs.

The replacement of lamps is a routine but essential activity that requires a procedures manual written in consultation with the curators and conservators. There is little use in a museum policy requiring a low level of UV radiation (under 10 µW/lumen) if the maintenance worker replaces the lamps in the gallery with fluorescent tubes that do not have built-in levels of UV protection, or discards the sleeves that were supposed to control the UV emission levels. Similarly, the maintenance worker needs to know precisely which lamps are needed in which orientation in each display, or the effects contrived by lighting consultants may be lost after the first change of lamps.

An important principle of museum accommodation planning is to provide access for repair personnel that does not require them to pass through or near collection zones. Many repairs may be carried out after hours, so it is a simple security precaution (which places far less responsibility on the repair workers) to ensure that replacements or repairs can be undertaken without walking through or past galleries or collection stores. If the layout of the building makes such a provision impossible, it will be necessary for a member of staff to accompany repair and replacement personnel at all times.

Deferral of maintenance and repair is a chronic problem in museums. Expenditure on upkeep or improvements always appears to be easier to postpone than other budget items, with the result that relatively minor maintenance requirements become progressively more serious until they result in major capital costs for complete replacement. Such deferrals may also weaken the security system. Assiduous managers should avoid such long-term inefficiencies by maintaining regular budget commitments for maintenance and repairs.

The repair and replacement of exhibits provides an interesting question for museum managers: how much should the museum undertake directly, and how much should be contracted out? The staff of some museums, particularly in continental Europe, have traditionally included exhibit designers or architects, and some museums have operated extensive workshops where new exhibits can be built and old ones repaired or replaced. The result in some cases was a 'house style' of exhibits – for better or worse. Today, many museum managers prefer to contract exhibit design and fabrication out – choosing a different designer or fabricator for each project, thereby reducing their design studio and workshop needs to the minimum. Even framing may be more cost-effective if carried out by contractors, rather than dedicating space, facilities and trained staff to a function that is required only intermittently.

The advent of electronic, video and computerised exhibition components, especially in science centres or children's museums, points to another need: the requirement for relatively quick and easy replacement of equipment, with weekend as well as weekday staff trained to fix exhibits before too much 'downtime' accumulates. Failure to provide for such replacements results in too many of the 'Sorry, this exhibit is not working today' signs that frustrate the museum public, especially those who are visiting for the first time. Admission charges have been one important factor in stimulating museums to ensure that malfunctioning exhibits are quickly repaired or replaced. It has also led many to calculate the anticipated life span of exhibits, and the projected cost of their upkeep, when preparing an exhibit plan.

### 3.4.2.3 SECURITY

Planning and managing security for museums is of primary importance, and should be the museum manager's first concern in a new posting. 'Security' here refers to the entire range of activities concerned with the protection of the public, staff and others in the museum, and the protection of the collections from all threats to them.

Like building operations, security affects and is affected by both the collections and public activities aspects of the museum, so the chief of security should meet regularly with those responsible for these functions, as well as with the operations manager, to ensure that security provisions are effectively in place at all times. The security chief should also meet regularly (at least annually) with local police, fire and hospital officials to ensure that the museum is up to date with current practices in these jurisdictions, and to acquaint the officials with the museum building's layout and recent or proposed changes to it.

Security is an area where policy and procedures manuals should be utilised fully, and updated regularly. Thus the management of security includes a continual process of planning and policy formulation, and review of procedures manuals. A security policy should include:

- risk analysis
- health and safety precautions
- insurance coverage and valuation procedures (see subsection 3.5.4)
- security equipment – present and recommended
- an emergency procedures manual

A RISK ANALYSIS involves seeking answers to four basic questions:

- *What is to be protected?* The collection should be analysed in terms of monetary value – classified by value categories of over or under certain monetary levels – and in terms of interest to thieves or vandals. Famous works of art or artefacts may be particularly vulnerable, and objects made of precious metals are always of interest to thieves because they can be melted down. Some artefacts are politically controversial or involve religious values that may attract attacks. Others may be of lower monetary value, but may be of great value to the museum and the community for other reasons.

- *What are the threats?* An explicit identification of the risks will help to focus the security plan on reducing or eliminating them.

- *What level of risk is acceptable?* Many threats cannot be eliminated entirely, but may be reduced to a level that the museum's security policy can accept. Purely from a security viewpoint, the museum could remain closed to the public to maximise the safety of its collections; but since the museum is a public institution, its management must determine the degree of risk that is acceptable. For example, there might be a policy against open displays of any kind, or against open displays of objects with the highest monetary value.

- *What countermeasures are appropriate?* Again, museum policy must determine acceptable standards among security options. One very busy museum in Manhattan, for instance, encourages its warders to be strict and even officious with the public, because it prefers to err on the side of security, rather than putting its emphasis on a visitor-friendly atmosphere. Other museums set different priorities.

The threats to be evaluated in a risk analysis include:

- *natural disasters*, such as earthquakes, hurricanes, tornadoes, floods, forest fires or power cuts;
- *building faults*, such as electrical or heating system deficiencies, or structural weaknesses;

- *theft* – art theft in particular is said to be second only to the drug trade as a source of revenue to criminals, and a distressingly high proportion of museum thefts are 'inside jobs' connected with or committed by underpaid staff;

- *fire*;

- *vandalism*;

- *accidents* on the part of staff or visitors;

- *social or political hazards*, such as bomb threats, strikes or demonstrations.

Risks may be evaluated in terms of their:

- *probability*, from least to most likely to occur;

- likely *frequency* of occurrence;

- seriousness of *consequences* for the museum.

Risks may be:

- *eliminated*, for example by changing staff procedures to stop causing a hazard;

- *reduced*, by installing detection or response equipment;

- *transferred* to an insurer;

- *accepted* as necessary to the fulfilment of the museum's public mission.

The museum's security policy should accordingly identify the following range of countermeasures (the 'four Ds'):

- DETECTION: Methods of determining whether a threat is occurring include surveillance by warders or guards, intrusion alarms, smoke detectors, display case alarms and closed-circuit television.

- DETERRENCE: Methods of reducing the likelihood of threats may range from perimeter fences to case locks. The perception of deterrence may be just as important as the reality – most museums now recognise the value of making security obvious, ensuring that visitors can see closed-circuit television screens near the entrance, for example.

- DELAY: If a threat arises, the intention of security is to retard its progress. Fire walls are a typical example, as is the practice of restricting egress from the building to one guarded exit.

- DEFENCE: An *emergency procedures manual* should detail appropriate staff responses in the event of a threat. All staff and volunteers should be provided with this manual – not just security staff – and there should be regular drills and rehearsals. In addition to fire drills, vandalism, theft, visitor illness and accident scenarios should be enacted, with staff being tested on their ability to respond in accordance with the museum's security policy, as detailed in the emergency procedures manual. All staff should know when and how to call for an ambulance, fire or police protection, and should understand the legal implications of liability for actions taken or not taken, both for the museum and for themselves. After-hours response should also be covered in the manual, especially for those who will receive telephone calls if the intrusion alarm or the fire alarm is activated. An *emergency team* of those employees empowered to co-ordinate responses to emergencies should be identified in the manual, and should meet regularly (at least twice a year) to review the museum's readiness.

It is possible to develop a risk analysis for individual objects, groups of objects, or an entire collection. An arbitrary scale of 1–10 for degrees of *criticality* and *vulnerability* may be devised, with 'criticality' defined as how important the object is to the museum, and 'vulnerability' measuring the extent to which it is at risk. Then:

$$\text{Risk} = \text{Criticality} \times \text{Vulnerability}$$

Thus if an object of prime importance to the museum (high criticality) is moved from inside a case to an open exhibit, its risk factor would be greatly increased – so the chief of security might suggest to the curators or the director that the relocation should be reconsidered.

The museum's security policy might define three levels of security for exhibition galleries:

- *high security* for exhibitions of highly valuable items, with special provisions, possibly including constant surveillance during open hours;
- *moderate security* for exhibitions of original works of art, artefacts, specimens or original archival material, for which the museum's routine security patrols and surveillance should be maintained;
- *limited security* for exhibitions that do not contain original works of art, artefacts, specimens or original archival material; these might be supervised by a person with duties other than those of a warder, and might be mounted in a corridor or foyer.

Seven levels of security may be distinguished for the stores:

- *alarmed vaults:* with internal masonry-reinforced walls, ceilings and floors, heavy metal doors operated by a combination lock, and with all visits accompanied by authorised staff and recorded – required for gems, stamps, coins and other relatively small items of high value;
- *high security store:* also with internal masonry walls, ceilings and floors, but with steel doors and frames with at least a six-pin tumbler lock and key control – required for works of art, weapons, furs and other objects of high value;
- *permanent collection stores:* the museum's main stores, of robust construction and with solid doors under key control – required for the main body of the museum's permanent collection;
- *transit stores:* with sturdy walls and doors under key control in a non-public area adjacent to the crating/uncrating area – required for temporary loans to the museum, or other works of art, artefacts, specimens or archival materials in transit; these areas must resemble the permanent collection stores, since they are likely to be visited by couriers accompanying loans from other museums;

- *storage cabinets:* these may be located in non-public areas, or under or above exhibit cases in the galleries; key control is critical, and objects stored should not be of high value;

- *off-site stores:* key control, alarm response and patrols of these areas present particular challenges, and should be appropriate for the nature of the collections in such storage – often required for larger items, such as vehicles or military equipment;

- *hazardous materials stores:* non-flammable and fire-retardant structures (at least a lockable metal cabinet with key control) should be used to store hazardous materials used in the museum (such as some conservation laboratory supplies); some collection materials are themselves hazardous, such as certain types of photographic negatives in archival collections.

In considering security planning for the museum site and building as a whole, it is useful to think of it as a series of concentric circles of protection, with the COLLECTION at the centre, and the following layers of protection, from the outside inward:

- *Museum grounds:* Landscaping can enhance security by eliminating overhanging trees or shrubbery near buildings. Car parks should be separated from the building by an access area subject to surveillance. Exterior lighting is an important consideration. Closed-circuit television (CCTV) systems may be used for surveillance.

- *Building fabric:* Walls and roofing materials should resist intrusion; fire ratings should in general meet building code requirements, but for walls surrounding collection zones should be at least two hours. Doors and door frames are a particular concern – their fire rating should be similar to the walls, and they should have a solid core; doors in historic structures may require discreet reinforcement. Hinges should be interior, and secured by non-removable pins. Exterior openings should be protected with magnetic switches and glass breakage detectors, with doors secured by six-pin tumbler deadbolt locks with a minimum throw of 25 mm. Windows, especially ground floor windows, present a major challenge: interior blocks (not visible on the exterior), bars or shutters that descend over the openings when the museum is closed may all be considered. Roofs should be examined carefully, since entry is very often gained through skylights or service doors there. Basement or half-basement windows or doors must also be reinforced.

- *Perimeter alarms:* Intrusion alarms should be installed at all entrances, and on all windows, including any skylights or other roof access points, with direct telephone connection via dedicated lines to either a police station or the security company, whose response to an alarm should be detailed in the emergency procedures manual. A verified passive infra-red detection system should extend to all interior spaces, with the same telephone connections. The closed-circuit television system should utilise close-coupled discharge colour cameras, which should be positioned to record the faces of persons entering and exiting the building at all points; computer software programs now integrate closed-circuit surveillance with computerised plans of the building, so that warders can select or record images of interest and store them in computer memory. Pressure-pad detectors on the roof should also be installed.

- *Security stations:* Most museums have at least two security stations, where warders operate and observe CCTV systems and monitor alarms. One should be visible to visitors entering, and should allow warders to intercept anyone attempting to enter or leave. The other station should be adjacent to the loading bay and the shipping and receiving door, with control over the personnel door which all delivery personnel must use to gain access to the museum; CCTV and an intercom system should be provided at this entrance, so that warders may interrogate delivery personnel before allowing them access even to the controlled area within the personnel door. The personnel door should lead only to a foyer, from which further access to the museum is also controlled by the warder within the protected security station. This entrance for delivery personnel may also function as the staff entrance; if not, a similar arrangement must be provided at the staff entrance.

- *Warders (guards):* This force makes up the largest single group of employees in many museums. They are also the people with whom the public has the most frequent and sustained contact. It is therefore crucial that they be well trained and well motivated, especially since they are seldom well paid. They are traditionally uniformed; this need not be para-military in style, but can simply consist of an official but not intimidating jacket and trousers or skirt. Attempts to mix education or interpretation functions with security responsibilities have generally not been successful: warders must focus their attention on security. But they should be trained in the nature and value of the collection, and in museum visitor service policy. Their operations manual should include their postings schedule, routines for opening and closing the museum, after-hours patrols, handling deliveries and other property control procedures, key control measures, locking and lock checking routines, exhibition gallery surveillance requirements, crowd control measures, and maintaining security during construction or exhibition replacement. Procedures for removing objects from exhibitions and for displaying a card notifying the public that an object has been temporarily removed should be controlled and recorded. An important change in warders' lives is the welcome and long-overdue tendency to consider them as members of the museum staff who can, in some cases, develop into other positions, rather than isolating them from other functions; this approach, implemented with success at museums in Glasgow, for instance, means that warders are likely to be far more involved in and aware of customer care as well as security issues. Requirements for higher educational qualifications (and rewarding them accordingly), providing training and offering personal development opportunities are all part of a changing work environment for warders as museums enter the 21st century.

- *Interior alarms:* The system should include alarms to alert warders if visitors approach exhibits too closely, as well as intrusion alarms that activate in response to any movement after hours, connected to the police station or security company in the same way as the perimeter alarms.

- *Display cases:* Case design is an issue not only for the exhibition designer, the conservator and the curators, but also for the chief of security, who should be consulted when display cases are being planned. Their location should be examined, to ensure that they do not block emergency escape routes, and that they do not offer an easy exit for a smash-and-grab thief. Proximity to fire exit doors is a serious concern. Polycarbonate glass or plastic should be used, and can be laminated to include clear ultra-violet light filters. Small, free-standing cases should be avoided; display cases should be substantial, well anchored to the floor or wall, and their locks should be tamperproof.

Sliding glass panels are not recommended, since they are difficult to protect from intrusion; lockable access panels should be hinged, preferably horizontally, with non-removable pins. Corners and joints should be tight-fitting. Display materials, whether within cases or not, should be fire-resistant; the security department (as well as conservators) should always test any new materials proposed. Works of art, artefacts or specimens should be discreetly but securely fastened within the case; the Asian Art Museum of San Francisco has gone much further and has developed support systems to protect its collections from earthquakes, both in display cases and in stores.

- *Security screws:* Pictures are sometimes suspended by chains or rods from hanging rails, the focus of security concern being to anchor both the chain or rod and the point of attachment of the picture to the chain or rod. Far preferable – and often required by lenders – are security screws, which pin a 'fishplate' to the wall behind the picture and to its stretcher (rather than the frame). Security screws can be turned only by special screwdrivers, as their heads are more complex than the usual slot or cross design. Unfortunately, well-equipped thieves stock a wide selection of security screwdrivers, so security screws are not foolproof, but they are a substantial deterrent.

Three 'concentric circles' form three levels of security for the building as a whole, which incorporate the security levels described above for the exhibition galleries and the stores:

- *outer level 1:* the perimeter, exterior lighting, locks, the intrusion alarm and interior space surveillance systems, most of which are inactive during public hours and activated only when the museum is closed;

- *median level 2:* the non-public non-collection zone and some non-public collection work areas, which would always be alarmed when the museum is closed, and may be alarmed during public but non-working hours;

- *inner level 3:* non-public collection zones such as the stores, which are always protected by alarms that can be deactivated only by authorised personnel, or on their instruction.

FIRE SAFETY presents another range of concerns that must be addressed by the museum's security policy. Fire presents the most serious threat to museums everywhere, not only to those housed in historic wooden structures, but in many more recent structures as well. Although theft or vandalism may remove or damage specific items, fire often ravages whole collections, and may destroy them completely.

- *Smoke detectors* are the preferred means of detection of fire, except in kitchens, where heat detectors should be used. Ionisation, photo-electric or projected-beam photo-electric smoke detectors may be used.

- *Sprinkler systems* were once resisted by museum managers, due to the risk of water damage, but widespread experience of fire response times, along with technical advances in sprinkler design, have rendered such fears outmoded, especially when compared with the very real destruction that even a few seconds' fire can cause. Individual-action on-off sprinkler heads (that turn off when the heat level drops), with copper, thermoplastic or internally galvanised iron pipes and water cleaned to potable or boiler water standards, should be specified. Dry pipes (which only carry water when the sprinkler system operates) are not recommended, due to the risk of corrosion products being spewed out with the water when activated; however, some lenders may not allow their objects to be displayed under pipes carrying water; a valve may be installed on pipes serving temporary exhibition galleries, so that the pipes may be drained during the period of the loan, *if* this is allowed by local fire officials.

Halon fire extinguishing systems are no longer legal in many jurisdictions, for environmental reasons. The best remaining options for fire extinguishers appear to be a combination of pressurised water extinguishers for non-electrical fires and carbon dioxide extinguishers for all others. All staff should be tested regularly (at least annually) on their ability to utilise the museum's fire extinguishers, and the test certification tags on the extinguishers should be checked regularly (at least quarterly) to ensure that they carry dated initials of authorised inspectors.

Accommodations planning should include *fire walls* (with fire ratings of two hours for collection zones, complying to the building code elsewhere); *doors* should match these fire ratings, and *fire compartmentalisation* should be incorporated in the building design, especially in the stores. Large storage rooms should be divided into compartments by fire walls at regular intervals, rather than designed as one continuous area. Atriums and stairwells are other danger areas, especially where they must be retained as an authentic feature of an historic building; they usually require enclosure on the landings, with fire doors for access. Renovation projects should be welcomed by the chief of security as opportunities for provision of additional fire walls or doors, and accommodations planners should include extensive security consultation as part of the planning process.

There is an inherent conflict between two aspects of security – the desire to control egress from an area, and the need to provide fire or other emergency exits. The latter requirement usually dictates panic hardware ('break bars') on fire doors, which must allow direct access to the outside. Yet these fire exits may provide a thief with a convenient exit from a gallery, sometimes directly to a car park. All fire exits should have audible alarms, and in some jurisdictions the opening of doors at the bottom of fire escape stairwells may be delayed for some seconds. The chief of security needs to consult with fire and police officials, and to balance fire safety requirements against the museum's concern to prevent theft.

Finally, it should be noted that good security depends on good housekeeping. Efficient cleaning and maintenance procedures, clear signage (including 'No Smoking', and a discreet but firm 'Do Not Touch' for open exhibits), sound preventive conservation practices and an alert and informed staff of warders will contribute to both improved security for the collection and enhanced safety for visitors.

# 3.5 | Financial Management

As the organisation chart developed in Chapter 2 and the job descriptions provided in the Appendix to this book indicate, the administration division of a museum is responsible for a wide range of functions including financial management, which is the subject of this final section.

For museums operated by independent non-profitmaking associations, financial management has always been a central concern. In the past few decades, with governments around the world emphasising increased self-reliance, even for museums that are wholly integrated with their own line departments, ensuring the financial well-being of the museum has become a major responsibility for museum management. The job descriptions and qualifications of museum directors increasingly focus on the skills necessary to manage the finances of the institution, especially fundraising abilities.

For museum directors especially, the challenge is to provide for the institution's financial needs while maintaining its creativity and scholarship. Finance officers should view their positions as facilitating research and public service, while development officers should see their roles as providing the means for building the collection and furnishing the facilities for people to enjoy and learn from it. Directors and trustees must ensure that the mission of the museum is paramount, and that the museum's financial arrangements support it, *not* vice versa. This is why this section on financial management follows all others, rather than preceding them. The apparent loss of sight of these priorities was what disturbed many people about the famous Victoria and Albert Museum advertisement of a few years ago: 'An ace caf', with a rather nice museum attached.'

This section begins with a consideration of the annual cycle of drafting and monitoring museum budgets (3.5.1) as the primary method of financial control. Revenue generation (3.5.2) follows, being the most urgent requirement for many museums today, although controlling expenditure (3.5.3) can also be critical. Risk management (3.5.4) – adequate insurance of the museum's assets – is an indispensable method to protect the institution against loss, while financial planning and development (3.5.5) can ensure a positive future in the long term.

## 3.5.1   BUDGETS

A budget is a plan with money attached. An annual budget attaches monetary values to the year's goals, which are the quantified, short-term applications to the budget year of the museum's longer-range, qualitative objectives. There should be a discernible continuity from the goals and objectives of the museum's long-range corporate plan through the objectives of the current year's action plan to the amounts allocated in the current year's budget. In recommending the budget to the museum's governing body, the director should be able to demonstrate this continuity.

In particular, the director should point to *variances*: the fluctuations in allocations due to the influence of the museum's current action plan goals. Some governments require *zero-base budgeting*, which requires museum managers within their line departments to justify each allocation in relation to the programmes it facilitates, as if it had no history. In most museums, however, it is assumed that many allocations will continue because those functions must be sustained, and it is only the variances – the increases or reductions in these amounts – that are of interest.

In practice, budgeting is usually carried out within individual departments, but budgets may also be organised by programme, objective or function:

- The *departmental* approach is the most common – each department is asked to review its past year's allocations, adjust for current objectives and tasks, and recommend next year's figures.

- Alternatively, or in addition, budgeting can be carried out by *programme* – each department identifies the programmes or services it provides, and allocates funds to each in accordance with the priority or emphasis given to that activity in the current year's plans.

- Budgeting by *objective* can be a useful review process, in which fluctuations in the current year's proposed allocations are evaluated in relation to the objectives identified in the museum's corporate plan and the outcomes they are intended to achieve.

- *Goals* of the current action plan should be reflected in the fluctuations of allocations – checking budget changes against agreed goals or longer-term objectives should form part of every budgeting process.

- It is also useful to review allocations in terms of the fundamental museum *functions* (as illustrated by the triangle of essential museum functions in fig. 1.2). How much of the museum's financial resources is devoted to collecting? How much is budgeted for documentation, preservation, research, display or interpretation? How much is allocated to administration? The answers can be revealing, and can point to a need for changes in the balance of allocations, in view of the museum's mission and corporate plan.

Museums may budget for various funds and purposes:

- OPERATING BUDGET: the annual revenue and expenditure for the museum's collection care, public activities programme and operation of its site and building;

- ACQUISITION FUNDS: the amount retained for purchasing objects for the collection, or for the expenses associated with acquisitions;

- ENDOWMENT FUNDS: usually donated moneys that are invested, with all or only a portion of the interest earned being spent, either on operations (in the case of 'unrestricted funds') or for specific purposes such as acquisitions, exhibitions, or lecture series ('restricted funds');

- CAPITAL BUDGET: an amount retained for planned development of the museum's site or buildings, such as renovation, relocation, new construction or exhibition renewal;

- GRANT PROJECTS: government or foundation grants often require separate accounting of the projects their contribution is intended to support;

RESERVES: amounts retained for contingencies, or for future development projects.

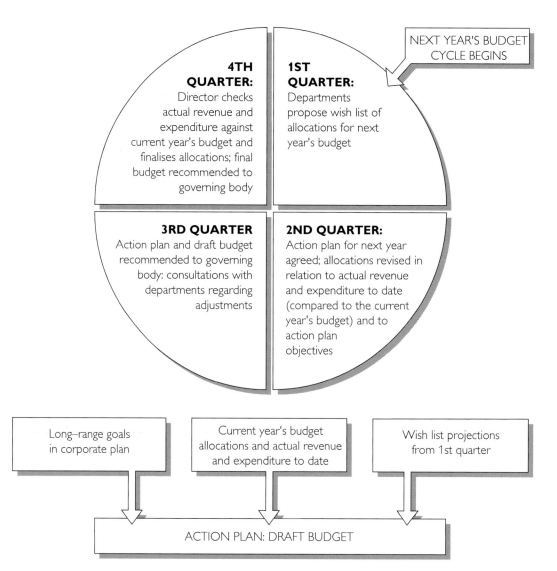

Figure 3.2  The Budget Cycle

The operating budget should be the end result of an annual budgeting process. This should be a constant cycle, with the progression to next year's budget beginning immediately after this year's has been approved. Figure 3.2 suggests a year-round approach to budget generation by quarter.

The annual budget cycle proceeds in this way:

1ST QUARTER: During the first three months after the passage of the previous year's budget, it is important to encourage those responsible for each department to 'dream anew' – to project a 'wish list' of all desirable (but reasonable) programmes and activities that the museum should undertake, so that new ideas and projects may be given full consideration. The director and the financial officer should be concerned to *stimulate creativity* and to resist cynicism during this phase. Although many of the ideas and projects may not be realised in the immediate future, it is vital that the museum's management should be challenged by new ideas, taking full account of them before budget limitations are addressed.

These 'blue sky' budgets should not, however, be irresponsible: each activity or project should be costed with reasonable order-of-magnitude estimates, with all attendant revenues projected; if possible, projects should be phased so that consideration can be given to entering into at least the first phase of projects, programmes or activities that are subsequently approved. It is also valuable to keep these projections ready to respond to grant-aid opportunities as they arise; many of the projects may be eligible for grant funding.

2ND QUARTER: During the second three-month period, the director, the financial officer, the relevant divisional deputy director and the officers responsible for each department should meet to develop next year's action plan. The *action plan*, as shown in fig. 3.2, aims to reconcile the input from three documents: the long-range, qualitative objectives relevant to this department in the museum's corporate plan; the current year's budget allocations for both revenue and expenditure compared with actual figures to date; and each department's 'blue sky' budget proposals from the first quarter. Variances from last year's allocations (increases or reductions) should be drafted to reflect the agreed action plan for that department.

3RD QUARTER: During the following three-month period, it is the responsibility of the finance officer and the director to recommend the action plan and its accompanying budget implications to the museum's governing body, generally through the finance committee. The governing level of the museum's administration or the trustees should review this draft budget and action plan in relation to the museum's long-term interests, and should ensure that the museum's mission and all of its functions are being adequately served. For example, an over-commitment to exhibitions or other public activities might reflect a director's priorities, but the interests of the institution may require more balanced funding of research or collection care. Another consideration is the extent to which revenue-generating activities may not only pay for themselves, but may also generate funds which can be dedicated to other functions, thereby justifying allocations to revenue-generating activities.

The governing body or the trustees have the responsibility to raise additional money to fill the 'income gap' if they agree with the recommendations of the director that the expenditures are required to fulfil the museum's mission and goals. Following on the governing body's reaction to the proposed action plan and draft budget, the director and the finance officer should return to the departmental level, and work out the necessary adjustments to the departmental allocations.

4TH QUARTER: The finance officer should report to the director on the comparison of actual revenues and expenditures to the expiring year's budget figures after three quarters (nine months) of activity, and both should issue any instructions required to keep the museum within budget, or as close to it as possible. The director should then determine the final allocations for the coming year's budget, making adjustments to the action plan and its draft budget in view of anticipated shortfalls or overspending, and return to the governing body for approval of the final budget.

Monitoring the current year's actual revenue and expenditure in relation to budget allocations is important, both as a means of control within the current year and as a vital part of the preparation of the coming year's budget. Figures should be refined in accuracy as the budget cycle proceeds, reflecting the museum's experience of the current year's figures, and any deficits or overspending to be carried forward. As soon as the budget is approved, of course, it becomes the subject of further monitoring, as the next budget preparation cycle begins.

## 3.5.2  REVENUE GENERATION

Many museum administrations used to be considered, and used to consider themselves, primarily as cost centres, expending government funds to provide public services. Although a few in some parts of the world remain in this position (not always comfortably), a very large number of museums in the past few decades have been obliged – or have wished – to focus much more on their potential as generators of revenue. We will therefore consider revenue generation before proceeding to the question of operating expenses in subsection 3.5.3.

In recent years much attention has been paid to museums' capacity for generating funds from their operations. This section examines the potential of self-generated revenue (3.5.2.1), but also considers the proportionately far more important subject of contributed funds (3.5.2.2), and ends with a brief discussion of the management of fundraising campaigns (3.5.2.3).

### 3.5.2.1  SELF-GENERATED REVENUE

'Self-generated revenue' refers to the museum's capacity to earn revenue from its operations, in contrast with government funding, endowments, sponsorship or donations, all of which may be termed 'contributed revenue'. Self-generated revenue includes the following sources of funding, most of which derive from services to visitors, which is why these categories of revenue are often referred to as 'visitor-generated'.

- admissions (3.5.2.1.1)
- retail sales (3.5.2.1.2)
- catering (3.5.2.1.3)

- memberships (3.5.2.1.4)

- rentals (3.5.2.1.5)

- films, performances and special events (3.5.2.1.6)

- educational programmes (3.5.2.1.7)

- publications and media (3.5.2.1.8)

- contracted services (3.5.2.1.9)

## 3.5.2.1.1 Admissions

Charging for admission to public museums has been, and remains, controversial. The argument put forward by opponents to charging is that museums are a public service and should be financed by taxes; advocates of charging observe that the quality of museum service often improves when staff and visitors know that admission is being charged, and that relatively affluent tourists, who often account for half of museum visitors, do not contribute to the cost of free museums, which are borne by the taxes imposed on their host communities. The imposition of admission charges on formerly free museums generally results in an immediate decline in attendance by approximately one-third, which is sometimes (but by no means always) recovered over the following five to ten years, depending on the extent to which the museum follows up their introduction with effective programming and marketing.

There has been much research and debate concerning the impact of charging on the demographic characteristics of visitors. Some studies demonstrate that low-income and minority group visitors value the visit more when there is a charge, and others indicate the opposite – that these populations visit less frequently when there is a charge. There are so many variables in the museum attendance 'equation' that it is impossible to isolate just one of them: the admission charge. One such variable is the type of museum: art museums are generally thought of as places to drop in to frequently to see favourite pictures or current exhibitions, while science museums tend to offer a 'day out'. A high admission charge would discourage short-stay return visits to the art museum and require a complete rethinking of the visitor experience, which may or may not be a good idea, depending on the museum's mission and philosophy of interpretation. On the other hand, free or low-cost admission alone does not guarantee broad public participation in the museum – therefore *both* charging and non-charging museums must examine how they communicate with the public, whether they are welcoming to the broad spectrum of people in the community, and what their programmes have to offer them. Further, since there are many ways to charge and many ways not to charge – as will be seen – what is needed is an *admissions strategy* appropriate to the specific situation of each museum.

It is sometimes said that admission revenues do not justify the cost of collecting them, but most museums that charge find that 10–20 per cent of their total net revenue can be derived from this source. Admission rates must be commensurate with those for other attractions in the area, and are usually scaled for adults, children, families and groups, often with reduced admission for senior citizens, pensioners or the unemployed. There are numerous ways to reduce the cost for frequent visitors, such as offering free entry to members, or free or discounted entry for everyone on particular days or evenings. One recent study has suggested that at least 7 per cent of the museum's opening hours should remain free of charge in order to serve the entire community. However, a programme of visitor research and evaluation would be needed to determine whether that outcome was being achieved.

An alternative approach which may be equally effective, or even more effective in attracting attendance from cultural minorities and low-income groups, is to extend invitations offering free or reduced admission through these groups' own community and social organisations. This approach avoids offering free admission to those who can easily afford to pay, and helps to build partnerships between the museum and the community or social organisations.

Another admissions strategy is to charge only for special exhibitions and events, but to offer free admission to the exhibition of the permanent collection. This has proven successful in many jurisdictions around the world, both in maintaining revenue and in providing a free, basic level of museum service to both tourists and residents. For example, Britain's 1996 Museum of the Year, the Buckinghamshire Museums Service in Aylesbury, offers free admission to its County Museum galleries, but charges for entry to its delightful Roald Dahl children's gallery. In some circumstances, this strategy may result in higher levels of income from the shop, programmes and food services as a result of higher attendance levels than if there were a general admission charge and fewer visitors.

Museums in major metropolitan areas with a large attendance base of over one million visits have been successful in introducing a 'discretionary admission charge' – there is a 'recommended' admission charge, but visitors may pay what they wish so long as they pay something. This approach may be distinguished from the so-called 'voluntary admission charge', which is neither voluntary nor really a charge.

Museums charging for admission have, in recent years, benefited greatly from the application of computers to ticketing. The combination of such software programs with visitors using charge cards for ticket purchases has resulted in a growth of mailing lists of patrons among those museums that retain the names and addresses of ticket purchasers. Membership recruitment programmes (by mail or by telephone) may be targeted at these visitors. These ticketing records can also be used to facilitate visitor surveys, which may be based on postal code prefixes, cross-referenced to demographic data. Of course, any such usage must comply with such legislation as the UK's Data Protection Act or similar laws elsewhere.

## 3.5.2.1.2   Retail sales

While admission charges may remain contentious, little controversy surrounds the almost universal provision of museum shops, which have been identified as one of the fastest-growing sectors of the retail trade world-wide. Visitor surveys in recent years indicate that growing numbers among the museum-going public expect a high-quality museum shop, and complain when they feel that the range and quality of stock, its presentation or customer service are inadequate. The shop offers visitors an opportunity to take home a product that will remind them of their museum visit, and if it is a book, catalogue, reproduction, video or CD-ROM, it will provide further opportunity for study: therefore, the quality and educational value of the retail offerings should be consistent with the mission and goals of the museum.

Smaller museums often make their shops cost-effective by combining volunteer retail clerks with paid retail managers. Some larger institutions, such as the Victoria and Albert Museum, are not only totally professional in the operation of their shops, but have also been successful in extending their profitable on-site operations into mail-order sales via catalogues and a parcel delivery service around the world. The Victoria and Albert Museum has also copyrighted patterns from its collection (such as William Morris wallpaper), and licensed them for reproduction.

To reduce crowding and improve service, it is sometimes worthwhile to separate children's shops and book shops from the general retail offerings. Prices in all shops may range from relatively expensive items, best suited to charge card purchase, to low-cost souvenirs, including some items intended for purchase by children or their grandparents. The mark-up may be only 40 per cent for books or museum postcards, but is usually 100 per cent, or may be even more, for other items.

The amount spent per visitor is usually about US$1 in smaller shops to around £1 (about US$1.50) in larger institutions, but can be much higher if the stock is well matched to the market and the attraction (preferably changed for each major temporary exhibition), and if the shop is well located and advertised. Spending also varies with the type of museum, art museums tending to be at the high end of the spectrum.

Location is critical to museum shops, as in all retailing. Accommodations planning should provide for a shop that is visible to visitors entering the museum and *inescapable* to those leaving. If possible, the shop should also be visible to passers-by, and accessible to shoppers who are not even visiting the museum (if this can be arranged while maintaining museum security). The ideal museum shop is positioned so that it can open and close independently of the museum, operating even when the museum is closed, if necessary, in order to meet market demand – especially during holiday shopping seasons.

Most museum shops combine a site-specific line of publications, media products, reproductions and souvenirs with a more generic stock of books, toys, jewellery, crafts and other gifts that are more or less unique in that community, and may provide an important sales outlet for local artists or artisans. The production of special lines of merchandise for major exhibitions (so-called 'blockbusters') is a means of both increasing retail revenues and promoting the exhibition. All new stock should also be submitted to curators for approval, on aesthetic as well as intellectual grounds, and the curators and director should approve all reproductions or replicas of objects in the collection. Some museum shops have improved their effectiveness by changing their stock significantly for each temporary exhibition, ensuring that the stock is relevant to the current one. To do so, of course, the retail manager must be included in the exhibition planning process.

*Picture rental schemes*, usually operated by volunteers, are often combined with museum shops, or run from premises adjacent to them. They serve both artists and the public by circulating works of art on monthly hire to homes and offices.

*'Production for sale'* by museum demonstrators on industrial heritage properties – such as ceramics produced at a historic pottery – can be an attractive addition to interpretation at a living history site, but attempts to combine it with wider distribution and truly industrial levels of production have proven more problematic. The museum's priority of interpreting the heritage slows production, in most cases to a pace that is not cost-effective in industrial terms.

With a few such exceptions, most museum shop initiatives have proven successful, so that retail sales remain one of the most promising of the museum's revenue options. Costs of sales are generally in the range of 50–60% of total sales, leaving a gross profit of 40–50%. Taking staffing and other overheads into account leaves a net profit of 10–20% of gross sales. Gift shop operations often contribute 5–10% of total museum revenues. Museums are increasingly extending the success of their retail operations through such means as catalogue sales, satellite shops (in other countries, as well as elsewhere in the same city), placement of the museum product line in other museum shops and in suitable commercial outlets, and sales on television 'shopping channels' and through the Internet.

### 3.5.2.1.3   Catering

Unlike shops, museum-operated cafeterias and restaurants generally do not produce high levels of income for the museum. The museum manager must understand the objectives of the food service (visitor comfort, extending the length of stay), and attempt to ensure that it does not lose money (although many museum-operated food services *do* lose money, when all relevant staffing and overhead costs are attributed to them).

While it is advisable for museums to operate their shops directly in order to maximise revenues, most now prefer to contract catering out, and to receive either a share of proceeds from the caterer, or a rental fee, or both. Catering companies can often achieve economies of scale by operating several food services and through special events catering. This can be a satisfactory arrangement as long as the museum maintains a 'quality control' provision in the contract with the caterer, whereby the museum may cancel the contract, after appropriate notice, if quality does not meet the museum's standards. This is a crucial contract provision, since a poor or overpriced lunch or an unsatisfactory snack can be more memorable than an otherwise outstanding museum experience for many museum visitors.

This quality control provision should address not only cooking, ambience and customer service, but also nutrition and the use of natural foods, as opposed to a strictly market-driven reliance on artificial and junk foods. The caterer and the museum should agree in the contract a policy regarding the type of food to be offered.

Decor is also important, especially if the museum opts to have the cafe themed in a period style. The contractors' compliance with the theming may extend to uniforms, and should be maintained in detail if it is adopted at all, since visitors may very well judge the museum's authenticity by the consistency of theming in the cafe. Attempts to cook and serve food in historic settings are even more problematic, due not only to concerns about the preservation of the heritage building and its furnishings, but also because of the caterers' need to use modern equipment to meet customer expectations and environmental health and safety regulations.

Most smaller museums find that a good-quality cafe with a light snack service, with or without a warming kitchen to heat pre-cooked meals, is sufficient for their visitors, and for after-hours rentals. Larger institutions may offer a full restaurant as well. Some very busy museums have evolved three levels of service – a franchised fast food service, a cafe for light refreshments, and a full-service dining room, with the latter two appropriately themed. The Metropolitan Museum in New York now features live music in both its cafe and fine dining areas during its very successful evening openings.

As with the museum shop, the location of the museum cafe dramatically affects its profitability. Many art museums like to include a courtyard, where sculpture can be enjoyed by diners seated outdoors in clement weather, or at least viewed from behind glass. More important commercially is a location that facilitates access after museum opening hours, if there is a market for that level of food service in that location. The museum's lavatories, or a separate set of washroom facilities for diners, must also be accessible if the cafe is to be open after the museum's public hours.

If a museum is located in a commercial area with convenient access to food services, it may choose not to invest the capital funds in a food service area, but to develop admission policies that encourage visitors to use neighbouring restaurants and cafes and to re-enter the museum as often as they wish during the day. Tickets and posters could reassure visitors that they can return as often as they like, and provide a map of nearby food facilities. This is sometimes helpful in establishing good relations with nearby restaurants, especially for a new museum in a relatively small commercial area. The restaurants and their operators may then be encouraged to become corporate or individual members or sponsors.

The museum must also provide for its other catering needs – refreshments for exhibition openings and other special events, food services for its function room (especially if rentals are involved), and tea services for the staffroom and the members' lounge. These activities may be included in the caterers' contract. Care must be taken in accommodation planning to ensure that food supplies and refuse circulation routes do not cross areas in which the collection is normally held. Refreshments for exhibition openings should not be served in the galleries themselves, of course, but in an adjacent function room that does not hold artefacts, specimens or works of art, if such space is available; space planners should include such an area in their priority list if it is not.

Another level of provision is a *school lunchroom* for school parties who bring packed lunches. Many museums find that a dedicated space for this purpose frees their cafes from large numbers of low-spending schoolchildren whose drinks or other refreshment needs can be adequately served by automatic dispensing machines – although again, the concern for nutrition and natural foods should be borne in mind. The area allocated for the school lunchroom need not be left empty at weekends or during evenings – instead, it can become a revenue earner by hiring it out for children's birthday parties.

### 3.5.2.1.4  Memberships

Even in the relatively recent past, many museum managers expected membership fees only to cover the cost of providing services to members. Today many museums are becoming much more ambitious about their membership programmes, both as a source of revenue and as a means of extending their support from the traditional membership base of high-income individuals to one that reflects the social, economic and cultural diversity of the community.

Membership is built and maintained by offering tangible benefits geared to the interests of frequent visitors, supporters and donors, such as: free admission, free or reduced admission to major exhibitions, discounts at the museum shop, a regular newsletter, priority access to museum activities and programmes, and special activities such as travel expeditions guided by museum experts and behind-the-scenes tours of the museum conducted by curators. For many members, however, the motivation of membership is as a form of philanthropy or expressing civic pride, rather than 'value for money', and this should be recognised and appreciated. Categories of membership should include not only adults, students and families, but also several donor and corporate membership levels, each with a graduated level of increasing support, with commensurate benefits. Corporate membership should include benefits for the member company's employees, both as a means of creating a closer relationship with the corporation and as means of expanding the museum's audience.

# Membership and Audience Development at the Art Institute of Chicago

BY CHRISTINE O'NEILL

The Art Institute of Chicago is committed to a co-ordinated, integrated approach to audience development which results in audience-based museum planning. This approach had its genesis in a trustee-initiated strategic planning process which established over-arching goals for the institute: to bring more – and more diverse – people face-to-face with original works of art, and to provide a meaningful, engaging experience for visitors, while maintaining the Art Institute's commitment to the highest professional, scholarly and educational standards.

This direction required a renewed focus on audience expansion. As a result, the *Audience Development Plan* was created to foster visitor attraction and retention, and to enhance the visitor experience. The success of the plan will ensure financial stability through increased admissions, membership, shop, restaurant and special event revenue, and, most importantly, philanthropy.

Three major objectives guide the plan:

● to diversify and expand the museum audience;

● to integrate planning efforts cross-functionally across the traditional museum departments involved with visitors – public relations, marketing, communications, membership and development;

● to allocate resources according to audience-based priorities, as well as collection needs.

These objectives have resulted in a comprehensive strategy to convert:

● infrequent visitors, within targeted market segments, to frequent visitors;

● frequent visitors to members;

● members to highly-committed participants, through involvement and philanthropy.

This strategy means rethinking and improving several aspects of the museum infrastructure – the interaction of various functionally-organised museum departments, the technology supporting those departments, and the variables in programming which can be realigned with audience expansion in mind. It also means reorienting procedures and processes in these areas with the objective of expanding the visitor base.

This translates into an approach described as the *Visitor Value Chain*, which moves a potential visitor from mere awareness of the Art Institute:

● to interest in making a first visit;

● to making sure that all aspects of that visit are positive;

● to making a repeat visit;

● to membership purchase;

● to additional usage of museum offerings;

● to a first contribution;

● eventually, to major philanthropic commitment, if possible.

A lively example of the Visitor Value Chain approach is the creation of the 'After Hours' programme, based on market research, to interest the target market segment of young professionals in a first-time visit. 'After Hours' is a monthly Thursday evening event at the museum that offers live jazz, complimentary hors-d'oeuvres, a cash bar, tours of the galleries, discounts on museum membership and special promotions or gifts, combining social interaction with an opportunity to become familiar with the collection. The programme includes print and radio advertising, direct mail, publicity and promotions to convey an appealing message and image specific to this market. Names of those who attend are recorded, on-site membership conversion is extremely successful, and initial visitor tracking indicates that those who attend 'After Hours' are making return visits. Only time will tell the level of future financial support.

This programme and all audience development plan strategies depend upon:

● adequate and accurate market research and programme evaluation – both pre- and post-programme;

● recording the visitors' details and database maintenance;

● inventive, if not necessarily expensive, promotion and advertising;

● front-line staff participation and training;

● trustee and managerial commitment to audience development goals.

Considering audience development as an interactive process between the museum departments and the audience keeps the focus on the desired end – lifetime involvement with the Art Institute. Each person who walks through the door of the museum is regarded as a future benefactor. Marketing decisions are checked against the possibility of future philanthropic support. Membership is viewed as a critical transition period from public at large to 'family'. Visitor and member/donor experience, both within the museum and in all aspects of the lifetime relationship with the institution, is highly significant. The most important factor in that relationship, at any point, is quality and presentation of the collection and programmes, not parties, gift shop offerings or free offers.

The result is a dynamic, diverse, financially viable museum, accessible to its varied and complex audiences, where new ideas and experiences from within and without are welcomed and incorporated into the life of the institution.

*'After Hours' at the Art Institute of Chicago, 1995.*
*Photograph by Steven Arazmus, courtesy of the Art Institute of Chicago.*

### 3.5.2.1.5 Rentals

Hiring out function rooms to groups or companies who wish to associate their event or their image with the museum has become another source of self-generated revenue. This practice depends upon well-located function rooms, accessible when the museum is closed as well as when it is open.

Since museums require such facilities for openings, special events or receptions anyway, it is economically attractive to offer these rooms for hire. Very often the function room is called 'multi-purpose', and is equipped with video and projection facilities, and with movable chairs (kept in an adjacent chair store). It may also be adjacent to the museum's theatre or auditorium facilities, which will usually have fixed seating and lecture room facilities, and may also be made available for hire. Catering and refreshments of adequate quality are crucial, as is access to the museum's public toilets. To enable it to be used for exhibition openings, the multi-purpose area must also be adjacent to the galleries.

Some museums, especially those that are government-supported, provide such facilities to specialist groups or community organisations primarily as a public service. However, the cost of security, and possibly other personnel, can be significant, so there is considerable interest in converting this service into a revenue centre. Some institutions, such as the Netherlands Railway Museum, have found that the best approach is to provide a high-quality facility, and to charge accordingly.

### 3.5.2.1.6 Films, performances and special events

Film programmes and performing arts presentations, such as dance and theatre, can complement a museum's exhibitions. Special events may be of any kind, including festivals during holidays. Some smaller museums welcome half their visitors on a dozen special-event days during the year, for which special admission rates may be charged.

The capacity to offer such attractions is, of course, dependent on the provision of adequate facilities. For many museums, a lecture auditorium with film projection and video facilities is sufficient. Again, access after the museum galleries' opening hours is important to make such facilities cost-effective, including access to the museum's public toilets.

Some larger museums have had success with *large-screen format film theatres*, including the very large IMAX and OMNIMAX theatres. At least one science centre in Asia derives a greater proportion of its revenue from such a theatre than it does from admission to its exhibitions. Although the capital investment may be relatively high for some museums, these facilities can be lucrative if they are well positioned in the market, and if they have access to other film programmes in addition to the site-specific or 'dedicated' film that the museum may commission about itself, its locale or its story-line. It is interesting that attempts to operate such theatres independent of museums or equivalent attractions have not to date been successful; they function best when seen as part of a larger experience.

*Simulators* have added another dimension to museum exhibitions, which can form yet another revenue centre if an additional admission fee is charged for their use. This adaptation of technology (originally developed for aviation training) to the needs of the leisure industry has been successfully used in science centres, and especially military and aviation museums. Many try to make do with archival footage (such as a First World War 'dogfight'), but the experience is vastly improved if the funds are raised to develop a new programme more directly related to the story-line of the museum or the exhibition.

Other entertainment formats are available to museums. Many have been successful with multimedia theatre programmes, including such features as moving screens and computerised lighting effects, with or without live actors or animatronic figures. Some of these shows may be *object theatres*, in which the museum's collections or replicas appear as 'stars' in the spotlight as a voice-over and/or projected imagery brings them to life, while others may be more conventional film, slide or video presentations. Another option is live theatre, which may be attractive for a summer season when student actors are available, or as part of an employment grant scheme. Historic sites may opt for 'first-person' interpretation, in which costumed actors play their parts in period, and answer visitors' questions from within the time and space limitations of the historic setting. If possible, all such attractions should be included in the general museum price of admission, but it may be preferable, depending on their scale and location, to present them as additional cost features, on offer at the original point of sale when the museum admission is purchased, as well as at the theatre door.

More problematic to date have been attempts to extend *virtual reality* experiences to the museum. Initial endeavours have foundered on the labour-intensive nature of the technology, not only for its successful presentation and use by the public (which requires constant staff attention), but also to cope with the extensive need for repairs and the resultant 'downtime'. One attraction found that its original virtual reality equipment was under repair three-quarters of the time! Future development, especially of the more social 'virtual reality caves', may find museum applications, but at present, most institutions view the applications found in amusement arcades, video arcades and world's fairs with caution. One happy exception has been the application of 'blue screen' technology, adapted from television news programming, in which visitors' images are superimposed into other contexts, allowing visitors to play 'virtual' ball games, throw virtual snowballs or guide virtual parachutes to a safe landing.

### 3.5.2.1.7 Educational programmes

Educational programmes are usually considered as cost centres, especially if the museum provides guided tours free of charge to school parties as part of its mandate. In such cases, however, the museum often receives a government subsidy which is partially or wholly justified by its educational service.

However, educational services can also be revenue centres. Museums may contract with schools to provide a certain number of guided tours to designated classes, or may charge school parties a special admission rate. Sometimes admission is free for school parties, but charged when museum staff provide special programmes or guided tours. Some museums have 'time-sharing' agreements with school boards or local authorities, whereby school parties have exclusive access during certain hours (certain mornings, for instance) when the museum is not otherwise open; the museum provides guided tours or other educational programmes during those hours, and receives a set fee from the school board or education authority.

Separate entrances with lay-bys for school buses are often provided for school parties, so that they may come and go without interfering with other visitors. Separate cloakrooms and a school lunchroom are also helpful. Classrooms have become common, and may be useful for orientation prior to a visit, or for discussion afterwards, as long as both museum staff and schoolteachers remember that the museum is the ideal setting for informal, not formal, education, and that the affective learning which the museum can provide can be experienced best in the galleries, not in a classroom.

Slide-illustrated adult education lectures may be a revenue source, and are usually more successful in museums if they are offered as series or courses. Such series can also be a means of building membership or recruiting volunteers. An auditorium with basic projection facilities and a sound system is usually sufficient for this level of programming.

Some art museums have studios in which they can teach both fine and applied arts, ranging from informal weekend or evening sessions for families (often booked a year or two in advance) to more structured courses for every level of serious interest in the arts. Artists' demonstrations and artists in residence can be accommodated in the same studios, or the spaces can be made available for hire when not in use for classes. One southern American art museum has studios booked until after midnight each weekday night!

Travel programmes for members, with museum staff as expert guides, can also be profitable. The imagination and energy of management and staff are the only limitations to well-marketed educational activities – always assuming that the museum's priorities allow for the dedication of staff time, materials, equipment and other resources to these ends.


## 3.5.2.1.8   Publications and media

The publication of catalogues and books about museum collections and exhibitions has long been an important source of revenue for museums, although in many instances, print runs were not related to the foreseeable target market, resulting in massive, long-term storage requirements for unsold copies. The production of video discs or CD-ROM discs may supplement such publications with more sophisticated media that can reach a world-wide audience at competitive prices.

The development of such media has put a premium on the museum's control of the imagery of its collection – an issue that is particularly important for art museums. Although cash-poor museums are naturally tempted to hand over to others the development of multimedia services in return for immediate financial gain, considerations of control over subsequent usage of the imagery and copyright provisions may lead museum managers to be cautious about leasing rights to digitised images of objects in their collections, while remaining positive about extending their images and information to new and much larger audiences through these new media.

Charging for the use of museum sites, buildings or collections in films, television programmes or advertising is another revenue source that has multiplied in frequency and value in recent years. Museums need policies that set differential rates for educational films, entertainment or advertising. These should take into consideration not only rights to the imagery and safeguards concerning ethical uses of it, but also the real costs to the museum of providing access to the film-makers, most of whom will need to work in the museum when it is closed, often through the night.

### 3.5.2.1.9   Contracted services

Museums themselves may undertake contracts to provide research or technical services to other museums, to government agencies, or to the private sector. Many museums are mandated to provide archaeological services within their geographical areas, while natural history curators may identify pests (or, for example, in Western Australia, snakes) for appropriate regional agencies or municipalities.

Museum conservation departments, in individual institutions or within regional museum services, have attempted to offer conservation services on contract to other museums and to private collectors. These have sometimes been moderately successful, although they have often proven to be more problematic than the optimism of their initial business plans would suggest. The type of equipment, personnel and practice required for such a regional service is likely to be quite different from what the conservation department normally provides.

One difficulty with all such contracts is that they divert time and attention away from museum priorities towards the imperatives of the revenue-generating contract. Another can be conflict with the private sector, which may complain of unfair competition from a partially (or wholly) subsidised museum staff. Such contracts are therefore best developed in consultation with the private sector, with publicly-funded museum management aiming to provide services that do not duplicate private sector capability or impinge on commercial enterprises. It is then more crucial than ever for the museum to conduct a market analysis and draw up a business plan before embarking on the provision of such a service.

Another more fundamental challenge to museum management in the provision of such services under contract is to preserve the spirit of shared scholarship and freedom of access to information that has always been a hallmark of museums. Even more important than the preservation of the collections as the museum's *raison d'être* is the provision to the public of information about them. As museum managers strive to develop more revenue sources by tendering for contracts for research or other services, it is important that they ensure that academic freedom of information about the collections is not forfeited in the process.


## 3.5.2.2   CONTRIBUTED REVENUE

Contributed revenue is given by others in support of the museum's mission. Therefore, despite the current emphasis on self-generated funding, contributed revenue remains of the utmost importance, including:

- government subsidies and grants
- grant aid
- endowments
- sponsorship
- donations

Having considered the many options for self-generated funding in subsections 3.5.2.1.1–9, we may now turn to these five sources of contributed revenue, which remain more important on the balance sheets of most museums around the world.


### 3.5.2.2.1   Government subsidies and grants

Governments at all levels contribute to the financial support of museums for a wide range of reasons, but principally because they provide three main services:

- PRESERVATION OF THE COLLECTIVE HERITAGE: Any community of people, whether they constitute a nation, a state, a province, a county or a municipality, inherits a *natural heritage* – the land, air and sea they inhabit or use – and a *cultural heritage* – the archaeology and history of their ancestors and those who came before their ancestors in that place, or wherever their history has taken them. They are constantly adding to their cultural heritage, as well as affecting their natural heritage. If they are or have become multicultural populations, the collective heritage will be accordingly diverse. Museums are charged with the preservation of the entire collective heritage, past and present, natural and cultural. Government subsidy is justified primarily by museums' fulfilment of this vital function.

- EDUCATION: Museums are a most effective means of informal education of the public, especially in the values and meaning of the collective heritage, both natural and cultural. Informal education is an important adjunct to formal education institutions, not only because it makes abstract lessons concrete, but even more so because it provides affective rather than merely cognitive learning. Affective learning is far more important in conveying and retaining values than mere cognitive comprehension of them. In countries with limited literacy or multicultural populations, such an affective learning institution can be even more important, because it can unite generations with widely differing formal educational backgrounds in the common experience of an exhibition or demonstration.

- CULTURAL TOURISM: Museums are a key part of any area's tourist attractions. Cultural tourism is the most dynamic sector of this vital industry (the world's largest), even in countries whose tourist appeal has formerly relied on the now universally suspect 'sun, sea and sand'. Governments must find ways to redirect taxes levied on this industry to make tourism a 'renewable resource'. Providing subsidies to museums is one way of contributing towards the preservation of the natural and cultural heritage, the principal resource for the cultural tourism industry.

As governments and people continue to re-evaluate the role of government, we may expect that the reasons for supporting museums may change, and the degree of support may also change. Museums will increasingly have to make a compelling case for government support, and this may involve museums changing to meet new community needs.

Government subsidy remains the most important single source of revenue for museums around the world. It accounts for 90–100 per cent of many national, provincial and state museums' revenue, and for 60–70 per cent of all museums' revenue, even in many countries (such as the UK or Canada) where museums have become active in increasing self-generated revenue. Even in the USA, the comprehensive *Data Report from the 1989 National Museum Survey* (Washington, DC, January 1992) – the 'decade survey' conducted by the American Association of Museums – indicates that government funding of all museums taken together amounted to 39 per cent of total revenue at that time.

To what extent should governments subsidise museums? The study that the authors conducted with our partner, John Nicks, for the UK Office of Arts and Libraries, *The Cost of Collecting* (London: HMSO, 1989), indicates that about 67% of all museum expenditure can be directly and indirectly attributed to care of the museums' collections. The figure for American museums is somewhat lower, at about 56%. One might take the view, therefore, that government subsidy or a combination of government subsidy and revenue from endowments should amount to approximately 55–70% of museum budgets if the collective heritage is to be preserved for future generations. A government with high educational priorities should go further, providing an additional 10–15% to ensure that the museum fulfils its educational objectives for the population.

In some jurisdictions, generous government assistance has been instrumental in stimulating higher standards of professionalism among museums. Annual contributions have been made contingent by some governments on the recipient museums' adoption of desired policies or the preparation of long-term plans. In some cases these requirements have been imposed directly by government cultural or heritage departments, in others by agencies established or encouraged by governments to impose registration or accreditation schemes, compliance with which then becomes a criterion in deciding whether to grant subsidies at all, or subsidies above a certain minimal subsistence level. The overall effect of such requirements has been positive for the recipient museums, and for the museum profession.

### 3.5.2.2.2    Grant aid

While government line department museums and some 'arm's length' institutions may enjoy government subsidies, independent, non-profitmaking associations – and many of the 'arm's length' and government line department museums as well – are more likely to receive government and foundation support in the form of grants. These are distinguished from subsidies primarily by the fact that they are not assured allocations, but are subject to application by the recipient museums to programmes established by government or its appointed agencies. In many countries, lotteries are the sources or administrators of grant-aid.

Grants may be of two types:

- OPERATING GRANTS: These are grant programmes that provide contributions to museums annually, so they are similar to subsidies, except that the recipient museums must apply for them and often cannot predict the amount of the annual grant. These are often made subject to their recipients' compliance with professional standards, which may be indicated on the application form. Funds granted for operating purposes may usually be expended on a wide range of activities, or for any running costs.

- PROJECT GRANTS: These are grant-aid programmes that have specific objectives, and therefore make funds available for particular purposes. Although some of these may be museum-specific, others may arise from agencies or government departments (or foundations) with very different concerns; among the most common are employment grants. Funds provided under these programmes must be expended on the projects for which they have been approved, and separate project accounts are usually required.

In many museums the preparation of grant applications has become a specialised function within the development office or performed by a contractor. The person responsible for this function needs to meet with the museum personnel who will execute the programmes or projects seeking funding before preparing the application, to ensure that all costs – in time, space, personnel, facilities and materials as well as money – have been considered. Failing to allow for the cost of administering successful grant-aid applications is one of the more common errors of over-enthusiastic museum managers.

Grant projects also need to be carefully correlated with the museum's long-term policies and priorities. Winning a grant from a government employment programme is of little value if it conflicts with the museum's personnel policies, or requires far more time for training than is justified by the progress realised on a museum project. Even more important is to ensure that grants are secured because they accord with museum priorities, rather than allowing grant programmes to determine the museum's programme.

Some government departments administer grant programmes directly, whereas others establish agencies, such as the National Endowment for the Arts, the National Endowment for the Humanities, the National Science Foundation or the Institute of Museum Services in the USA, or the Museums and Galleries Commission in the UK. Some of these specialised agencies have been instrumental in stimulating higher levels of professionalism among recipient museums.

Private philanthropic foundations are increasingly important sources of grant aid. Some, like the Gulbenkian Foundation, the Getty Foundation or the Pew Charitable Trusts, have major programmes specific to museums, whereas many have more general cultural or educational objectives that museums can fulfil.

## 3.5.2.2.3   Endowments

Many museum managers outside the USA have the impression that American museums largely 'pay for themselves' through self-generated revenues. This is rarely true. A much more important aspect of American museum funding is the tradition of philanthropy through endowments. These endowments are invested, with some of the interest earned by the investments being devoted to the museum's running costs. Investment decisions may be made by trustees with expertise in that area, or investment counsellors may be encouraged to volunteer, or may be commissioned. Income from endowments often accounts for 10–20 per cent of American museum operating budgets, and some American museum officials have set 20–30 per cent of the total operating budget as a target for this category of revenue.

In museums with current or planned endowment funds, raising contributions to the endowment becomes an important aspect of fundraising in itself. Museum trustees and members in particular should be encouraged to make donations or bequests to the endowment as the most effective way of helping the museum achieve financial stability in the long term.

The best opportunity to raise contributions to unrestricted endowment funds that may be used for operations arises during capital development campaigns, when endowment requirements can be presented as part of the overall development need. The difficulty in raising endowment funds is that they appear to be too long-term and too diffuse in application, so that potential donors do not feel in control of, or responsible for, the results of their philanthropy. For this reason there are restricted endowment funds with specific aims and uses, such as acquisitions.

### 3.5.2.2.4 Sponsorship

Sponsorship of exhibitions and other museum programmes is one of the most productive ways in which the private sector can be involved in museums. Unfortunately, some advocates of government cutbacks have formed the notion that such sponsorship can somehow supplant grants and subsidies. However, sponsorship, even where it has been enthusiastically pursued, usually remains a relatively minor source of revenue in proportion to museum requirements in general.

Nevertheless, private sector sponsorship has taken its place as a significant revenue source, particularly as it can be combined with corporate memberships. Museums should prepare *sponsorship policies* that articulate the institutional mission and ensure that control over the content and style of exhibitions or other programmes is retained by the museum. Company executives are usually relieved to learn of such provisions, since they ensure that the sponsorship does not risk subsequent public criticism for alleged interference. Acknowledgements of sponsors' contributions should include a statement of the museums' responsibility for, and control of, all issues of content and style.

Growing numbers of companies regard contributions to museums as part of their public relations or marketing strategy, rather than as philanthropy. Museums can respond to this orientation (which usually places significantly larger amounts of funding at their disposal) by targeting potential sponsor companies with interests in the content of museum projects, or with a marketing focus on the target market for specific exhibitions or other programmes. Thus companies with products or services directed at children and their parents may be interested in sponsoring a children's gallery or an educational programme, while others may be particularly drawn to a programme directed at encouraging multicultural participation in the museum. The museum management should consider the sponsor as a partner, and aim to develop mutually beneficial relationships. Sponsorships need not involve large amounts; some smaller museums have found it most effective to recruit exhibition sponsors among relatively small local companies, such as accountancy, law, medical, dental or architectural practices, which can afford relatively small amounts of sponsorship on a regular basis, and enjoy being included in the opening festivities as a reward.

### 3.5.2.2.5 Donations

Gifts and bequests of artefacts, specimens or works of art, and related donations of money by relatively wealthy individuals, have historically been responsible for the development of many major museums. For the most part these were made before the donations earned significant tax advantages for the donors; rather, this kind of philanthropy aimed to establish a lasting memorial that would have cultural and educational value for many years to come.

Such donors still exist, and it is very much in the interest of museums to seek their support, where it is available. Income tax deductions for donations to museums in the form of acquisitions or cash remain an attraction in some jurisdictions, but have been substantially reduced in many others. Another motivation may be to reduce or escape capital gains taxes or estate duties, or to comply with cultural property export and import legislation, which usually restricts sales abroad and makes donations to national institutions more attractive. Museum trustees should include among their number at least one authority on inheritance law, who can give informal advice to prospective donors.

Museums are increasingly finding that they may be more successful in attracting donations of goods or services from corporations, rather than asking for money. Such donations in kind may be especially valuable at a time of capital development, whether of new buildings, new facilities or renewed exhibitions. Computer or audio-visual hardware and software are other frequent donations in kind.

An important consideration for both museum and donor to understand is that donations or bequests of acquisitions convey to the museum the *liability* of caring for the donated material. The donation of a collection, or even of a few works of art, artefacts, specimens or archival materials, should be accompanied by a cash contribution to the museum's operating funds for the care of the donated material. These funds will be expended on providing the stores, display space, security, conservation, documentation, curatorial research and many other costs associated with the addition of the donation to the museum's collection. The larger the collection donated, the more important such financial support of the museum's running costs becomes.

Proposed donations of acquisitions should be acknowledged with temporary receipts while under consideration. The permanent receipt for an accepted gift or bequest must make clear that the transfer of ownership is total and in perpetuity, and is unconditional. Under no circumstances should the museum be persuaded to accept donations 'with strings attached', such as stipulations that the donation should be placed on permanent display, or that it cannot be loaned to other museums. If such arrangements have been inherited, the museum should move to re-negotiate them with the heirs or executors, if possible. Such commitments can hamper the museum's scope of operations severely, especially its ability to change displays or to participate in loan exhibitions, and dissolving such constraints is not easy, as the trustees of the Barnes Foundation in Pennsylvania or the Burrell Collection in Glasgow can attest.

### 3.5.2.3 FUNDRAISING CAMPAIGNS

Fundraising campaigns are the means of organising donations. They range from once-in-a-lifetime capital fundraising drives to annual solicitations, but usually follow a similar pattern:

FORMING A FUNDRAISING COMMITTEE: Raising money is a social enterprise, and is best undertaken by a committee of people who can be convinced that it is not only valuable but necessary to raise the required funds because they believe in the project or programmes for which the funds are to be raised. Each member should join the committee by making whatever donation he or she can afford; the trustee or development officer forming the committee should determine in advance the amounts each committee member might donate, and invite them to join with a suggestion of a suitable amount.

Committee members who have not contributed appropriately themselves cannot convince others to do so; but those who have already contributed are usually strongly motivated to persuade others to join them. In addition to their willingness to give according to their means, committee members should be selected as representative of the groups of people who are considered to be the most likely donors – if a certain industry has a special interest in the museum or the exhibition, for instance, then a leading person in that industry should serve on the committee.

The most active and most committed members should be considered as possible chairpersons. In addition, a 'figurehead' chair may be named – a well-known person who is willing to add his or her name as an endorsement to the campaign; in the UK these are often members of the royal family, but they may also be well-known figures from the arts, sports, entertainment, or sometimes retired (and therefore non-partisan) former political leaders.

The committee may also wish to appoint professional fundraising consultants, and to agree on a campaign budget, which should be at least 10–12 per cent of the amount to be raised. Fundraising consultants can be helpful in providing planning and sound advice, especially about realistic objectives, but unfortunately, they cannot do the work of the committee, who must undertake the actual fundraising themselves.

DRAFTING THE CASE STATEMENT: The first rule of fundraising is 'If you don't ask, you don't get.' But the museum must be sure that the use to which the funds will be put is made clear, not only in terms of what will be done with the money, but more importantly, *why* the museum needs the funds. This is usually articulated in a case statement, in which the museum management makes the case for the project, or for the continuation of the programmes to be funded. Drafting a persuasive case statement and publishing it attractively is crucial to a successful fundraising campaign.

PLANNING THE CAMPAIGN: Successful fundraising is three-quarters planning, one-quarter execution. The campaign plan must identify an adequate but realistic *target*, the anticipated groups of *donors*, and attainable amounts to be sought from each group, adding up to the overall target. Remembering that people give money to other *people* (not to projects or causes), the plan should also identify the *fundraisers*, pairing those who will ask with those who it is hoped will give. The representative of the industry selected to serve on the committee should help to develop a list of leaders in that industry who are likely to donate. *Timing* is crucial: the campaign plan should schedule the best times to make requests to corporations and private individuals, to be followed by a public campaign. The spring is often considered ideal for individual giving, whereas school holidays are obviously not a good time to approach individuals with families. For corporations, knowing when the public relations budget is being considered is essential.

PACE-SETTING DONATIONS: Up to 80–90 per cent of the target amount is often donated by only 10 per cent of donors. The campaign should begin with a relatively quiet phase in which key donors are approached with the case statement, with a view to obtaining 'pace-setting' donations – amounts that can then be cited (anonymously or not, as the donors prefer) when approaching subsequent donors in that group. The other donors may then be persuaded to make their contributions in proportion to the pace-setter. The pace-setting donations should all be sought by personal appeals; the committee can decide whether subsequent appeals may be made by telephone or mail, or should also be made in person.

PUBLIC CAMPAIGN: A well-publicised campaign to secure relatively small amounts from a large number of donors (often only 5–10 per cent of the total to be raised), complete with fundraising events, should follow after the pace-setting contributions have been secured, as the rest of the private donations are being made. The value of this part of the campaign is to demonstrate the degree of public support for the museum or the project to be funded.

COLLECTING: Many campaigns seek *pledges* of amounts to be given over time. Wherever possible, automatic payment methods such as post-dated cheques, standing orders, covenants, direct debits or charge card commitments should be arranged, but however it is organised, it is crucial that the campaign includes the collection of the money pledged.

THANKING DONORS: It is vital for the museum to acknowledge donors in a suitable way – which might range from throwing a party in celebration of a successful campaign to erecting a plaque acknowledging a major donor. Even small contributors must receive acknowledgement and the museum's thanks in some tangible way.

EVALUATION: Whether completely or only partially successful, the campaign should not end without a formal evaluation by the committee of the lessons learned. These should be written in a detailed report that can serve as the 'script' for the next campaign committee. Mailing lists should also be updated in preparation for the next time.

## 3.5.3  CONTROLLING EXPENDITURE

The adage 'a penny saved is a penny earned' certainly applies to the financial management of museums. Given the challenge of combining the many sources of revenue listed in subsection 3.5.2 – or the equally demanding challenge of living within the constraints of a government line department budget – museum managers need to keep close control of their expenditure.

In addition to administering the budget cycle outlined in subsection 3.5.1, the museum's director and the finance officer may facilitate such control by establishing financial *responsibility levels* for each position in the organisation chart. Each financially responsible museum officer should have an authorisation level, below which each is authorised to commit the museum's resources. Departmental commitments above that amount must be referred to the next higher responsibility level, or beyond. Within his or her responsibility level, each officer should be empowered to make *requisitions*, which should be directed through the finance office. Actual *purchase orders* should be issued only by the finance office, and should be counter-signed by both the relevant department head and the finance officer.

Museum *contracts* with suppliers of all kinds – from exhibit fabrication to cleaning or catering – should be administered according to a tendering or bidding policy that meets the standards of the governing body and those of granting authorities from which the museum has received, or hopes to receive, funding. Given these constraints, museum management should, if possible, avoid commitments to automatic selection of the lowest bidder. Very often – in security services or exhibit design, for example – it is crucial that the museum be free to select higher bidders in order to ensure that museum standards are maintained.

Monitoring departmental expenses against the budget throughout the year is now usually carried out by referring to computer print-outs that show *variances* from projected expenditures to date. Variance statements should be reviewed with departmental officers monthly, with reports to the chief executive officer on any that exceed a pre-set level of tolerance – say, 10–15 per cent. Very often, such variances may be due to unforeseen opportunities, so they need not necessarily be viewed with alarm; however, a plan for congruence with budget projections should always be in the hands of the director and the finance officer. These often involve balancing under-expenditure in one department, or one section of one department, against over-expenditure in another; again, such changes may represent an entirely positive adjustment of plans as long as they are recorded and agreed by all concerned, and fed into the budget cycle.

Almost all museums are required to undertake an annual *audit* of both revenues and expenditures. The balance sheets that result from such audits usually do not show the true value of the museum's collections, which are often assigned only a nominal value for accounting purposes. There has been considerable resistance to evaluation of collections, because it is felt to be unwise for security and other reasons. Our book, *The Cost of Collecting* (London: HMSO, 1989), provides a basis for evaluation that is related not to some imagined auction room, but to the real, worked-up value of collection care dedicated to the objects over the years they have been in the museum's keeping, which may be called the 'opportunity cost' of retaining collections.

Museums in a number of countries are exempt from many taxes, usually because they are either government agencies or charitable organisations. Many are able to reclaim value-added taxes or sales taxes. In the USA, museums are now taxed on unrelated business income arising from revenue-producing activities that are not directly the result of their core operations as non-profitmaking or charitable organisations. For example, museum shop proceeds from the sales of items not directly related to the museum's collections may be subject to tax.

The running costs listed in museum budgets and financial reports can usually be classified according to the following line items:

- salaries and benefits
- occupancy costs
- curatorial and conservation costs

- public programming costs

- marketing expenses

- administrative costs

SALARIES AND BENEFITS: Museums are labour-intensive institutions. Hence, despite the relatively low wages often paid to each employee, salaries and benefits often amount to 50–65% of total expenses. Proportions even higher than that – ranging up to 70–80% – are not unknown, particularly in some government line department museums where civil service pay levels are subject to annual increments, whilst government budget allocations for museums are being cut. Proportions higher than 65% may be regarded as unhealthy, since they leave too little money in the rest of the budget for the staff to accomplish its tasks. A target of 55% might be taken as an attainable goal for many institutions. The benefits proportion in many countries accounts for 15–20% of total employment costs.

OCCUPANCY COSTS: By 'occupancy costs' we mean expenses incurred by the operation of the museum's site and buildings. These may include rent or taxes (if applicable), utilities, groundkeeping, maintenance and repairs, the operation of security systems, and insurance on the building, but not the cost of major renovations, which is a capital expense. Maintaining environmental controls and security to museum standards is expensive, so occupancy costs in museums usually account for 15–20% of total expenses, unless some functions are being provided by the museum's governing body as part of some centralised government service.

CURATORIAL AND CONSERVATION COSTS: Most collecting institutions should aim to reserve 5–10% of their total budget for direct collection management costs other than salaries. Lesser reserves are often encountered, usually indicating neglect of the museum's most important resource. Yet these direct curatorial and conservation expenses are by no means all the costs of maintaining a collection. They do not include acquisition costs (which are not part of the operating budget), nor the wide range of salaries (all the warders, for instance) made necessary by the collection, nor the indirect administrative and building occupancy costs connected with maintaining a museum-quality environment for the collection. Our 1988/89 study of the total costs of collection care in 100 British museums, *The Cost of Collecting* (London: HMSO, 1989), indicates that when salaries and benefits are allocated to collection-related functions, fully 38% of the museum's budget is directly linked to collections care, and that when allowance is made for the indirect costs of administration and building operation that are due to the museum's retention of collections, the total rises to about 66.5%, which with the median cost of acquisitions added rises still further to approximately 69% of all museum expenditure.

PUBLIC PROGRAMMING COSTS: Museums serving the public with a lively and well-researched programme of exhibitions, education and other services should aim to reserve about 10–15% of their running costs for the non-salary costs of such activities. When the proportion is lower than this, the museum is usually failing to serve its visitors. Since some of these public activities may be revenue-generating, it is likely to be in the museum's immediate financial interests, as well as serving its broader concerns with fulfilling its mission, to allocate adequate resources to these ends.

MARKETING EXPENSES: Failing to provide adequate funds for marketing is the most common lapse encountered in museum budgets. The managers of an art exhibition centre in Vienna recently found that they were able to substantially outdraw another Viennese art museum with a retrospective of the same artist, even though the other museum's retrospective had preceded theirs by two years, and therefore might have been thought to have 'saturated' the market for visitors interested in works by that artist; the difference between the two retrospectives was that the later and far more successful one had a significant marketing budget which was used creatively, whereas the earlier and less successful retrospective was given the minimal marketing treatment that is so common in the museum world. Many commercial attractions find that they need to allocate as much as 25% of the cost of admission in order to ensure that each paying visitor is replaced by another, with 10% considered an absolute minimum. By contrast, most museums' marketing budgets are far below this. The target for a sound museum marketing budget should be at least 5% of the institution's total running costs.

ADMINISTRATIVE COSTS: These are the routine running costs of communications, bookkeeping, auditing and other professional fees, office and other expenses, for which 5% or more of the budget should be reserved.

Figure 3.3 indicates the range of potential distribution of these running cost components.

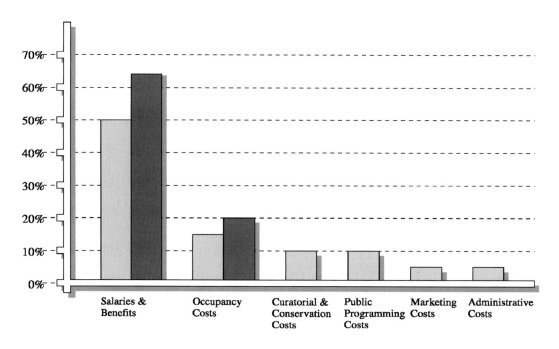

Figure 3.3    Range of Cost Distribution

## 3.5.4  INSURANCE

Several years ago, after eighteen months during which the authors of this book had served as curators of a major international loan exhibition, we came to the conclusion that the one thing we should have done differently from the outset was to hire an insurance and indemnity clerk – so challenging had those issues proved, from the negotiation of the loans through to their eventual return!

Although that staff position is not included among the job descriptions provided in the Appendix to this volume, curators, registrars and other professional museum personnel must be familiar with insurance or indemnity. Some government line department museums may be wholly or partially exempt because part or all of their property may be classified as government assets that are not subject to private insurance coverage. But in most museums the registrar is responsible for maintaining insurance on the permanent collection and on incoming and outgoing loans, while the chief of security and the operations officer and building engineer are concerned with insuring the building and equipment, and the finance officer takes care of liability coverage.

Insurance is a means of transferring risks from the museum to the insurer. Subsection 3.4.2.3 defines 'risk analysis' as one component of planning for security, and insurance is one form of 'risk management', transferring financial responsibility for the risk to the insurer. Museums generally require insurance of five kinds:

- insurance on the collection

- insurance on buildings

- insurance on equipment

- liability insurance

- insurance on loans

INSURANCE ON THE COLLECTION: Often called 'fine arts insurance', even for other types of museums, this type of policy is based on an inventory of the collection and valuations. The inventory should include an up-to-date location file – one European museum found that its insurer was unwilling to pay for an alleged theft when it was discovered that the inventory of the affected section of the collection had not been checked since the early years of this century! Evaluation is another challenge, but may be carried out by distinguishing between low-value items, those of moderate value and high-value objects: values may be assigned on a routine basis for large quantities of similar low-value objects, or for items that are agreed to be below a certain valuation; objects of moderate value may be evaluated by the curators; high-value items, however, should be re-evaluated regularly, preferably by an authority independent of the museum. Curators should monitor auction prices and other sale values, and a review of valuations should be undertaken by the registrar in consultation with curators every year. Condition reports on all works of higher value can be used to demonstrate their prior condition if objects in the collection should suffer damage. Documentary photographs are essential in case of theft. Reports of thefts should be made not only to local police but also through the various international agencies that reproduce pictures of stolen items. An 'all risks' policy is preferable to one that is restricted to 'named perils'.

INSURANCE ON BUILDINGS: Fire insurance is the most common form of protection for museum buildings, but some form of 'fire and extended coverage' policy should be considered, to extend to such risks as earthquakes, hurricanes, tornadoes, storms, floods, explosions, sprinkler accidents, vandalism or civil disturbance. Here again, valuation is a concern, since it is crucial that the insurer should pay not merely for replacement or repair of any building lost or damaged, but for a comparable building of museum quality. (Of course, if the insurer declines on the grounds that the present building is not of museum standard, that is one more argument for upgrading it.) It is also important for the chief of security to ensure that the insurer is kept informed of improvements made in the building, changes in the permanent collection exhibits, or even of relocations of the fire extinguishers.

INSURANCE ON EQUIPMENT: This may include vehicle insurance, boiler insurance, plate glass insurance, warranties and other policies protecting the museum against loss, damage or malfunction of its equipment.

LIABILITY INSURANCE: In most countries, public institutions such as museums assume responsibility for the safety of their users and those persons' property from the moment they open their doors until they close. The museum – and in some jurisdictions, its governing body – may therefore be liable for any damage suffered by its visitors. Public liability and property damage insurance is therefore required. The museum's liability also extends to the people who work in the museum: many governments provide workers' compensation for injuries to paid staff while on duty, but the museum will also need employer's liability insurance if volunteers are to be covered as well. 'Bonding' of those employees responsible for handling money or valuable objects may also be considered. Legal liability coverage should also be carried, to protect the museum in case of legal proceedings, justified or not, taken against the institution.

DIRECTORS' AND OFFICERS' LIABILITY INSURANCE: Often called simply 'D&O', this is a type of liability insurance that museums can secure in order to protect board or trust members, so they are in a position to attract and retain high-quality and dedicated trustees, whose anxieties might otherwise cause them to consider resignation due to real or perceived notions of their potential personal exposure. It is noteworthy that museums that have D&O insurance report that 90 per cent of claims under it are employment-related: alleged discrimination, wrongful dismissal or harassment are the most common grounds for D&O claims.

INSURANCE ON LOANS: The registrar should ensure that all outgoing loans are fully covered by insurance, either by extension of the museum's own policies, or by insurance taken out by the borrower (a copy of the policy on the loaned items should be checked and kept on file). Incoming loans may be most efficiently insured by an 'all risk fine arts floater' attached to the insurance on the permanent collection; even if the value of the borrowed exhibition is very high, it will only be a modification of the insured value of the permanent collection. The floater should provide 'nail-to-nail' coverage (as it is called, referring to the nails on which pictures hang), extending from the moment it is removed from the lender's gallery or stores until it returns there. Condition reports are imperative each time a borrowed work of art or artefact is packed or unpacked.

The cost of insuring large, permanent collections of high value is, in some cases, prohibitive, while the cost of insuring travelling exhibitions of high value has become a major impediment to their organisation. In order to protect their major national museums and to maintain the feasibility of nation-wide or international exhibitions, various governments have developed programmes of *indemnity*, under which the government indemnifies the museum or the lender against loss. The main challenge of establishing indemnity programmes for temporary exhibitions lies in the government, the museum and the lender arriving at a mutually satisfactory valuation. In the event of dispute, the borrowing museum may be obliged to purchase additional insurance to cover the value above the ceiling set by the government.

## 3.5.5  FINANCIAL PLANNING AND DEVELOPMENT

Despite their widespread success and growing public, and notwithstanding the list of revenue sources described in subsection 3.5.2, museums almost everywhere are struggling to cope with government cutbacks on cultural funding, and demands that they should be more self-reliant and less dependent on subsidy. Although relatively few museums have closed for financial reasons, many are obliged to postpone important tasks, or to close to the public for some hours or days each week.

The financial constraints on museums in the long term can only be increased by the fact that one of their primary activities – collecting – results in constantly growing demands on space and facilities. Hence even financially healthy museums are constantly faced with capital fund requirements for expansion, renovation or relocation.

Another dimension of the crisis is rooted in museums' success with the public. Visitors, better informed than ever by travel and television, are constantly raising their expectations of exhibitions, media programmes, even of museum shops. In an effort to meet rising expectations, museums constantly need fresh development capital, and the requisite additional operating funds.

Trustees and museum directors therefore have the responsibility to rise above the constant scramble to meet current operating, capital and acquisition costs, in order to plan the long-term financial future of their institutions. This may be addressed as part of the strategic planning process, or when the corporate plan is being reviewed. The principles of such a long-term financial plan may be suggested here, as a useful conclusion to this consideration of the financial management of museums:

- The museum's long-term financial plan should aim to secure financial *stability* for the institution. Wherever possible, funding should be put on an assured rather than a contingent basis, as a regular allocation rather than grant aid. This may require strenuous representation to government or other funding sources.

- The museum must become, and should endeavour to remain, part of the institutional framework of *education,* another area that is subject to government cutbacks, but one that, in the long term, will experience continuity of funding.

- Trustees and senior museum staff should promote the museum as a vital part of the *cultural tourism* industry, and lobby to make tourism a renewable resource through taxes on tourism operators or an equivalent arrangement that channels part of the revenue from tourism back to the institutions that are its fundamental resource. Some cities and states in the USA have imposed a 'hotel tax' of this kind.

- An *endowment fund,* or some equivalent form of return on investments, should be established. Donors should be persuaded to address the long-term interests of the institution, so that contributions and especially bequests may be made to such a fund. Providing for a growing proportion of the museum's needs with the interest earned by such a fund is one way to secure greater financial independence.

- The long-term plan should be integrated with a *visitor development programme* that extends the museum's appeal to those sectors of the community which are currently under-represented among museum visitors. Government or other support should be sought to institute such a programme, and should then lead the museum to a still more widespread base in the community, which in turn can serve as the foundation of further funding.

- Since the museum is an information-based institution entering an information age, the plan should give careful consideration to the museum's ability to gain substantial funding through control of its *image* and *information database* as new media for education and entertainment are developed.

None of these principles in themselves will suffice to ensure long-term financial stability for museums. Together, they may form a basis for the future. In any event, managing the financial future of museums will continue to require diligence, ingenuity and – above all – courage.

# Afterword

This book indicates why museum management is challenging, inspiring and demanding, and becoming so much more so that some have said the post of museum director is among the most difficult today.

It is our hope that this manual demonstrates that management and leadership can and should be exercised by professional staff, trustees and volunteers and by security and visitor services staff, as well as by curators, educators and administrators. For the challenges of being visitor-responsive and creative, of maintaining the primacy of scholarship and ensuring the preservation and security of the collection, while being of real value to the community and raising funds, can only be met by people working together – and that requires leadership and management skills to be activated throughout the entire museum organisation.

It is equally our hope that new generations of museum managers will succeed as leaders of these remarkable institutions that communicate meaning through objects in space and time. Museums of the 21st Century will be exploring new levels of meaning, yet continuing to find it in their specimens, artefacts, records and works of art. May their managers realise the full extent of the principles of museum management noted here, and extend them to new horizons, serving ever-growing numbers of their public in relevant, stimulating and inspiring ways.

# Appendix: Job Descriptions

The following job descriptions have been developed from a list prepared as part of a planning study for an American museum by Lord Cultural Resources Planning and Management Ltd. No museum is likely to need all these positions, and there may well be other specialised jobs at some museums. Nevertheless, we have tried to make the list as inclusive and as representative as possible.

Positions listed here have been assigned a letter and a number for reference. The letters indicate the division in which the post is located:

- D – Director's Office
- C – Collection Management Division
- P – Public Programmes Division
- A – Administration

The positions accord with the organisation chart developed in Chapter 2.

# Director's Office

**D-1    CHIEF EXECUTIVE OFFICER (DIRECTOR)**

The chief executive officer (CEO) of a museum is usually called a director, but may be a chief curator, curator or director/curator, especially in smaller museums.

The CEO reports to the board or trust, and is responsible for:

- realising the museum's mission;
- conceptual leadership through specialised knowledge of the museum's mandate;
- recommending policies and plans, and their revision, to the board;
- implementing policies and plans approved by the board;
- reporting on the implementation of policies and plans to the board;
- planning, organising and staffing;
- directing and co-ordinating day-to-day operations through the staff;
- financial management and funding;
- liaison with all relevant levels of government, the academic community and the private sector in the interests of the museum.

Qualifications

- advanced degree in an area of the museum's specialisation;
- extensive experience and proven ability in management and administration in the cultural sector;
- demonstrated knowledge of financial development and the ability to manage fiscal responsibilities;
- knowledge of the legal aspects of museum operation and legislation affecting museums.

**D-2    DIRECTOR'S SECRETARY**

The director's secretary reports to the chief executive officer (director) and is responsible for:

- reception and dealing with enquiries;
- secretarial support services to the director and the board, including transcription of meeting notes, general clerical duties, word processing and correspondence.

Qualifications

- secondary school education;
- proficiency in communications media, especially word processing;
- excellent human relations and personal communications skills.

# Collection Management Division

**C-1**  **DEPUTY DIRECTOR (COLLECTION MANAGEMENT) OR CHIEF CURATOR**

With either title, this position reports as part of the management committee to the director and is responsible for:

- the collection development and management programme;

- the security, preservation, documentation and interpretation of all collections;

- recommendations for acquisition and de-accession;

- design and implementation of a collection research programme;

- general and object-specific research, and the publication of that research in a form which is accessible to visitors and other users of the museum;

- consultation in the creation of permanent and temporary exhibitions;

- consultation in the creation of public programming;

- co-operative and joint venture research projects and exhibitions;

- supervision of the collection management division and its staff;

- selection of software programs to meet collection management requirements;

- financial management of the collection management division.

## Qualifications

- advanced degree in an area of the museum's specialisation;

- proven ability in management and administration;

- management experience in a museum or related institution;

- specialised knowledge of at least one area of the collections;

- evidence of scholarly research and writing;

- ability to interpret the collections and communicate knowledge relevant to the collections;

- knowledge of the techniques of selection, evaluation, preservation, restoration and exhibition of objects;

- knowledge of the current market, collecting ethics, and current customs regulations in the area of specialisation.

## C-2   CURATOR

The curator reports to the deputy director (collection management) or chief curator and is responsible for:

- research and documentation of the collection in one discipline or area;
- care of the collection in that discipline or area;
- responding to public enquiries and requests for information on the collection in that discipline or area;
- participation in the creation of exhibitions and public programmes in that discipline or area;
- preparation of publications resulting from research;
- acquisition and de-accessioning in the curator's or archivist's discipline.

### Qualifications

- degree in an area of the museum's specialisation, or equivalent experience;
- specialised knowledge and demonstrated excellence in one discipline or area of the museum's collection;
- evidence of scholarly research or publication;
- knowledge of the techniques of selection, evaluation, preservation, restoration and exhibition of objects;
- knowledge of the current market, collecting ethics and current customs regulations in the area of specialisation.

## C-3   CURATORIAL ASSISTANT OR TECHNICIAN

The curatorial assistant or technician reports to the curator and is responsible for:

- safe and secure storage and ongoing care of the collections;
- accessioning and cataloguing materials and condition-reporting;
- dealing with enquiries and requests for information as directed by the curator;
- preparation of artefacts, specimens or works of art for exhibition.

### Qualifications

- certificate in museum registration techniques, or equivalent experience;
- experience and proven ability in carrying out standard cataloguing procedures;

- two years' experience in a museum or related organisation in the registration area;
- knowledge of specialised collections areas or disciplines.

## C-4　REGISTRAR

The registrar reports to the deputy director (collection management) or chief curator and is responsible for:

- creating and maintaining orderly systems for the management of collections in keeping with standard museum practice;
- supervising, numbering, cataloguing and storing the museum's collections;
- co-ordinating all aspects of borrowing and lending objects;
- integrating the museum's information database on its collections with national or international networks;
- providing catalogue information on the collection to print or other media;
- insurance of the collections.

### Qualifications

- degree in an area of the museum's specialisation, or in liberal arts or museum studies;
- two years' service in a museum registration department;
- knowledge of standard practice in registration techniques;
- knowledge of conservation and storage practices;
- knowledge of legal matters, including contract law and copyright as they relate to collections, as well as policies governing rights and reproductions;
- knowledge of records management and data processing systems;
- knowledge of insurance requirements for collections, packing and transportation;
- knowledge of the museum's collections.

## C-5　CATALOGUER (OR CURATORIAL ASSISTANT)

The cataloguer reports to the registrar or to a curator, and is responsible for:

- support services to the registrar, including numbering, cataloguing and storing the collections;
- helping to define procedures for description and indexing and to devise vocabularies;
- dealing with enquiries, both internal and external, including liaising with curators.

## Qualifications

- certificate in museum registration techniques or equivalent experience;
- experience and proven ability to carry out standard cataloguing procedures;
- experience in a museum or related organisation in the registration area.

## C-6 DIGITISING TECHNICIAN (OR DATA ENTRY CLERK)

With either title, this position reports to the registrar and is responsible for:

- entering descriptive and indexing information into the collections management database;
- performing periodic database maintenance in the form of vocabulary consistency checks and data validation.

### Qualifications

- certificate in museum registration techniques, or equivalent experience;
- knowledge of database management;
- experience in a collecting institution in the area of collections management;
- knowledge of data processing systems.

## C-7 PHOTOGRAPHER

The photographer reports to the registrar and is responsible for:

- producing documentary prints of the collections and details of objects on loan or in the collections for the museum's records;
- producing prints of the collections for curatorial research and publications;
- producing prints for educational materials and publications, promotions and public requests for information;
- imaging for all media.

### Qualifications

- secondary school education and certified technical training in photography and processing, with emphasis on studio work;
- studio experience as part of experience in commercial photography and processing;
- portfolio of past work;
- familiarity with digitising of imagery.

## C-8   LIBRARIAN

The librarian reports to the deputy director (collection management) or chief curator and is responsible for:

- the development, management and operation of the museum library;
- provision of library services to curatorial and all other staff;
- the performance of services such as selection, purchase or acquisition, cataloguing and classification, circulation and maintenance of print materials and material in all media;
- co-ordinating visitor access and use of the library, including school field trips and other groups (if the museum library is public);
- co-ordinating on-line remote users of museum databases;
- possibly co-ordinating exhibitions of material from the library collection;
- liaison with related institutions and information services;
- provision of a reference and readers' advisory service.

## Qualifications

- advanced degree in library science and course work in the area of the museum's specialisation;
- experience in a museum or specialised library;
- experience with information retrieval in a research-oriented cultural or arts organisation;
- knowledge of the needs and purposes of resources relevant to the museum in all media;
- knowledge of all required support services, with a strong emphasis on electronic resources as well as print material;
- knowledge of storage and retrieval systems for printed materials, audio tapes, discs and manuscripts.

## C-9   LIBRARY TECHNICIAN/LIBRARY ASSISTANT

With either title, this position reports to the librarian and is responsible for:

- cataloguing, circulation and maintenance of library materials and services;
- dealing with public enquiries, use of multimedia, reference and reader services;
- support services related to all aspects of the museum library.

## Qualifications

- secondary school education, and certified technical training in library science;
- good communication skills and excellent customer service attitude.

## C-10 Archivist

The archivist reports to the deputy director (collection management) or chief curator and is responsible for:

- research and documentation of the museum archives;
- care of the archival collection in all media;
- dealing with public enquiries and requests for archival information;
- participation in the creation of archival exhibitions and public programmes;
- preparation of catalogues or other publications resulting from archival research in all media;
- acquisition and de-accessioning of archival material in all media;
- linking museum archives with national or international networks or databases.

Qualifications

- degree in an area of the museum's specialisation, or equivalent experience;
- archival training or experience, including experience in all archival media;
- evidence of scholarly research or publication;
- knowledge of the techniques of selection, evaluation, preservation, restoration and exhibition of archival materials of all media.

## C-11 Chief conservator

The chief conservator reports to the deputy director (collection management) or chief curator and is responsible for:

- preservation of all works in the collection;
- examination of all acquisitions and loans, and preparation of condition reports on them;
- treatment of works in need of cleaning or restorative conservation;
- maintenance of the optimum conditions possible in the building for preventive conservation aimed at minimising deterioration of the collection;
- reporting on the condition of all exhibition materials prior to and immediately after display, whether the property of the museum or on loan;
- research on the methods and materials of the collection;
- administration of the conservation department.

## Qualifications

- higher education degrees, preferably in both one area of the museum's collections and in chemistry or conservation science;
- several years' experience as a conservator in a museum;
- administrative experience.


## C-12   CONSERVATION SCIENTIST

The conservation scientist reports to the chief conservator and is responsible for:
- research into the conservation methods and materials of objects in the collection;
- research into environmental conditions to enhance preservation of the collection;
- research into display and presentation methods appropriate to the exhibitions;
- publication of the results of this research in all media.


## Qualifications

- higher education degrees in both one area of the museum's collections and in chemistry or conservation science;
- several years' experience as a museum conservator;
- experience as a research scientist.


## C-13   CONSERVATOR

The conservator reports to the chief conservator and is responsible for:
- preservation of works of a particular material or type in the collection;
- examination and treatment of works of that material or type;
- maintenance of environmental conditions to preserve works of that material or type;
- preparation of condition reports on works in the collection, proposed acquisitions or loans of that material or type.


## Qualifications

- higher education degree in one area of the museum's collection, and/or in chemistry or conservation science;
- experience as a museum conservator.

## C-14 CONSERVATION TECHNICIAN

The conservation technician reports to the conservator and is responsible for:

- monitoring and recording environmental conditions of the collection;
- treatment of works in the collection under direction of the conservator;
- preparation of condition reports for works in the collection and on loan.

### Qualifications

- technical college qualification in conservation technology;
- experience in museum conservation or other scientific laboratories.

# Public Programmes Division

**P-1** **DEPUTY DIRECTOR (PUBLIC PROGRAMMES)**

This position reports to the chief executive officer (director) and is responsible for:

- the development and management of exhibitions and audio-visual programming, activities, materials and events which attract and serve a wide range of audiences, including schools;
- liaison with the school system to increase awareness of the museum as an educational resource;
- liaison with exhibit designers and fabricators, technical programme suppliers, and artists;
- meeting revenue and attendance targets as set out in the marketing plan;
- supervising the performance of staff within the public programmes division.

## Qualifications

- advanced degree in an area related to the museum's specialisation and/or in museum studies;
- experience in a management position in a cultural attraction;
- proven management ability;
- knowledge of visitor behaviour and needs;
- knowledge of the museum's collections;
- knowledge of evaluation methods;
- entrepreneurial orientation.

**P-2** **PROGRAMMES SECRETARY**

The programmes secretary reports to the deputy director (public programmes) and is responsible for:

- reception and dealing with enquiries related to public programmes;
- administrative support services for the public programmes division;
- co-ordinating space bookings for visitors and other users of the museum.

## Qualifications

- secondary school education;
- knowledge of and experience in word processing, scheduling software and general office procedures;
- familiarity with the operation of cultural institutions;
- good communication skills.

## P-3 EXHIBITIONS OFFICER

The exhibitions officer reports to the deputy director (public programmes) and is responsible for:

- planning and producing, in collaboration with the curators, a programme of exhibitions which meets the museum's exhibition objectives;

- setting design and communication standards;

- planning and implementation of audio-visual and interactive components of exhibits and public programming;

- production and budgeting of exhibitions including proposals, design costing, construction, scheduling, maintenance and repairs;

- circulation of travelling exhibitions, and achievement of revenue targets associated with these exhibitions;

- evaluation of exhibitions in collaboration with the evaluation officer;

- contact with technical suppliers and creative producers;

- evaluation of all system, product and service proposals;

- supervising the performance of exhibition staff.

### Qualifications

- degree or certificate in graphic design, industrial design, commercial art, architecture, interior design, theatre design or studio arts, preferably with course work in typography and media use;

- experience and proven ability in exhibition design, preferably in a museum or cultural attraction;

- experience in project management, exhibit fabrication, related construction work;

- demonstrated ability in the use of audio-visual and interactive techniques;

- knowledge of the museum's collections and standard conservation and security practices.

## P-4 EXHIBIT DESIGNER

The exhibit designer reports to the exhibitions officer and is responsible for:

- translating curatorial and educational staff ideas into permanent, temporary or travelling exhibitions through renderings, drawings, models, lighting and arrangement of exhibit materials;

- supervising and participating in fabrication and installation of exhibits, setting schedules and budgets, meeting opening and maintenance deadlines and keeping within budget;

- dealing with outside contractors and providers of services as required for exhibition production;

- working with the exhibitions officer to integrate and implement technical systems and media operations and to update all warranty requirements;
- drafting, selecting and monitoring exhibit design and fabrication contracts.

## Qualifications

- degree or certificate in graphic design, industrial design, commercial art, architecture, interior design, theatre design or studio arts, with course work in typography and media use;
- experience and proven ability in exhibition design, preferably in a museum or cultural attraction;
- experience in project management, exhibit production, related construction work, model-making or media;
- demonstrated ability in the use of audio-visual and interactive techniques;
- knowledge of the nature of the materials to be displayed and standard conservation practice.

## P-5  PREPARATOR

The preparator reports to the exhibitions officer and is responsible for:
- preparation, installation and removal of all objects and materials in displays;
- preparation and packing of travelling exhibitions;
- preparation of cases and mounts for objects and exhibit materials;
- daily maintenance and operation of all permanent and temporary exhibitions, including audio-visual components;
- updating the designer on details of systems and operations, and updating warranty requirements;
- maintenance of electronics, audio-visual and computer-driven components of exhibits and shows;
- maintenance of lighting systems in exhibits and shows;
- developing and testing new display techniques for security and conservation.

## Qualifications

- experience in the fabrication and installation of exhibitions;
- knowledge of and ability in carpentry, metalwork, plastic forming;
- knowledge of and ability in electronics, audio-visual exhibit applications and computer-driven exhibits and shows;
- knowledge of standard conservation and security practices;
- knowledge of lighting systems and applications.

## P-6 GRAPHIC DESIGNER

The graphic designer reports to the exhibit, designer and is responsible for:

- design and production of graphic elements of exhibits, including signage and labels for all permanent, temporary and travelling exhibits in keeping with the museum's established design standards;

- design and production of general orientation and circulation signage within and outside the museum.


Qualifications

- degree or certificate in graphic design or commercial art;

- experience in exhibit design, preferably in a museum or cultural attraction;

- experience in exhibit fabrication, installation and in media.


## P-7 MUSEUM THEATRE MANAGER

For museums with theatres, the museum threatre manager reports to the deputy director (public programmes) and is responsible for:

- co-ordinating all performances, activities and special events in support of the museum's overall programming and revenue goals;

- preparation of promotional copy and programme notes in co-operation with other programme staff;

- liaison with the education officer to schedule school visit-related performances;

- scheduling, box office operation, ticket sales, front-of-house operations;

- operation of the museum theatre to maintain acoustic standards and ambience.


Qualifications

- certificate in arts administration, theatre or performing arts, or equivalent experience;

- experience and proven ability in theatre operations and management;

- good supervisory skills;

- knowledge of computerised ticketing systems;

- entrepreneurial orientation.

## P-8    FILM PROGRAMMER

For museums with extensive film programmes, the film programmer reports to the theatre manager or the deputy director (public programmes) and is responsible for:

- developing and managing a series of film programmes in support of the museum's programming and revenue goals;
- preparation of promotional copy and programme notes;
- co-ordination of scheduling, sales of tickets and programme delivery in collaboration with the theatre manager and education officer;
- liaison with schools and other target audiences.

### Qualifications

- degree in film, communications, or the equivalent experience;
- experience in film programming at a museum or cultural institution;
- proven ability to develop audiences and meet revenue targets.

## P-9    PROJECTIONIST (LIGHTING AND SOUND TECHNICIAN)

This position reports to the exhibitions officer and is responsible for:

- projection of slides, film, video and other audio-visual programmes;
- technical support services for all exhibitions, performances and productions;
- maintenance and upkeep of museum theatre equipment;
- maintenance and repair of all audio-visual components of the museum's exhibits.

### Qualifications

- certificate or other training in electronics;
- demonstrated ability to maintain and operate sophisticated lighting and sound systems.

## P-10  MEDIA OFFICER

This media officer reports to the deputy director (public programmes) and is responsible for:

- planning, design and production of public programmes in all media, including film, video, electronic, computer and multimedia programmes;
- operation and maintenance of these programmes;
- research and development of applications of imaging and graphic technology to the museum's public programmes;
- evaluation of the museum's media programmes, in consultation with the evaluation officer.

### Qualifications

- experience in media planning, design and production;
- familiarity with multimedia programmes;
- knowledge of the collection or of the museum's subject matter.

## P-11  EDUCATION OFFICER

The education officer reports to the deputy director (public programmes) and is responsible for:

- managing and developing partnerships with schools to offer curriculum-based programmes related to the museum's collection, in the museum and/or in schools;
- setting standards for all educational programming;
- liaison with schools, community groups and other target audiences to arrange a programme of field trips, consisting of guided tours and/or demonstrations;
- contributing to the design of exhibitions and other public programming to enhance its educational value;
- achievement of school attendance and revenue targets;
- preparation of publications or media-based products for schools;
- preparation of promotional copy for all aspects of the educational programme;
- developing and implementing adult education programmes related to the museum's collection;
- developing training programmes for volunteer docents.

## Qualifications

- advanced degree in education or in an area related to the museum's specialisation, or in museum studies;
- experience in the education and/or programme area of a museum or cultural attraction;
- ability to design and implement educational programmes, including the preparation of exhibits and publications;
- demonstrated ability in communications and museum education techniques;
- knowledge of the objectives and curricula of the school system;
- knowledge of the museum's collections;
- knowledge of evaluation methods.

## P-12   BOOKINGS CLERK

The booking clerk reports to the education officer and is responsible for:
- booking school groups and public group tours;
- booking paid staff or volunteer docents to meet group tours;
- liaison with schools, community groups and tour operators.

## Qualifications

- secondary school education;
- knowledge of and demonstrated ability in word processing, data entry and scheduling software;
- excellent accuracy and communication skills.

## P-13   STUDIO MANAGER

For museums with visual arts studios, the studio manager reports to the education officer and is responsible for:
- development, implementation and evaluation of a programme of after-school and weekend classes for all ages in a variety of arts and technical disciplines;
- recruitment and co-ordination of professional technicians and artists to instruct in this programme;
- achievement of attendance and revenue goals established for the programme;
- liaison with schools, community groups and other target audiences;
- preparation of all support materials;
- preparation of promotional copy.

Qualifications

- degree or certificate in visual art, or visual art studio experience;

- experience in a museum or related institution;

- proven ability to design and implement educational experiences for students and families.

## P-14 SCHOOL PROGRAMMES MANAGER

This position reports to the education officer and is responsible for:

- design and delivery of programmes for school groups;

- preparation of school kits and resource materials;

- liaison with teachers and schools;

- co-ordination of part-time museum teachers;

- training and evaluation of volunteer docents;

- field trip programmes.

Qualifications

- degree in education or museum studies;

- experience in a museum education department or related institution;

- knowledge of objectives and curricula of the school system;

- knowledge in the area of the museum's collections;

- knowledge of evaluation methods.

## P-15 EDUCATOR/DOCENT

This position reports to the education officer, or to the school programmes manager, and is responsible for:

- planning and provision of tours of the museum's galleries for schools and other groups, for both the permanent collection and temporary exhibitions;

- planning and provision of other museum educational programmes;

- collaboration with teachers on educational use of the museum.

## Qualifications

- undergraduate degree (at least) in the museum's subject matter, or in education;
- experience as a teacher, docent or in other educational work;
- excellent communications and language skills;
- knowledge of the collection.

## P-16    SPECIAL EVENTS MANAGER

The special events manager reports to the deputy director (public programmes) and is responsible for:

- the design and delivery of lecture series, demonstrations, film series, festivals and other special events to complement exhibitions and other programmes;
- recruitment and co-ordination of speakers, instructors and facilitators;
- achievement of attendance and revenue targets for the unit.

## Qualifications

- degree or certificate in adult education or museum studies, or the equivalent experience;
- experience in a museum or related institution in the area of public programming;
- demonstrated ability to create programming in this format and an entrepreneurial orientation.

## P-17    OUTREACH MANAGER/COMMUNITY LIASON OFFICER

This position reports to the deputy director (public programmes) and is responsible for:

- developing and implementing outreach programming aimed at bringing under-represented groups into the museum as visitors, and/or at extending museum services into the community;
- liaison with community groups and other community services.

## Qualifications

- experience and ability in the outreach or community development area of a museum or related institution;
- knowledge of the school system and of community organisations and services;
- excellent communication skills.

**P-18    VOLUNTEER CO-ORDINATOR**

The volunteer co-ordinator reports to the deputy director (public programmes) and is responsible for:

- recruitment, training and supervision of volunteers in collaboration with all programme co-ordinators and activities which require volunteer staffing;
- placement, scheduling and booking of volunteer assistance;
- maintenance of records and mailing lists;
- creation of a benefit programme for volunteers, such as a newsletter.

Qualifications

- degree in museum studies, or an area related to the museum's specialisation;
- demonstrated supervisory skills, preferably with volunteers in a museum setting;
- experience in and knowledge of the field of volunteerism;
- excellent communication skills.

**P-19    MARKETING MANAGER**

The marketing manager reports to the deputy director (public programmes) and is responsible for:

- design and implementation of the museum marketing plan;
- advertising strategies and their implementation;
- media relations strategies and their implementation;
- assessment of public and visitor perception of the museum's image and its services and products;
- management of the marketing budget;
- achievement of attendance and revenue targets;
- creation of relationships with the museum's various publics.

Qualifications

- university degree in business, marketing, communications or journalism, or equivalent experience;
- experience and proven ability in marketing and communication in a museum or cultural attraction.

**P-20** **PUBLIC RELATIONS OFFICER**

This position reports to the marketing manager and is responsible for:

- the public image of the museum;
- relations with all media;
- promotion of all museum products and services;
- community relations;
- monitoring trends, interests and issues so the museum can respond to developments in areas affecting it.

Qualifications

- university degree in public relations, communication or journalism, or equivalent experience;
- proven experience in public relations in a museum or cultural attraction and in journalism or communications;
- extensive knowledge of the media and of writing, editing and standard media formats;
- ability to collaborate effectively with other staff in the implementation of effective public relations programmes;
- knowledge of the appropriate use of photography.

**P-21** **EVALUATION MANAGER**

The evaluation manager reports to the deputy director (public programmes) and is responsible for:

- measuring and documenting the public's perception of the relevance of the museum's products and services;
- designing and implementing the museum's evaluation plan;
- designing and implementing visitor and non-visitor surveys;
- gallery and exhibition evaluation;
- programme and special event evaluation;
- participation in the design of exhibitions, public programming and other public products and services.

Qualifications

- university degree in psychology or psychometry, or equivalent experience;
- knowledge and proven ability in the design, implementation and interpretation of visitor studies and surveys;
- experience in evaluation in a museum or other cultural attraction.


## P-22 PUBLICATIONS MANAGER

The publications manager reports to the deputy director (public programmes) and is responsible for:

- co-ordination and supervision of all printed materials produced by the museum, such as annual reports, books, catalogues, guide books, film and lecture materials, newsletters, research journals, and all historical, photographic and graphic reference works;
- editing all material, and maintaining editorial standards of language, grammatical and stylistic form;
- ensuring that all graphic design projects the museum's desired image;
- achievement of revenue targets;
- publications in non-print media, such as videotape, CD-ROM or on network;
- distribution of materials and determining print runs.


Qualifications

- degree in journalism, public relations, communications or marketing;
- proven ability and extensive experience in all aspects of publishing, editing, print or other media production and distribution;
- experience in working in a museum or related organisation.

# Administration Division

## A-1    DEPUTY DIRECTOR (ADMINISTRATION)

This position reports to the director and is responsible for:

- establishing financial objectives, in collaboration with the director and board;
- financial management, including budgeting, accounting, purchasing, human resources, salaries and benefits, insurance, taxes and contracts;
- operation of physical plant and security;
- visitor services.

### Qualifications

- degree in accounting, business administration or public administration;
- experience in administration;
- experience in a non-profitmaking cultural organisation or related institution;
- knowledge of fund accounting and general fiscal practices, including grants administration;
- knowledge of legal aspects of museum operation;
- knowledge of human resource procedures;
- knowledge of insurance requirements;
- knowledge of office and museum equipment, data processing systems, physical plant management and security, and visitor services.

## A-2    ADMINISTRATION SECRETARY

The administration secretary reports to the deputy director (administration) and is responsible for:

- reception and dealing with enquiries;
- administrative support services for the division.

### Qualifications

- secondary school education;
- previous experience in an office environment and knowledge of cultural organisations;
- word processing skills;
- excellent communication skills.

## A-3   Finance officer

The finance officer reports to the deputy director (administration) and is responsible for:

- financial management of the museum, including budgeting, accounting, purchasing, salaries and benefits, and insurance;
- contracts;
- taxes;
- membership, endowment and fundraising records;
- investments and interest-earning accounts;
- external and internal auditing;
- revenue-generating activities, such as the shop and food services;
- supervision of bookkeeper and finance clerk.

### Qualifications

- degree in business administration, public administration or accounting;
- experience in administration in a non-profitmaking organisation;
- knowledge and proven ability in all aspects of accounting and fiscal practices.

## A-4   Bookkeeper

The bookkeeper reports to the finance officer and is responsible for:

- maintaining and monitoring accounts;
- regular reporting on accounts.

### Qualifications

- certificate in bookkeeping, and related experience in a non-profitmaking organisation.

## A-5   Finance clerk

The finance clerk reports to the finance officer and is responsible for:

- support services to the finance officer and the bookkeeper.

Qualifications

- secondary school education, and previous experience in the financial administration department of a non-profitmaking institution.


**A-6     BUILDING OPERATIONS MANAGER (ESTATE MANAGER)**

This position reports to the deputy director (administration) and is responsible for:

- planning, managing and operating the building's plant;
- managing contracts for maintenance and repair services;
- managing contracts for security services and cleaning, if these are contracted out;
- managing rentals of the building for revenue-generating purposes;
- supervising maintenance staff.


Qualifications

- engineering background preferred;
- knowledge of building management and maintenance systems;
- proven ability in the management and operation of a large, multi-use facility;
- excellent communication and supervisory skills.


**A-7     MAINTENANCE WORKER**

The maintenance worker reports to the operations manager and is responsible for:

- cleaning all non-collection items in the galleries;
- cleaning all other areas of the building;
- removing refuse;
- replacing lamps;
- replacing supplies to toilets and first aid stations.


Qualifications

- knowledge of cleaning equipment and techniques to meet museum standards;
- experience in maintaining museums or other public facilities.

**A-8    RENTALS MANAGER**

The rentals manager reports to the building operations manager and is responsible for:

- promoting and operating a programme to rent the museum's facilities for functions such as meetings, conferences, parties and receptions;
- dealing with enquiries and bookings;
- liaising with caterers and furniture rental companies;
- liaising with tour operators, corporations and other target client groups;
- co-ordinating security and cleaning staff for events.

Qualifications

- secondary school education;
- previous experience in the management of functions in a non-profitmaking organisation;
- entrepreneurial orientation;
- knowledge of the museum's potential, as well as its limitations, as a physical setting for functions.

**A-9    VISITOR SERVICES MANAGER**

This position reports to the deputy director (administration) and is responsible for:

- visitor reception and orientation;
- information in the form of maps of the building or other media;
- dealing with visitor enquiries about events and programmes;
- operation of amenities such as the cloakroom, toilets and catering;
- disabled access and assistance;
- scheduling and supervising visitor service staff;
- dealing with visitor comments and complaints;
- monitoring the overall quality of the visitor experience in collaboration with public programme staff;
- first aid, safety and emergency planning and provision for staff and visitors.

Qualifications

- degree in public relations, communications, museum studies, or equivalent experience;
- proven ability to manage visitor services functions in a cultural attraction or museum setting;
- excellent public relations, communication and supervisory skills.

## A-10  CLOAKROOM SUPERVISOR

This position reports to the visitor services manager and is responsible for:

- daily management and operation of the cloakroom;
- supervising staff;
- first aid and safety for visitors.

### Qualifications

- secondary school education, or equivalent experience;
- previous experience in the operation of cloakroom functions;
- training in first aid.

## A-11  RECEPTION/TICKETING/INFORMATION DESK CLERK

This position reports to the visitor services manager and is responsible for:

- welcoming visitors;
- providing orientation and other information to visitors;
- recording information about visitors;
- selling tickets (if required) and admitting visitors.

### Qualifications

- secondary school education, or equivalent experience;
- excellent communication skills;
- knowledge of and interest in the museum's field;
- retail or cashier experience.

## A-12  CATERING (FOOD SERVICES) MANAGER

Catering is often contracted out, but whether a member of staff or a contractor, the manager reports to the visitor services manager and is responsible for:

- planning and providing food and refreshments to visitors;
- supervising catering staff;
- meeting catering revenue targets;
- procuring catering provisions;
- providing ancillary catering services to receptions, openings, members' lounges or staffrooms;
- maintaining catering equipment.

Qualifications

- catering experience at a level of quality appropriate to the food services intended for the museum;
- administrative experience in catering;
- knowledge of dietary and culinary principles;
- familiarity with equipment appropriate to the level of food services intended for the museum.

## A-13    CATERING STAFF

Catering staff report to the catering manager and are responsible for:

- preparing and serving food and refreshments to visitors;
- maintaining the cafe or restaurant and kitchen.

Qualifications

- food preparation or service experience at a level appropriate to the catering provided at the museum;
- knowledge of dietary and culinary principles;
- familiarity with equipment appropriate to the level of service provided at the museum.

## A-14    CHIEF OF SECURITY (HEAD WARDER)

This position reports to the deputy director (administration) and is responsible for:

- security of the collections and the building;
- safety of visitors, staff and others in the building;
- maintaining of security records and tapes;
- operating and monitoring closed-circuit television surveillance systems;
- maintaining intrusion alarm contract and system;
- maintaining fire detection, alarm and deterrent systems;
- planning and implementing responses to emergencies of all kinds;
- supervising and rostering warders (security guards).

Qualifications

- secondary school education, or equivalent experience;
- experience in security, police, fire or a related area of work;
- administrative experience;
- experience in museums or other public facilities;
- knowledge of closed-circuit television, intrusion alarms and fire detection, alarm and suppression systems.

**A-15**  **WARDER (SECURITY GUARD)**

This position reports to the chief of security (head warder), and is responsible for:

- invigilation of galleries;
- surveillance of visitors and all others entering the museum;
- monitoring the closed-circuit television screens;
- admission of visitors, staff and delivery personnel;
- providing security records;
- responding to emergencies.

Qualifications

- experience in security, police, fire or related areas of work;
- knowledge of the operation of closed-circuit television, intrusion alarms, fire detection, alarm and suppression systems;
- good communication skills.

**A-16**  **PERSONNEL (HUMAN RESOURCES) MANAGER**

This position reports to the deputy director (administration) and is responsible for:

- contributing to the creation of policies concerning the employment and safety of all staff, and the terms and conditions which apply;
- developing and managing payment systems in co-ordination with the finance officer;
- negotiating with, hiring and placing paid staff;
- liaising with unions and employee associations;
- developing and administering professional training and development policies and procedures;
- developing and managing training and development;
- managing and monitoring the health and benefits package;
- organising programmes for all museum staff to stimulate a 'learning organisation';
- assisting managers with regular employment review processes.

Qualifications

- degree in human resources management, or equivalent experience;
- previous experience in managing a personnel department in a museum or other non-profitmaking organisation;
- knowledge and ability in all areas of human resource management, including data processing systems.

## A-17 PERSONNEL CLERK

The personnel clerk reports to the personnel (human resources) manager and is responsible for:

- reception and dealing with enquiries regarding personnel matters;
- support services for the personnel or human resources manager, including record-keeping, correspondence and circulating relevant information to employees.

Qualifications

- secondary school education;
- previous experience in the personnel or human resources area of a cultural or other non-profitmaking organisation;
- word processing skills and knowledge of data processing systems.

## A-18 DEVELOPMENT OFFICER

The development officer reports to the deputy director (administration) and is responsible for:

- co-ordinating and directing the fundraising activities of the museum, including capital projects, endowments, membership drives, sponsorships and grant applications to government, corporations and foundations;
- planning and supervising special fundraising events;
- supervising membership and retail staff.

Qualifications

- university degree in business, arts administration or marketing;
- experience in fundraising on a scale consistent with the needs of the museum;
- experience in development in a museum or cultural attraction;
- knowledge of financial management, record management and data processing systems;
- ability to motivate and train staff and volunteers in the implementation of membership programmes.

## A-19   DEVELOPMENT SECRETARY

The development secretary reports to the development officer and is responsible for:

- support services to the development officer, including correspondence, scheduling of meetings and record-keeping.

Qualifications

- secondary school education;
- knowledge of software and database programmes;
- excellent communication skills.

## A-20   RETAIL MANAGER

The retail manager reports to the development officer and is responsible for:

- meeting objectives for sales and revenues;
- promotion and sales of museum merchandise;
- all aspects of the operation of the shop, including record-keeping of sales and expenditures, inventory development and maintenance, monitoring sales and promotions, shop display and organisation;
- acquisition of stock, subject to curatorial approval;
- hiring and supervising sales staff and volunteers.

Qualifications

- extensive experience and proven ability in the management of retail operations in the cultural sector;
- strong entrepreneurial orientation and excellent financial management skills;
- knowledge of effective display and promotional techniques;
- proven supervisory skills.

## A-21 SALES CLERK

This position reports to the retail manager and is responsible for:

- customer sales;
- inventory maintenance;
- stocking and pricing of merchandise.

### Qualifications

- experience and proven ability in customer sales, preferably in a cultural attraction or related setting.


## A-22 MEMBERSHIP MANAGER

The membership manager reports to the development officer and is responsible for:

- attracting and maintaining the interest and support of target audiences;
- developing and implementing strategies for recruiting members;
- planning, promoting and co-ordinating special events, services and benefits for the members;
- maintenance of records and mailing lists;
- supervising the membership clerk.

### Qualifications

- university degree in business, public relations, marketing or liberal arts;
- two years' experience in membership development and management in a museum or related institution;
- ability to carry out programming for members and sponsors;
- knowledge of techniques used to attract, maintain and benefit members;
- knowledge of media;
- knowledge of financial management, record management and data processing systems.

## A-23  MEMBERSHIP CLERK

The membership clerk reports to the membership manager and is responsible for:

- reception and dealing with enquiries;
- maintaining records and mailing lists;
- support services in co-ordinating special events.

Qualifications

- secondary school education;
- knowledge and proven ability in word processing, data entry and record-keeping;
- excellent customer relations and communication skills.

# Glossary

The following is a glossary of commonly used terms in the field of museum management. Most of these terms are more fully described in the text.

ACCOMMODATION PLAN: projection of the space and facilities required for the collections in store and on display, for the public programmes and amenities, and for the necessary support facilities and work space for staff.

ACQUISITION FUND: the amount allocated for purchasing objects for the collection, and in some cases for the expenses associated with acquisition as well.

ACQUISITIONS COMMITTEE: a group of trustees delegated by a museum's board to consider issues of collection policy and collection development strategy, as well as recommendations for additions to the collections (and de-accessioning), which should be made only by the relevant curators.

ADMINISTRATION: co-ordination of museum functions in order to realise the museum's mission.

ADVISORY BOARD (OR VISITING COMMITTEE): a non-governing group appointed to represent the public interest and empowered only to recommend policy, usually to the governing authority of line department museums.

AESTHETIC DISPLAY: a mode of exhibition of works of art, specimens or artefacts arranged to stimulate contemplation of the museum objects for their own sake.

ANIMATRONICS: mannequins, figures or three-dimensional human, animal or imagined characters with mechanical, electronic, audio-visual or multimedia applications to facilitate lifelike motion, sound and other special effects.

ARM'S LENGTH: the metaphorical distance between a museum and the political authority allocating or granting funds to it.

ATTENDANCE, REVENUE AND EXPENSE PROJECTIONS: a forecast of all sources of income and all categories of expenditure.

AUTOMATION: the process of converting manual records (e.g. collection records) to computerised form.

BEST PRACTICE STUDY: comparative analysis of outstanding successes in specific programmes or activities in other institutions.

BOARD (OR TRUST): a fiduciary body to whom the public interest in the museum may be committed to be administered with the same diligence, honesty and discretion as prudent people would exercise in managing their own affairs.

BRIEF: instructions for the architect or designer from the client or user pertaining to the requirements for space, facilities or exhibitions.

BUDGET: a plan with money attached; funds allocated to attain the museum's objectives.

BUDGET BY DEPARTMENT: the most common method of projecting revenue and expenditure, whereby each department is asked to review its past year's allocations, adjust for current objectives and tasks, and recommend next year's figures.

BUDGET BY FUNCTION: a method of reviewing allocations in terms of the fundamental museum functions – collecting, documentation, preservation, research, display, interpretation and administration.

BUDGET BY OBJECTIVES: a review process in which fluctuations in the current year's proposed allocations are evaluated in relation to the objectives identified in the museum's corporate plan and the outcomes they are intended to achieve.

BUDGET BY PROGRAMME: projection of revenue and expenditure in terms of activities or services to be provided, in accordance with the priority given to that activity in the current year's plans.

BUILDING CODE: standards for built space, as defined by the government authority in a particular jurisdiction.

BUILDING COMMITTEE: a group appointed by the museum's board to oversee and control a construction or renovation project.

BUILDING MANAGEMENT (OR AUTOMATION) SYSTEM (BMS OR BAS): a computerised system of controlling and monitoring atmospheric conditions throughout a building.

BUILDING TEAM: a group of professionals – architects, engineers, landscape architects, building contractors, construction managers and other technical specialists – who meet with the project manager and endeavour to meet the requirements of the functional brief by means of technical drawings and specifications, and through the construction of the building.

BUSINESS PLAN: a document that projects the viability of a project under certain conditions or assumptions, which, in the museum context, may include: a collections analysis; a public programming plan; statements of mission, mandate and purpose; recommendations regarding institutional status and structure; space and facilities requirements; staffing requirements; market analysis; marketing and operational recommendations; projections of capital and operating expenditures and revenues, and an implementation schedule.

CAPITAL BUDGET (OR FUNDS): financial resources retained for planned development of the museum's site or buildings, such as renovation, relocation, new construction or exhibition renewal.

CAPITAL COST PROJECTION: the amount needed to upgrade or build the space required to provide furnishings and equipment, or to build the planned exhibits.

CAPITAL COSTS: the one-time costs of acquiring a site and building or renovating a facility.

CASE STATEMENT: a document that articulates the rationale for donating funds for a particular project, or for the continuation of the programmes to be funded.

CATALOGUING: curatorial recording of works of art, artefacts or specimens (more extensive than registration), aiming to record a full sense of each object's significance in relation to other objects in the collection, in other collections and in the world at large.

CHANGE ORDER: a contract document issued by the client to the contractor, authorising an alteration in the original design or specifications of a building or exhibition under construction or being installed.

CLOSE-COUPLED DISCHARGE CAMERAS: cameras, black-and-white or colour, used in surveillance systems that employ a solid-state device rather than a picture tube which burns out and requires replacement. Most good quality cameras used in surveillance are now solid-state type.

CODE OF ETHICS: a set of principles for trustees and staff of museums in relation to the museum they serve, intended to avoid conflicts of interest, and to respect relevant international conventions and national, state, provincial or local laws pertinent to artefacts, specimens or works of art.

COLLECTION ANALYSIS: quantitative and qualitative study of the contents of a museum collection in meaningful groups or classifications, and of the spatial and facilities requirements of the collection, including projection and provision for its future growth over a stated period, and for the security, documentation and preservation of the collection.

COLLECTION DEVELOPMENT STRATEGY: projection of both qualitative and quantitative growth of the collection.

COLLECTION POLICY (OR COLLECTION MANAGEMENT POLICY): the museum's fundamental document governing the scope and limitations of its intended collection, together with standards for its acquisition, documentation, preservation, security and management.

COLLECTIVE BARGAINING AGREEMENT: a set of principles, policies and practices affecting the working conditions of personnel in museums where the staff are unionised, approved by both the unions and the museums.

COLOUR RENDERING INDEX (CRI): the degree to which perceived colours of objects illuminated by a light source conform to the colours of the same objects as illuminated by the reference standard of daylight at the given colour temperature. The CRI of a light source comprises two elements: the colour temperature that establishes the daylight reference standard, and a number that indicates how closely the illuminant approaches that standard.

COLOUR TEMPERATURE (CT): a means of measuring the heat produced by a light source by reference to a scale established by heating a black, light-absorbing body so that it glows with different colours as temperature rises or falls. Heat-producing light sources are thus compared to the CT scale to determine their approximate colour temperature.

COMMISSIONING: provision of the completed building (or exhibition) to the client by the contractor and architect (or exhibit fabricator).

COMPETITIVE BIDDING: comparison of tenders submitted by contractors for work specified; the tender selected is usually the lowest in other sectors, but not always in the museum field, due to the need for museum standards of quality.

CONDITION REPORT: a document prepared by a conservator to record the state of a work of art, artefact or specimen at the time of the report.

CONNOISSEURSHIP: the intimate knowledge of a collection rooted in an acquired ability to perceive, to make distinctions, and above all, to make judgements about the works of art, artefacts or specimens in the collection.

CONSERVATION: maximising the endurance or minimising the deterioration of an object over time, with as little change to the object as possible.

CONSERVATION POLICY: a document establishing the museum's long-term qualitative standards for both preventive conservation and conservation treatment.

CONSERVATION TREATMENT PLAN: a detailed guide to how to treat a work of art, artefact or specimen, aiming to enhance its preservation through reversible procedures.

CONTEMPLATIVE MODE: a style of presentation most commonly used in art galleries (but also found in other museums), in which works of art, artefacts or specimens are presented in an aesthetic mode, enhancing the visitors' affective experience or aesthetic appreciation of them.

CONTEMPORARY COLLECTING: acquisition of artefacts or works of art of today with a view to their future appreciation as the heritage of later generations.

CONTEXTUAL, THEMATIC OR DIDACTIC DISPLAY: a mode of presentation in which artefacts, specimens or works of art are placed in context so that their significance may be better understood, often in relation to an interpretative theme.

CONTRACTING (OR CONTRACTING OUT): agreements with individuals or companies to undertake specific functions for the museum (e.g. security, cleaning, catering) as an alternative to employing permanent staff.

CONTRACTOR: an individual or company which undertakes to fulfil a contract.

CONTRAST RATIO: the difference, expressed in terms of light readings, between light reflected from two objects: for example, a background and an object set against it.

CONTRIBUTED REVENUE: funds allocated, granted or donated to the museum by individuals, governments or agencies in support of its mission, including government subsidy, grant aid, endowments, sponsorship and donations.

CONTROL: a function of management, monitoring budgets and schedules to ensure that resources of time and money are utilised in accordance with allocations.

CORPORATE PLAN (OR BUSINESS PLAN): a document focusing all museum functions towards fulfilment of the museum's mission and goals within a specific planning period and financial framework.

CORRELATED COLOUR TEMPERATURE: for non-heat-producing light sources, only an approximate colour temperature can be determined by correlation or reference to the CT scale, to find the temperature of the black body whose chromaticity most closely matches that of the test source (see *Colour temperature*).

COST-EFFECTIVENESS: a measure of the qualitative and quantitative extent to which the museum's expenditures achieve the intended result.

CRITICALITY: correlation of the probability of a security risk and the degree of its impact (vulnerability), used to determine priorities among security requirements.

CULTURAL TOURISM: travel away from home to experience the arts, heritage or lifestyle of people and places.

DAMPERS: devices used to vary the volume of air passing through an outlet, inlet or duct

DEFENCE: a countermeasure identified in the museum's security policy which should be detailed in the emergency procedures manual as the appropriate response by staff in the event of a threat.

DELAY: a countermeasure identified in the museum's security policy to retard progress of a threat.

DESIGN CONCEPT: the initial drawings of a building or exhibition, which are generally based on a brief.

DESIGN DAY: a day of good (but not peak) attendance for which space and facilities are to be provided.

DESIGN DEVELOPMENT: the stage in exhibition or building design in which the design concept is elaborated into detailed drawings, sometimes called 'information drawings' (see also *Schematic design*).

DESIGN TEAM: the group of practising professionals who plan the disposition of spaces, materials and facilities of a museum building or exhibition based on the approved brief or programme.

DESIGN YEAR: the year for which a long-range plan, such as a master plan or a collection development strategy, aims to provide – usually about twenty years in the future.

DETECTION: countermeasures identified in the museum's security policy to determine whether and when threats occur, including surveillance by warders or guards, intrusion alarms, smoke detectors, display case alarms and closed-circuit television.

DETERRENCE: a countermeasure identified in the museum's security policy to reduce the likelihood of a threat.

DIORAMA: a display method that presents a two- or three-dimensional environment, sometimes within a case but often as an open or even walk-in exhibit.

DIRECT DIGITAL CONTROL: computer-based monitoring and control of building systems via sensors on each piece of building system equipment that relay readings to the computer. Microprocessors, either at the sensors or at the central computer, translate the analog readings to digital format for analysis; the computer then transmits control decisions back to the system equipment to regulate operations.

DIRECTORS' & OFFICERS' LIABILITY INSURANCE (D&O): protection from liability claims that museums can take out to protect trustees; most claims are for employment-related grievances.

---

DISPLAY COLLECTION: a group of artefacts, specimens or works of art acquired primarily for exhibition and interpretation purposes with the intention of preserving them indefinitely.

DOCUMENTATION: preparation and maintenance of a permanent record of the collections and all transactions related to them.

DOCUMENTATION PROCEDURES MANUAL: explicit instructions for registrars, cataloguers and data entry clerks on how to register and/or catalogue the collection.

DONATION: a gift or bequest of artefacts, specimens or works of art and/or funds in support of the museum's mission.

DONATION IN KIND: provision of goods (other than collections) and/or services, rather than funds, in support of the museum's mission.

EDUCATION PLAN: a document setting out the goals and objectives of the museum's education services, together with the means of attaining them.

EFFECTIVENESS: a measure of the qualitative and quantitative extent to which the museum's efforts achieve the intended results.

EFFICIENCY: a measure of effectiveness in proportion to the effort required to achieve it – in the provision of person-hours, money, space, or in the use of facilities or equipment.

ELECTRONIC ELECTRODE DISPOSABLE-CYLINDER STEAM HUMIDIFIER: the type of steam humidifier often recommended for museum purposes because of its efficiency, effectiveness and lack of harmful effects associated with other options.

EMERGENCY PROCEDURES MANUAL: a staff handbook detailing actions to be taken in the event of threat, accident, illness, flood, fire, earthquake, hurricane, tornado or other disruptions of museum buildings or services.

EMERGENCY TEAM: a group of museum employees empowered to co-ordinate emergency procedures.

ENDOWMENT FUND: donations or bequests that are invested, with all or only a portion of the interest earned being spent, either on operations (in the case of unrestricted funds) or for specific purposes, such as acquisitions, exhibitions or lecture series (in the case of restricted funds).

ENVIRONMENTAL MODE: a style of presentation in which a room setting or large-scale exhibitry is used to re-create or evoke the atmosphere of the time and place in which the museum objects were used or developed.

ENVIRONMENTAL SCAN: the initial step in a strategic planning process, which aims to develop an understanding of changes in the external environment affecting the museum or gallery directly and indirectly, such as economic, demographic, community, market and museological issues, taking into consideration local, regional, national and international trends and developments.

EVALUATION: qualitative and quantitative measurement of museum programmes in relation to their objectives.

EXHIBITION COMMITTEE: sometimes a group of trustees delegated to consider exhibition policy, but more often a specific staff committee or task force that combines the talents of all those responsible for the many aspects of an exhibition project.

EXHIBITION PLAN: a statement of the theme, objectives and means of expression of a proposed exhibition, which may be accompanied by a projected layout and budget (see also *Interpretative plan*).

EXHIBITION POLICY: a statement of the objectives of the exhibition programme, the philosophy of presentation, and the number, frequency, size and scope of temporary as well as permanent collection exhibitions.

EXTENSION: programmes that museums offer outside the museum building or site.

EXTERNAL ASSESSMENT: as part of a strategic planning process, an effort to see the museum as others see it, and to learn from this external perspective through such means as visitor surveys, community surveys, workshops, focus groups and interviews with knowledgeable persons in the field, community leaders, donors, sponsors and funders as well as frequent museum-users and – notably – non-users.

FACILITIES PROGRAMMING: a broad planning activity, usually undertaken by a specialist consultant, to determine the facilities required by an institution undergoing physical expansion or alteration, including the design and performance criteria of those facilities, as well as social and behavioural factors.

FEASIBILITY STUDY: a determination of the viability of a proposed or existing institution, or of the further development of an institution, including financial feasibility, marketing prospects, funding sources, visitation and revenue projections, structural suitability of an existing building, viability of various proposed sites, and other factors; this is usually undertaken by specialist consultants independent of the project itself, with a view to making explicit the conditions under which a proposed project may prove viable, usually not in terms of a profitmaking nor even a break-even budget, but in proportion to the requirement for subsidy, endowment or other sources of contributed income.

FIRE COMPARTMENTALISATION: the practice of dividing large spaces (such as a museum store) into smaller areas by means of fire walls, in order to contain the spread of fire.

FIRE RATING: a standardised projection of the length of time which a building material or construction can withstand fire without collapsing or allowing the fire to pass through.

FIRE WALL: a division between rooms that is resistant to fire for the length of time specified in its fire rating.

FIRST-PERSON INTERPRETATION: a method of interpretation in which costumed actors play their parts in period, and answer visitors' questions from within the time and space parameters of the historic setting.

FLAME SPREAD NUMBER: a numeric rating referring to the flammability or surface burning characteristics of a material as rated by a standard test such as the American Standard Test Method E84 for Surface Burning Characteristics of Building Materials. The lowest number is rated against pre-cast concrete, with ranges upward for more flammable materials.

FOCUS GROUPS: informal sessions, sometimes recorded or observed through two-way mirrors, in which representatively structured groups (usually of about six or ten persons) are directed by a facilitator to evaluate actual or prospective products or services, such as a new exhibition, qualitatively.

FORMATIVE EVALUATION: measuring the effectiveness of an exhibition while the exhibition is taking shape (or form) to ensure that the exhibition communicates accurately and effectively with its visitors.

FOUNDATION: a philanthropic organisation with educational, research or social service objectives that can be a source of contributed revenue for museums.

FUEL-CONTRIBUTED LEVELS: a numeric rating referring to the length of time a material continues to burn, or provide fuel for combustion. A material which provides no fuel for combustion would have a rating of 0.

FUMIGATION: a method for eliminating insect pests from museum objects.

FUNCTIONAL BRIEF (OR PROGRAMME): a systematic document written in the users' language, describing the functions required of a building and its systems and facilities, its circulation patterns and adjacency and access requirements, including a room-by-room identification of every technical variable (light, humidity, filtration, etc.) affecting each room in the building.

FUNCTIONS: the essential activities of a museum – collecting, documentation, conservation, research, display, interpretation – and the administration of these six core activities.

FUNDING STRATEGY: a plan which sets out ways to meet both the capital and operating fund requirements from public, private and self-generated sources.

FUNDRAISING: programmes or activities designed to stimulate contributed revenue.

GOALS: the long-range qualitative standards or levels of programme fulfilment or achievement towards which the museum is striving, usually articulated in a master plan or corporate plan.

GOVERNANCE: the ultimate legal and financial responsibility for a museum.

GOVERNING BOARD: the group of trustees appointed to assume responsibility for governance of the museum, reviewing and determining policy and long-range plans, and usually engaging, evaluating and, if necessary, terminating the employment of the museum's director.

GRANT PROJECT: a government or foundation funding programme with specific objectives.

GRIEVANCE PROCEDURE: a method of handling staff complaints about working conditions or treatment of personnel, usually defined in a collective bargaining agreement.

HALON FIRE EXTINGUISHER: a method of fire control by means of expulsion of halon gas from hand-held extinguishers, now being phased out due to environmental considerations.

HALON SYSTEM: a method of fire control by means of expulsion of halon gas from overhead, now illegal in many jurisdictions, and being phased out everywhere due to environmental considerations.

HANDS-ON MODE: a style of presentation whereby exhibits encourage visitors to learn by doing, especially popular in children's museums and science centres but also used elsewhere.

HAZARDOUS MATERIALS STORE: a storage cabinet constructed of non-flammable and fire-retardant materials and under key control for authorised users only, for storing hazardous materials used in the museum, such as some conservation laboratory supplies.

HIERARCHY: any organisational structure in which lower levels of responsibility and authority report to higher levels, resulting in a pyramidal structure culminating in the director.

HIGH SECURITY: a degree of security required for exhibitions of highly valuable items with special provisions, possibly including constant surveillance during public hours.

HIGH SECURITY STORE: a level of security for museum stores, typically with all-interior masonry walls, ceilings and floors, and with steel doors and frames with a minimum six-pin tumbler lock and key control, usually required for works of art, weapons, furs and objects of high value.

HUMIDISTAT: a device for both sensing changes in relative humidity (RH) and controlling the output of humidifiers and/or dehumidifiers in order to regulate the RH in an air-conditioned space or supply duct.

HYGROTHERMOGRAPH: a device for monitoring and recording fluctuations in relative humidity.

HYPERTEXT: a computerised link between one document and other related documents elsewhere in a collection, facilitating staff or visitor access to related museum documentation.

IMPLEMENTATION: deployment of time, money and staff to accomplish the museum's goals and objectives according to agreed priorities, assigning responsibility and re-allocating or acquiring new resources.

INDEMNITY: a provision in lieu of insurance of objects on loan for museum exhibitions, under which the government secures the museum or the lender against any loss.

INFORMATION MANAGEMENT: activities and programmes facilitating the effective production, co-ordination, storage, retrieval and dissemination of spoken and written text and images in all formats and from internal or external sources, leading to the more efficient functioning of the museum.

INFORMATION MODEL: a graphic illustration of the current tasks and consequent flow of text and image data, and desired improvements in these patterns.

INFORMATION POLICY: a commitment by museum management to standards of documentation of records about and interpretation of the collection, and public access to them, addressing issues of intellectual property and the museum's participation in databases or other means of dissemination of museum records, including images.

INFORMATION SYSTEM PLAN: an analysis of data-related functions, both text and imagery, with recommendations for their efficient integration, compatibility and future growth.

INSTITUTIONAL CONTEXT: issues related to the museum's relationship with other institutions and agencies, such as all levels of government, educational institutions, other museums, specialist groups, the tourist industry and potential donors or sponsors in the private sector.

INSTITUTIONAL PLAN: a strategic planning document that examines and makes recommendations for both the museum's internal organisation (its governance structure, and its statements of mission, mandate and purpose) and its external relations with its institutional context (government, educational institutions, other museums, the private sector, tourism, etc.).

INTERACTIVE MODE: a style of expression in museum exhibitions that involves the visitor in active physical and/or intellectual dialogue with the exhibition.

INTERACTIVITY: physical or intellectual interaction between the public and museum exhibits.

INTERNAL ASSESSMENT: a step in the strategic planning process, consisting of a review of the institution's programmes and operations using available documentation and discussions, with museum management, staff, volunteers, members and trustees to develop an analysis of a museum's strengths, weaknesses, opportunities and threats (a SWOT analysis).

INTERNET: a global network of databases and an informal computer service that links groups of computers from government, university and private or public service organisations all over the world.

INTERPRETATION: communication between the museum and its public about the meaning of its collections.

INTERPRETATIVE PLAN (OR EXHIBITION BRIEF): a strategy that articulates the objectives of the museum in interpretation and the quality of the visitor experience; it includes a component-by-component description of the exhibition which lists the communication objectives of each component, and the potential means of expression to achieve these objectives, along with diagrams of visitor flow patterns and concept sketches to indicate the 'feel' of the exhibition (see also *Exhibition plan*).

IONIZATION SMOKE DETECTOR: automatic fire detection that responds to an increase in combustion particles in the air entering the device, which produce an increase in current flowing between two charged surfaces, which triggers an alarm. These devices are very sensitive, and are used in incipient fire situations to sense an extremely low build-up of combustion materials.

JOB DESCRIPTION: a succinct statement of the responsibilities of a post, the qualifications required for it, and its reporting relationships. (See the Appendix.)

KEY ISSUES: in the strategic planning process, the fundamental questions which the museum must address in order to become a more effective and successful institution.

LEADERSHIP: the ability to inspire people with a sense of the museum's mission in order to achieve its goals.

LIABILITY: legal and financial responsibility for one's own or others' actions, especially for the actions of an institution such as a museum.

LINE DEPARTMENT MUSEUM: a museum administered as an integral division or agency of a government ministry, university or corporation, and funded primarily through allocations from the budget of the governing organisation.

LOW DRIFT FACTOR: drift is change in an output–input relationship over time, with the change unrelated to input, environment or load. A low drift factor thus indicates that operation of the equipment will be subject to a minimum of variation due to drift.

LUMEN: a measure of photometric power, or light power, as perceived by the human eye. One lumen is the amount of luminous energy (light) emanating from 1 square foot (metre) of the surface of a transparent sphere placed around a single candlepower source, at a distance of 1 foot (metre) radius from the light source. One candlepower produces 12.57 lumen of perceived luminous energy.

LUX: the metric unit for measuring the intensity of light (10.76 lux = 1 footcandle).

LUX LEVEL: the amount of visible light to which a museum object is being exposed; most accurately calculated as lux-hours per annum, being the lux level at any given time multiplied by the number of hours the lights with that lux level illuminate the object.

MANAGEMENT: facilitating decisionmaking in an organisation so that it can achieve its goals.

MANDATE: the range of material culture for which a museum assumes responsibility, which may be stated in terms of an academic discipline, geographical range, chronological range or specialisation, and may be qualified in relation to other institutions.

MARKET: the existing and potential public for a museum.

MARKET ANALYSIS: the process by which existing and potential audiences for a facility or programme may be understood and projected.

MARKET SEGMENTATION: analysis of the potential visitors to a museum into groups sufficiently homogeneous that the institution can effectively plan programmes to meet the needs of each segment, and prioritise its development of staff, facilities and budget accordingly.

MARKETING: promoting museum services to visitors by stimulating and increasing attendance, length of stay, visitor satisfaction, expenditure and return visits, not merely through advertising but through customer services and activities that will meet the museum's objectives and motivate visitors to return.

**MARKETING STRATEGY:** a plan which sets out ways in which the museum may enhance its communication with and service to its target audiences with the objective of boosting attendance and visitor spending, thereby building a closer relationship with its audiences, leading to return visits, increased membership and donations.

**MASTER PLAN:** organisation of museum functions and resources towards the achievement of a desired level of effectiveness, often reviewing all aspects of the institution and projecting requirements for additional space, staffing or finances, as well as means of attaining them.

**MATRIX:** an organisational structure in which functions are arranged on axes of interaction.

**MICRO-ENVIRONMENT:** a climate-controlled and secure space for the display or storage of artefacts or specimens within a sealed case or frame, used in buildings where such control is not feasible in entire rooms.

**MISSION:** an objective, brief and inspiring assertion of a museum's long-term reason for existence, which serves as the foundation of all policy development.

**MULTIMEDIA:** a mode of display which uses simultaneous methods of communication in one co-ordinated exhibit apparatus to appeal to multiple senses, usually employing computer and/or electronic technology.

**MUSEUM:** a non-profitmaking, permanent establishment open to the public and administered in the public interest, for the purpose of conserving and preserving, studying, interpreting, assembling and exhibiting to the public, for its instruction and enjoyment, objects and specimens of educational and cultural value, including artistic, scientific (whether animate or inanimate), historical and technological material.

**MUSEUM PLANNER:** a museum professional specialising in the planning of museum space, facilities, functions, services, operation and/or administration.

**MUSEUM PLANNING:** the study and practice of facilitating the preservation and interpretation of material culture by organising all those components that comprise a museum into a constructed or renovated whole that can achieve its functions with optimal efficiency.

**MUSEUM PROJECT TEAM:** the working group of museum personnel in a museum renovation or construction project whose task is to ensure that the museum's requirements are clearly stated in a functional brief or programme, and that those requirements are met by the architects, engineers and contractors.

MUSEUMS SERVICE: an organisation made up of museums and/or government agencies to serve a group of museums.

NOMENCLATURE: a structured and controlled list of terms organised in a classification system to provide the basis for indexing and cataloguing collections.

NON-PROFITMAKING (OR CHARITABLE) ORGANISATION: an institution registered with its government under letters of patent or a charitable tax number, allowing it to provide tax-deductible receipts for donations and to receive other benefits allowed by government policy within that jurisdiction.

NON-PUBLIC COLLECTION ZONE: an area of a museum in which environmental controls and security are provided for the preservation of the collection, but with a level of finish adequate for staff use only.

NON-PUBLIC NON-COLLECTION ZONE: an area of a museum requiring environmental controls adequate for staff comfort only, and levels of finish appropriate to staff use only.

OBJECT THEATRE: a mode of presentation to visitors in which artefacts, specimens, replicas or other apparatus may be featured, usually by means of spotlights or other illumination, with a voice-over script and projected imagery interpreting them by relating a thematic story-line in which they appear.

OBJECTIVES: short-term, quantified levels of achievement specified in plans and budgets as measures of fufilment of longer-term, qualitative goals.

OPERATING BUDGET: a projection of allocations for the museum's running costs, usually prepared annually.

OPERATING (OR RUNNING) COSTS: ongoing expenses of a museum, including salaries and benefits, building occupancy costs, maintenance, security, curatorial and conservation expenses, administration, marketing and the cost of public programming.

OPERATING GRANT: a grant-aid programme that provides contributions to the running costs of museums.

OPERATING SPAN: for any control sensor, the adjustable dead band around a set point, within which readings are allowed to float before equipment switches on or off. For example, if the set point for RH is 55% RH, the dead band may be adjusted so that a dehumidifier switches on only when the RH reaches 57%, and switches off when RH drifts back to 55%; if at the same time the humidifier were set to switch on when RH falls to 52%, the operating span would be between 53% and 56%.

ORGANISATIONAL CHART: a diagram of an institution's management structure.

ORIENTATION: information provided to visitors regarding where they are, what services are available and where, in what languages services are provided, what there is to see and do, and how to find it.

OUTREACH: museum activities that are designed to appeal (or 'reach out') to new or non-traditional audiences, whether offered in the museum or at another location.

PACE-SETTING DONATION: a gift that can be cited (anonymously or not, as the donor prefers) when approaching other potential donors.

PARTNERSHIPS: co-operation with other museums, institutions, agencies and attractions by sharing resources.

PERFORMANCE INDICATORS: statistics, ratios, costs or other ways of measuring the museum's or museum workers' progress in achieving the aims and objectives of the museum – for example, cost per visitor or revenue per visitor – to be used with caution, since they normally do not include reference to the quality of the visitor experience.

PERFORMANCE REVIEW: evaluation of an employee's effectiveness and efficiency in the accomplishment of museum functions in relation to the museum's goals and objectives.

PERIMETER ALARM: an intrusion alarm that should be installed at all entrances, and on all windows, including any skylights or other roof access points, preferably with direct telephone connection via dedicated lines to a police station or security company.

PERM: the equivalent to 1 gram of water transmitted through 1 square foot of surface in one hour, when the vapour pressure on the high side is 1 inch of mercury greater than the vapour pressure on the low side.

PERMEABILITY RATING: a measure of the rate at which moisture is transmitted through a substance, expressed in Perms. A vapour barrier is a material with a water vapour transmission rate of less than 1 Perm.

PERSONNEL POLICY: a statement of the museum's expectations, and a commitment, within the museum's means, to its staff in relation to working conditions.

PHOTO-ELECTRONIC SMOKE DETECTOR: an automatic fire detection device which can detect a fire moving into the second, or smouldering, stage of combustion. When sufficient smoke obscures a beam of light directed onto a photosensor, the flow of current in the photosensor changes and an alarm is triggered. More advanced models depend on a beam of pulsed LED light, and both a supervisory photocell sensor and a shielded sensor. Smoke does not affect the supervisory sensor but causes the light beam to be refracted so that it reaches and activates the shielded sensor. This type is less subject to false alarms.

PICTURE (OR ART) RENTAL: a service to visitors which involves providing works of art for monthly hire to homes or offices, sometimes restricted to museum members only.

PLANNED GIVING: donations and bequests scheduled to meet the needs of the donor and his or her estate, as well as those of the museum.

POLICY: a statement of the museum's commitment to its mission, mandate and purposes in relation to a particular museum function (such as a collection policy, conservation policy, security policy, exhibition policy, research policy, interpretation policy, etc.), and to the achievement of specific levels of quality in fulfilling this commitment.

PREPARATOR: a museum worker whose task is the preparation of works of art, artefacts or specimens for display or loan, and their installation and dismounting.

PREVENTIVE CONSERVATION: the applied science of providing an environment that minimises the deterioration of works of art, artefacts or specimens.

PRIVATE OWNERSHIP MUSEUMS: museums owned and operated by individuals, foundations or companies, either for a profit or as private charities.

PROCEDURES: the systematic means of accomplishing museum functions in such a way as to achieve the museum's objectives.

PROCEDURES MANUAL: a document codifying and communicating the systematic means of conducting museum functions and related tasks in order to realise the level of quality specified in the museum's policies.

PRODUCTION FOR SALE: manufacture through traditional methods by museum demonstrators, often on industrial heritage properties, of products that are offered for sale, either directly to visitors or by distribution to other vendors.

PROGRAMME BUDGET: the estimated cost of an activity, reflecting the performance and quality criteria indicated for that activity.

PROJECT MANAGER: an individual or company, usually independent of the museum staff, whose function is to bring under a single co-ordinating authority all those involved in a project's implementation, in order to ensure that the project objectives are achieved, and that it is completed on time, within budget, to an agreed level of quality, and with minimal disruption to other functions.

PROJECTED-BEAM SMOKE DETECTOR: automatic fire detection device operating on the same principle as the photo-electronic smoke detector (see above). Instead of the light beam and sensor(s) being contained within a single device, the two elements are separated, so that the light beam is thrown across a considerable distance (up to several hundred feet) to reach the photosensor. This type of device is useful for large, unobstructed spaces such as the upper parts of high-ceilinged halls or galleries.

PUBLIC COLLECTION ZONE: an area of a museum with environmental controls and security designed for the preservation of the collection, and with a level of finish and durability appropriate to public use.

PUBLIC FUNDRAISING CAMPAIGN: the well-publicised aspect of a fundraising campaign that is usually directed at securing relatively small amounts from a large number of donors, often amounting to only 5–10 per cent of the total to be raised, but demonstrating to other funding sources the degree of public support for the museum or the project to be funded.

PUBLIC NON-COLLECTION ZONE: an area of a museum in which environmental controls need to achieve human comfort levels only, but in which levels of finish and durability must be appropriate to public use.

PUBLIC PROGRAMME PLAN: a strategy governing all activities that the museum wishes to undertake, or has been undertaking, to serve its visitors and other users, ranging from exhibitions through interpretation of its collection to education, publications, extension services, outreach and such public amenities as toilets, shops or catering, with reference to the museum's target markets.

PUBLIC TRUST: responsibility (in some jurisdictions, a legal responsibility) for the collective material heritage of others, which is assumed by the governing body of the museum, to care for that heritage not only for the present generation, but for their descendants in perpetuity with the same prudence that one would be expected to exercise if the property were one's own.

QUANTITY SURVEYOR: a professional consultant specialising in the estimation of quantitative requirements to achieve qualitative goals; his or her function involves projecting capital cost and occupancy cost estimates for buildings, systems, facilities and functions.

REDUNDANCY: the ability of building systems to sustain operation despite malfunction or power failure.

REGISTRATION: the process of numbering artefacts, specimens or works of art in a museum collection, and recording a range of data about each of them – such as name and function of the object, the artist or maker, its source and provenance, place and date of origin, materials, and so on.

RELATIVE HUMIDITY (RH): the ratio, expressed as a percentage, of the absolute humidity of sampled air to that of air saturated with water at the same temperature.

REPRESENTATIVE COLLECTION: museum objects selected to represent ideas, concepts or themes, or to be indicative of a time period or geographical area.

RESEARCH: academic or applied investigations in disciplines relevant to a museum's collection or public programmes.

RESEARCH PLAN: a proposal to undertake academic or applied investigations in a discipline relevant to part or all of a museum's collection or its public programmes, including a budget and time estimate for its execution.

RESEARCH POLICY: a statement of the museum's commitment to academic or applied investigations relevant to its collections and public programmes, the levels of quality and priorities sought, and budget limitations in providing the personnel, time, library, travel budget and other resources required.

RESERVE COLLECTION: those works of art, artefacts or specimens which are either pending assignment to display or study collections, are duplicate or secondary examples assigned to hands-on educational programmes, or are objects pending de-accessioning.

RESERVES: funds retained for contingencies, or for future development projects.

RESTORATION: returning a building or artefact, as far as possible or as far as desired, to an earlier condition or appearance, sometimes (but not always) its original state, through repair, renovation, reconditioning or other intervention.

RESTORATION POLICY: a statement of the museum's philosophical intent in restoring works of art, artefacts or specimens, specifying standards of quality and levels of responsibility, including requirements for reversible processes and clear directives in regard to manifesting lacunae or wear in the original objects.

RESTORATION PROCEDURES MANUAL: a document giving step-by-step guidance for the execution of the museum's restoration policy, including a statement of the responsibilities of curators or conservators, the roles of paid or volunteer workers, and requirements for both written and photographic documentation of all processes.

RETREAT: an extended meeting at which participants may consider long-term plans, often part of a strategic planning process.

RISK: the possibility of occurrence of an event that may adversely affect the normal functions of an institution, which may be measured for a museum by assigning values to the criticality of a loss and the museum's vulnerability to it, and multiplying the criticality index by the vulnerability index.

RISK ANALYSIS: calculation of the priority of security needs in terms of the possibility of all threats, the criticality of those threats and the vulnerability of the institution to them.

ROOM SETTINGS: a mode of presentation in which artefacts, works of art or specimens are grouped as they would have been found in their original setting.

SCHEMATIC DESIGN: the stage of planning a building or exhibition that follows the design concept phase by developing drawings that indicate the contours and character of the building or exhibition according to the general requirements of the functional brief, programme or interpretative plan, usually including floorplans and three-dimensional views (or presentation drawings) of each building or exhibition component (see also *Design development*).

SECURITY: the entire range of activities concerned with the protection of the public, staff and others in the museum, and especially the protection of the collections, from all threats.

SECURITY POLICY: a commitment by the museum to safeguard its assets, including a risk analysis, description and distribution of levels of security, health and safety precautions, security equipment (present and recommended), routine and emergency procedures, and insurance coverage and valuation.

SECURITY SCREWS: threaded metal connectors intended to fasten the stretcher (not the frame) of a painting to a gallery wall by means of a metal 'fishplate', operable only by screwdrivers specially designed to fit the heads, whose design is more complex than the usual slots or crosses.

SECURITY STATION: a post where warders (or guards) may operate and monitor closed-circuit television surveillance systems, monitor alarms, and regulate entry and exit to the building.

SELF-GENERATED REVENUE: funds earned by the museum's operations, including admissions, retail sales, catering, memberships, rentals, films, performances, special events, educational programmes, publications, media and contracted services.

SET POINT: the condition to be attained and maintained by environmental control equipment, such as humidifiers or dehumidifiers.

SIMULATOR: an apparatus which provides visitors with an experience of motion, usually related to moving images, which is often presented in a thematic context when used in museums.

SITE SELECTION: determination of the optimal location for a museum, based on weighted evaluation of such factors as availability, access, audience development potential, cost of acquisition and development, funding opportunities, security considerations, building type, size and layout, parking, visibility and compatibility of neighbouring facilities.

**SMOKE DENSITY:** a numeric rating referring to the relative number of combustion particles present in air, produced by the burning of a particular material. Standard tables are available for commonly used construction and finishing materials.

**SMOKE DETECTORS:** the preferred means of fire detection for museums, except in kitchens, where heat detectors should be used.

**SPECIFICATIONS:** a detailed statement of work to be carried out by each contractor, materials to be used, standards to be met, procedures to be followed, matters of jurisdiction between contractors, procedures to resolve jurisdictional disputes, procedures for change orders, and so on, relating to an exhibition or a building project.

**SPONSORSHIP:** contributions of funds or donations in kind by corporations or individuals towards a specific project, such as an exhibition or other programme.

**SPRINKLERS:** devices installed in the ceiling that respond to fire by releasing a deluge of water.

**STAFFING PLAN:** a projection of requirements for personnel in order to operate the desired level of public programmes with the collection resource identified.

**STATEMENT OF PURPOSE:** a concise identification of the functions of a museum in relation to the objectives defined in its mandate.

**STORY-LINE:** the consecutive theme of an exhibition or other museum programme, sometimes, but not necessarily, narrative (see also *Theme*).

**STRATEGIC DIRECTIONS:** in the strategic planning process, meaningful and memorable guidelines indicating the institution's approach or philosophy in resolving the key issues affecting that museum.

**STRATEGIC PLANNING:** determining the optimal future for an organisation, and the changes required to achieve it.

**STUDY COLLECTION:** a collection acquired for purposes of comparative or analytical research, usually intended for indefinite preservation.

**SUMMATIVE EVALUATION:** an assessment of the visitor experience of an exhibition or other museum programme that considers the outcome in the context of the original interpretative plan to determine whether or not the exhibition communicated what it planned to communicate, and if so, how effectively this was accomplished.

SYSTEMATIC COLLECTION: artefacts or specimens acquired to exemplify an entire range of significant types or variants within that collection category.

SYSTEMATIC MODE: a style of presentation of specimens or artefacts in which the comprehensiveness of the display and the information provided is intended to demonstrate all type variations.

TARGET MARKETS: those segments of the museum's actual or potential public that are identified as a priority on which the museum's programmes should focus in order to increase and enhance levels of visitation.

TASK FORCE: co-operation between a group of individuals, usually from several departments, to achieve a common aim, such as an exhibition.

TECHNICAL PROGRAMME: the plans, drawings and specifications of the architect and engineers that should meet the requirements of the functional brief or programme.

TENDER (OR BID): a proposal to undertake work on contract.

TENDER DOCUMENTS: the detailed designs and specifications that are issued to competing contractors, and which form the basis of the consequent contract to undertake the construction, renovation, fabrication, installation or other work necessary to complete a museum building or exhibition or operate services within it.

TENDERING: the process of issuing requests for tenders or bids on work to be contracted out, evaluating the bids, negotiating and awarding the contract.

TERMS OF REFERENCE: a statement of mandate and requirements for a committee, a planning process, a programme or a project.

THEMATIC (OR CONTEXTUAL) DISPLAY: a mode of exhibition of works of art, specimens or artefacts arranged to illustrate a theme, subject or story-line in order to facilitate comprehension of their significance in relation to that theme, often employing graphic or other interpretative devices to place the objects in context for the visitor.

THEME: a connective statement or relationship between works of art, artefacts or specimens that is articulated in an exhibition plan or interpretative plan as the core content that an exhibition or other museum programme is intended to communicate.

TIME-SHARING AGREEMENT: a partnership between a museum and a school administration whereby school parties have exclusive access during certain hours when the museum is not otherwise open, and the museum provides guided tours or other educational programmes, in return for a set fee from the school board or a subsidy allocation from the relevant level of government.

TRAINING AND DEVELOPMENT STRATEGY: a plan agreed between the museum and an individual employee, related both to the individual's needs in learning how to do his or her job to the requisite level of quality, and his or her programme to upgrade skills and capabilities for future advancement.

TRAINING PROGRAMMES: instruction for employees in how to do their job.

TRANSIT STORE: an area in which works of art, artefacts or specimens loaned to the museum for temporary exhibitions are to be held, with levels of security approximating those of the permanent collection store, since it is likely to be visited by couriers accompanying loans from other museums and must meet insurance and indemnity requirements.

TRUST: see *Board*.

TRUSTEE: a member of a board or trust in either a governing or advisory role.

TRUSTEES' MANUAL: a publication providing members of the museum's governing or advisory board with all relevant mission, mandate and policy statements and the board constitution, as well as a history of the institution, current plans, staff organisation charts, budgets and financial reports, board roles and responsibilities, and an outline of the committee structure.

ULTRAVIOLET (UV) LIGHT: rays beyond the visible spectrum of light that are the chief cause of colour fading and chemical changes due to exposure to light.

VAPOUR BARRIER: an impermeable barrier to prevent movement of water vapour into a building, having a water vapour transmission rate of less than 1 Perm.

VERIFIED PASSIVE INFRA-RED DETECTION SYSTEM: an intrusion detection device which incorporates two different technologies to 'verify' each other: a PIR (passive infra-red) detector, plus a second detector which may use microwave, ultrasonic, or other complementary technology. PIR detectors use sensors which are activated by radiation of infra-red energy from a source such as the human body.

VIRTUAL REALITY: a simulated environment, usually computer-generated, intended to provide the visitor with meaningful and exciting experiences with which he or she may interact.

VIRTUAL REALITY CAVE: a multimedia display in which an environment is projected onto the walls, floors and ceiling of a contained space, facilitating the involvement of visitors who may interact with the software environment without personal imaging goggles or sensor gloves.

VISIBLE STORAGE: provision of public access to part or all of a museum collection by means of systematic presentation of artefacts, specimens or works of art, as in closed storage, but presented in a public gallery, normally on shelves or in drawers behind or under glass, with publicly-accessible catalogues providing interpretation either by means of laminated flip-cards of entire catalogue entries, or computer terminals where similarly detailed information is available.

VISITOR ANALYSIS: quantitative and qualitative analysis of the museum's present visitors, usually undertaken to determine visitor need and perceptions of the museum.

VISITOR SERVICES: activities directed at accommodating the visitor, including admissions, orientation, wayfinding, retail and food services, toilets, rest areas and customer care policies that affect the quality of the visitor experience and communicate the museum's attitude to its public.

VISITOR-RESPONSIVENESS: giving due regard to the visitor experience in all aspects of the museum's programmes.

VOLUNTEER: an unpaid employee, whose rewards are in the form of personal development and social recognition for work done.

VOLUNTEER AGREEMENT (OR CONTRACT): a signed commitment by the volunteer to the museum, and by the museum to the volunteer, making reference to all working conditions and schedules.

VOLUNTEER MANUAL: a document that links the museum's mission and mandate to the museum's volunteer policy and to practical details pertaining to the daily work of volunteers, including all museum policies and procedures relevant to the volunteers' area of work.

VOLUNTEER POLICY: the museum's commitment to the recruitment, training, deployment, evaluation and social rewards of unpaid museum workers.

VULNERABILITY: the extent to which a work of art, artefact, specimen or an entire museum collection is at risk.

WARDERS (OR GUARDS): museum workers with responsibility for security of the collection and the safety of all persons in the museum.

WORK PLAN: a statement of objectives and resources, together with a budget and a schedule for achieving particular tasks.

WORLD WIDE WEB: a global network of computer networks, interconnected via phone lines and communications devices, facilitating a vast interchange of knowledge and information throughout the world.

ZERO-BASE BUDGETING: a method of projecting revenue and expenditures which requires museum managers to justify each allocation in relation to the programmes it makes possible without reference to historical levels of service provision.

# Index

Note: Case study photographs are listed in **bold**, by their page number.

*Index by Fiona Barr*